*I take great pleasure in applauding the advent of the Ubu Repertory Theater Publications. Devoted to bringing English versions of important contemporary dramatic works from French-speaking countries, this program could not be more important or timely when institutions such as the Eugene O'Neill Theater Center and the Milwaukee Repertory Theater have begun to embrace and espouse the cause of this key element of cultural exchange.*

*It is particularly important to realize that the plays chosen for translation and publication are not part of any specific genre, but rather are eclectic and are selected to inform the English-speaking public of the scope and richness of present-day French-speaking playwrights.*

*I cherish the hope that this marvelous project will spark a renaissance in professional collaboration between our French and English-speaking theaters and foster greater understanding between diverse national groups.*

George C. White, President
Eugene O'Neill Memorial Theater Center

# UBU REPERTORY THEATER PUBLICATIONS

# PREFACE

The five plays in this collection are representative of the wide range of themes and styles in contemporary French dramatic writing. Jean Tardieu, in *The Sleepless City*, creates a fantasy world that mocks modern man's obsession with efficiency and productivity. His fable gives our imaginations free reign and explores the powers of the unconscious. On the other hand, Jean Bouchaud's *A Birthday Present for Stalin* is a period piece: the drab offices of a communist party cell in 1949 are the setting for a light farce that turns poignantly sour in 1956. *The Rest Have Got It Wrong*, by Jean-Michel Ribes, blurs the boundaries between the real and the imaginary, the past and the present, to portray a woman crushed by tragic personal events and unfulfilled hopes. The two other plays are set in present-day France. *Trumpets of Death*, Tilly's scathing satire of class differences, is grounded in meticulous sociological detail in a style close to hyperrealism. Michel Vinaver's *The Neighbors* uses unpunctuated, elliptical dialogue to convey the non-linear complexity of human relationships. Vinaver's style forbids complacency or easy understanding; and the spectator or reader is forced to draw his or her own conclusions.

Fantasy, farce, satire and realism, traditional and innovative, playful, tender, poignant, caustic and serious, these plays challenge the skills and imaginations of directors, actors, readers and audiences.

Catherine Temerson  
Françoise Kourilsky

# The Paris Stage

## Recent Plays

UBU REPERTORY THEATER PUBLICATIONS

Ubu Repertory Theater Publications
Françoise Kourilsky
Catherine Temerson
General Editors

Printed in the United States of America 1988

ISBN 0-913745-25-1

*Jean Bouchaud*

# A BIRTHDAY PRESENT
# FOR STALIN

Translated from the French
by **Matthew Ward**

This English translation of *A Birthday Present for Stalin* was given its first reading, directed by **Charles Barber,** at the Donnell Library Center Bankers Trust Company Auditorium, on March 20, 1988, during the "Ubu International" festival.

**JEAN BOUCHAUD** is an actor and director as well as a playwright. He was born in Marseilles in 1936. After training as a professional actor in Paris, he appeared in productions directed by prominent French directors such as Jean Vilar, Roger Planchon and Antoine Bourseiller. In 1966 he began writing and directing his own plays, and he acted in seven of his own works during the following nine years: *Pop 4*, *Les Caisses qu'est-ce?*, *La grande fuite*, *Les Affreux*, *Les Poubelles*, *Akoiskonjoue?* and *Brocabric*. In 1978 he founded the Théâtre Puzzle and was awarded the Prix Courteline of the Société des Auteurs Dramatiques for *Gros Oiseau* in a production directed by Jean-Michel Ribes. A year later he directed the production of his play *C'était comment déjà?* It was subsequently broadcast on French television, starring Madeleine Renaud. *A Birthday Present for Stalin (Un drôle de cadeau)*, which he also directed, opened to unanimous critical acclaim in Paris in 1985. It received the prize of "Best French Production of the Year" as well as the Prix des "U." Bouchaud has also written four screenplays and several television scripts (including a weekly series co-authored with Jean-Michel Ribes and Roland Topor), and he has always continued to direct noteworthy productions of plays by other authors.

**MATTHEW WARD** is a poet, critic and essayist. He has translated works by Roland Barthes, Pablo Picasso and Colette, as well as plays by Bernard-Marie Koltès and Jean-Paul Aron for Ubu Repertory Theater Publications. Alfred A. Knopf has just published his translation of *The Stranger* by Albert Camus, the first American translation of the novel.

# CHARACTERS

Desiré Scartini
Heloise Scartini
Roger Blot
Josyane Terson
Jean Louis Sélavy
Leona Chalière
Marcel Feuillard
Suzanne Lalande

The action takes place in the small office of the Elisa Verlet Cell and the courtyard of the small apartment house in which the office is located. Stage right, the office itself is defined by two walls and a glass roof. Stage left, the glass-paned door of the concierge's lodge opens onto a small stoop, which is reached by a few stairs. Behind the staircase, a hallway leads to the upper floors of the house. At the back is a hallway leading to the street and in a corner of the courtyard, the W.C. In order to be visible at all, the cell's office has only one door at the back. The third wall, which separates the office from the courtyard, consists of piles of newspapers. The cell office is furnished with an old bureau beneath some shelves; an old stove, and a wooden plank and two trestles that serve as a table; an armoire; an old sideboard; and two stools, a chair and a bench. The furniture is mismatched and shabby. The shelves and cupboards are stacked with unsold books, leaflets and pamphlets not handed out and posters not pasted up. The office is cluttered with brushes, buckets of glue, banners and flags. Portraits of Lenin, Stalin, Thorez, etc., hang on the wall.

## ACT ONE

*(A Sunday in December 1949. The sounds of a radio can be heard coming from the lodge of the concierges, Desiré and Heloise Scartini. As he does every Sunday, Desiré, in a referee's uniform, bicycle in hand, is getting ready to go to the local stadium.)*

DESIRÉ: Are you sure you don't want to come?

HELOISE: And freeze my tail off all afternoon in some stadium just to watch you run around on some grass? No, thanks.

DESIRÉ: You won't be bored all by yourself, my lady-love?

HELOISE: Don't worry; there's no shortage of work to be done around here! *(She goes into the W.C. and pulls the chain.)* Here we go. . . . It's clogged again!

DESIRÉ: Of course it is; they'll throw anything in it.

HELOISE: Some people are really sick! What's the point of

putting squares of newspaper on the string, somebody always has to be different!

DESIRÉ:   They wouldn't have dared do it when the Germans were around!

HELOISE:   *(looking at her husband)* Poor Desiré, you really can be an ass sometimes. Really!....And to think I believed I was marrying a future police superintendent!

DESIRÉ:   You're not going to start that again, are you?

HELOISE:   My dream was to see you assigned to the colonies. Diego-Suarez,...Tizi-Ouzou,...Papeete....A cop's wife is somebody in the territories! And what do I get: Paris, Rue de la Tombe-Issoire and a mop!

DESIRÉ:   You know perfectly well that if it hadn't been for my accident in '35, anything would have been possible. For starters, I should have been named to Aubenas....

HELOISE:   You never did know how to handle things. Even during the war you were on the wrong side,...and yet you had a fifty-fifty chance!

*(Desiré gestures to her to be quiet. Roger Blot emerges into the courtyard. He heads toward the office of the French Communist Party.)*

ROGER:   *(entering the office)* Madame, Monsieur.

*(The concierges mumble a vague response.)*

DESIRÉ:   Are you crazy? Do you realize the risk we run having them here? The eye of Moscow...!

*(Heloise takes the key out of the door to the W.C. and holds it out to him.)*

What's this?

HELOISE:   The key to the john. Just in case they send the blueprint to the Russkies....We have to be careful!

*(Desiré walks away, shrugging his shoulders. Pause.)*

Aren't you going to be late for the match? You didn't forget your snack, did you?

DESIRÉ:   No.

HELOISE:   Do you have your whistle?

DESIRÉ:   I took two. I lost mine last time, so I thought. . . .

HELOISE:   As if it wasn't enough that you blow it all week long in the middle of some intersection!. . .You should give it a rest on Sundays!

DESIRÉ:   It's not the same! Sundays I referee!

HELOISE:   What kind of filth won't they scribble on these walls next? Look, here's a new drawing. . . . Looks like you!

DESIRÉ:   *(dubious)* You think so?

HELOISE:   Just read what it says.

DESIRÉ:   *(reading)* "Scartini-weenie-peenie."

HELOISE:   Well, seems they're pretty well informed!

DESIRÉ:   No need to ask where that came from! Well, see you this evening.

*(He leaves, pushing his bicycle, while Heloise goes back into her lodge. In the dimly lit office, Roger, his ear to the door, has been listening to the entire scene. Hearing Desiré leave, he starts to sing "Gloire au 17ᵉ" by Montehus.)*

ROGER:
"Hail, hail to you,
Brave soldiers of the 17th. . . ."

*(Heloise, hurrying out of her lodge, runs into the office where Roger is. She starts to sing.)*

HELOISE:
"Hail, brave soldier boys,
You are loved and admired by all."

*(Roger and Heloise do a few dance steps as they sing.)*

ROGER and HELOISE:
"Timela lamelou panpan timela,
Padilamelou cocodou labaia."

*(He ardently backs her up against a pile of unsold newspapers.)*

HELOISE:   Careful, Roger!

ROGER:   You know you're beautiful!

HELOISE:   Put something over the papers!

ROGER:   Why?

HELOISE:   I'll get ink on my dress. . . .

ROGER:   No, you won't!

HELOISE:   I'm telling you, it comes off! The other day I had a headline imprinted on my behind!

ROGER:   What?

HELOISE:   "General Strike," in capital letters! How do you think that sits with Desiré?

*(Running in from the street, as if pursued, Josyane Terson enters the courtyard. The couple, hearing the sound of footsteps, freeze. Roger quickly shuts himself in the cupboard. Heloise cracks open the door and, without Josyane seeing her, runs back into her lodge as fast as she can. Josyane then rushes into the office, locking the door behind her. Jean Louis Sélavy arrives next. He is the same age as Josyane, about twenty-five. He appears to be looking for her and stops at the door of the concierges' lodge.)*

JEAN LOUIS:   Are you in there? *(Pause. No answer.)* I know you're there! Open up!

*(He walks over to the door of the cell office, which he tries to open. Hearing him approach, Josyane backs into the shadows and knocks over a stool.)*

Oh, I heard you! Let me in!

JOSYANE:   Leave me alone!

JEAN LOUIS:   But it's Sunday!

JOSYANE:   So?

*(Brief silence.)*

JEAN LOUIS:   Sunday's the day to meet,...to discover other people....On Sundays I'm not the same person I am the rest of the week!

JOSYANE:   Well, I am!

JEAN LOUIS:   Is this your place,...in there, where you are?

JOSYANE:   No....Yes,...it's my fiancé's place....

JEAN LOUIS:   Oh, I see.

JOSYANE:   He's very big,...and crazy,...violent....Go away, quick; here he comes!

*(She makes the sound of footsteps, without seeing Jean Louis, who, perched on a trash can, watches her through the window in the door.)*

JEAN LOUIS:   Introduce me!

JOSYANE:   Leave me alone!

JEAN LOUIS:   If you don't open up, I'll howl....I'll make a scene!

JOSYANE:   Shhhhh!

JEAN LOUIS:   C'mon, open up.

JOSYANE:   No.

JEAN LOUIS:   *(singing at the top of his voice)*
"La petite diligence
Sur les beaux chemins de France
S'en allait en cahotant. . . ."

*(Heloise comes out onto her stoop, and Josyane comes out of the office.)*

HELOISE:   The howling has got to stop!

JEAN LOUIS:   I've been locked out.

JOSYANE:   It's nothing, Madame Scartini. . . . He's a friend.

HELOISE:   They wouldn't put up with this kind of thing in Moscow.

JOSYANE:   *(embarrassed)* Of course not. . . . *(She pushes Jean Louis into the office and shuts the door.)* That was clever! I hope you're happy; her husband's a cop!

HELOISE:   *(going back into her lodge)* If it isn't a disgrace to see such a thing!

JEAN LOUIS:   Why Moscow?

*(Josyane turns on the lights. He gets his first look at the premises: posters, fliers, pamphlets and, of course, the portraits of Lenin; Stalin; Maurice Thorez, head of the French Communist Party; etc.)*

JEAN LOUIS:   Oh, yes, I see.

JOSYANE:   Does this happen to you often?

JEAN LOUIS:   What? Finding myself in an office of the Communist Party while following a girl? No, never!

JOSYANE:   Well, now that you've had the experience, goodbye!

*(She pushes him toward the door.)*

JEAN LOUIS:    One second. . . .You can spare me one second, can't you?

JOSYANE:    Get out!

JEAN LOUIS:    *(playing for time)* I'm not asking that much. . . . Is it just me, or is it a little chilly in here?

JOSYANE:    We can't afford to put in central heating.

JEAN LOUIS:    And that there,. . .isn't that a stove?

JOSYANE:    Yes, but there's nothing to put in it.

JEAN LOUIS:    *(gathering some leaflets)* And what about all this?

JOSYANE:    Are you crazy! Give those to me! Leave those alone! *(She grabs the leaflets from him.)*

JEAN LOUIS:    *(pointing to the piles of leaflets)* You can't tell me you're going to use all these?

JOSYANE:    Yes, precisely!

*(He takes one from a stack of unsold newspapers.)*

Those too!

JEAN LOUIS:    *(reading)* "November 1949". . . .These are last month's. What are you doing with them?

JOSYANE:    Those are the unsold ones. They have to be sent back.

*(She takes the newspapers out of his hands. He plops down on the bench. Pause.)*

JEAN LOUIS:    I'll just sit here a few minutes; I'm beat. . . . You walk pretty darn fast.

JOSYANE: *(standing next to him, waiting)* Well, you didn't have to follow me, did you?

JEAN LOUIS: I've got something in my little toe. Whenever I start walking, after a minute...it starts pricking me.... It goes ti-ti-ti-ti....

JOSYANE: You're not going to take off your shoes right here, are you?

JEAN LOUIS: No....Did you like the movie? I....

JOSYANE: It was terrific!

JEAN LOUIS: Yeah, really! It really was amazing,...especially the color....

JOSYANE: Obviously, it's Sovcolor! It's far superior to American Technicolor.

JEAN LOUIS: For sure! I really had a very good time. *(Pause.)* It's the first time I've seen a Russian film...and, well, I don't think it'll be the last!

JOSYANE: Soviet!

*(He doesn't understand. Pause.)*

It's a Soviet film, not Russian.

JEAN LOUIS: It's the same thing!

JOSYANE: Not at all! The Soviet Union is made up of different republics; this film was shot in the Ukraine, so it's not a Russian film.

JEAN LOUIS: Oh yeah, right!...I mean, you could tell it was the Ukraine....Those vast expanses,...those huge fields of wheat must be beautiful! It's true, here, we're not used to seeing tractors, peasants while they work!

JOSYANE: That is the true face of socialism.

JEAN LOUIS:   Is that so? It doesn't surprise me. There were so many amazing things in that film!

*(A sneeze is heard coming from the cupboard where Roger is hiding.)*

Bless you!

*(She doesn't understand. He stands up.)*

If you have things to do, don't let me keep you. *(He looks at the pile of posters.)* If I can be of any help,. . . .

JOSYANE:   You just stick like glue, don't you!

JEAN LOUIS:   *(picking up a roll of posters)* Well, you're in luck. . . . I'm ready to do anything you ask.

*(She grabs the posters from his hands. While she's putting them back, he pulls a package out from under a chair.)*

Hey, look!. . .Some kindling; that's great!

JOSYANE:   *(trying to get the package away from him)* Leave it there! Maybe it's for something!

JEAN LOUIS:   No, no; you'll see, a little fire will do us good! *(Before she can stop him, he dumps the contents of the package into the stove; he grabs a leaflet, which he reads.)* "Let us denounce Tito's treachery, which follows the Trotsky-Doriot line.". . .Jacques Duclos. . . .

JOSYANE:   Give that to me!

JEAN LOUIS:   This is two weeks old! Don't you sell these leaflets?

JOSYANE:   No; we hand them out.

JEAN LOUIS:   Good, so none is unsold!

*(He lights the leaflet and throws it into the stove. Worn down, Josyane falls back onto a pile of newspapers.)*

You should come over here; it's starting to warm up.

JOSYANE:   Just how long are you going to make yourself at home here?

JEAN LOUIS:   *(pointing to a portrait on the wall)* Who's that...with the beard?

JOSYANE:   You don't know Lenin? The founder of the Soviet Union?

JEAN LOUIS:   *(catching himself)* Oh, yes,...of course,...now that you tell me....It must be the cap!...Now, Stalin, there's no mistaking him, is there? In the film he was practically in every shot! Either a bust, or a photograph, a painting, a medal, a statue....

JOSYANE:   He's a hero to all the peoples of the Soviet Union.

*(He picks up a magazine,* Soviet Union, *off the desk and flips through it.)*

JEAN LOUIS:   *Soviet Union,* is it a good magazine? *(She doesn't answer.)* They're really crazy about cows, aren't they?

JOSYANE:   Why?

JEAN LOUIS:   They're everywhere! Here,...here,...and here.

*(She walks over to him.)*

JOSYANE:   Did you see how sanitary the conditions in the stable are? All the women are in white; everything is sterilized. Wearing the smock is obligatory.

JEAN LOUIS:   A cow smock! *(He laughs and then, before Josyane has time to react, is serious again.)* Uh, yes, it all looks very clean. *(He fllips through the magazine.)* A phosphate treatment plant,... a sanatorium....

JOSYANE:   If you're interested in the economic progress of the Soviet Union, there's a very interesting subscription rate.

What's your name?

JEAN LOUIS: Jean Louis Sélavy. What's yours?

JOSYANE: Josyane Terson. You see, it's a fascinating magazine. *(She fills out a form.)*

JEAN LOUIS: It looks it! Well, I mean, skimming it like this, it's pretty impressive. . . .

JOSYANE: For one year, you get twelve issues for two hundred francs. It's a bargain, don't you think?

JEAN LOUIS: Oh, yeah!

JOSYANE: And, as a bonus, I'll give you a gift: this pamphlet by Jacques Duclos: "Who Is to Receive Funds from Abroad?"

JEAN LOUIS: Oh, I can tell I'm gonna have a ball reading this!

JOSYANE: People say all kinds of crazy things about us, about our politics.

JEAN LOUIS: Oh, yeah? I must say that until today, . . .well, for quite some time now, I haven't paid much attention. But now, I think I'll throw myself into it. You speak with such faith, . . .your eyes flash. . . . Anyone can see you're carried away by your subject, . . .you're transfigured, . . .you're very beautiful.

*(She stands up. A sneeze comes from the cupboard.)*

JOSYANE: *(her back to him)* Bless you!

JEAN LOUIS: Thank you! *(Absent-mindedly, he takes a handkerchief out of his pocket and wipes his nose. She holds out a book to him.)*

JOSYANE: Do you know this book?

JEAN LOUIS: I don't think so, no. . . . *(He reads.) Son of the People* . . .by Maurice Thorez. . .Oh, I knew he was head of the French Communist Party, but I didn't know he writes, too. . . .

I'll read it right after the pamphlet.

JOSYANE:   It really is a very good book.

JEAN LOUIS:   Good, good.

JOSYANE:   Indispensable for anyone who wants to know more about the workers' condition in France.

*(A pause. He rejoins her near the stove.)*

JOSYANE:   Actually, it does feel better in here now.

JEAN LOUIS:   It's the fire, it. . . it warms things, . . . so it feels better. . . *(He puts his arm around her waist.)*

JOSYANE:   What do you do for a living?

JEAN LOUIS:   Oh, a little of this, a little of that; I get by!

JOSYANE:   You do odd jobs?

JEAN LOUIS:   Yeah. . . .Well, no. . . .I like doing odd jobs too, but I'm just kidding. *(She doesn't understand.)* Secondhand furniture. An antique dealer, if you prefer.

JOSYANE:   Oh, you're a shopkeeper!

JEAN LOUIS:   Not exactly. I fixed up an old truck and a friend lets me set up in his stand at the flea market. I'm not complaining; I'm a free man!

JOSYANE:   That's what you think! Do you think that this system based on the exploitation of one man by another is capable of providing you with the means to grow in freedom?

JEAN LOUIS:   I don't know. . . .

JOSYANE:   What would you say to coming to one of our meetings?

JEAN LOUIS:   Sure! They must be fascinating, judging by. . .

what you've been telling me. . .just now. . .Yes, really, I'd be very tempted!

JOSYANE:   At the moment, we're preparing for our little celebration marking card renewal day, as we do at the end of every year, and for comrade Stalin's birthday too.

JEAN LOUIS:   Oh? It's his birthday?

JOSYANE:   His seventieth!

JEAN LOUIS:   He certainly doesn't look it!

JOSYANE:   Stalin is the man we most admire.

JEAN LOUIS:   And have you chosen a present for him?

JOSYANE:   Not yet. But we're starting up a fund, . . .and you can be the first to contribute! *(She goes and gets a list and a pencil.)*

JEAN LOUIS:   *(surprised)* Oh, really? That's nice, my being the first. . . .

JOSYANE:   We're not a rich cell. . . .

JEAN LOUIS:   *(digging in his pockets)* How much can I. . .?

JOSYANE:   From each according to his means!

*(He takes out a coin. She looks at it.)*

Stalin is the victor over Nazism. . . . It's thanks to him that we're still somewhat free. . . .

*(Jean Louis, embarrassed, replaces the coin with a bill.)*

JEAN LOUIS:   I only have a big bill. You don't have any change, do you?

JOSYANE:   No, but if you come back. . . . I'll also take the price of *Son of the People* out of it! *(She takes the bill.)*

JEAN LOUIS: Right, fine! So we'll do it that way;. . .we'll figure it all out together at the meeting, okay?

JOSYANE: Sign here; the amount can be filled in later.

*(He signs his name as Josyane puts the bill in a small metal box.)*

JEAN LOUIS: Have you thought about a small clock?

JOSYANE: *(surprised)* For Marshall Stalin?

JEAN LOUIS: Yes, but a nice small clock. They make real funny ones with Mickey Mouse. . . . *(He stumbles over himself.)* Or else a big one, a big country clock. . . . *(She's not listening.)* And what about you, what do you do?

JOSYANE: At the moment, I'm a salesclerk in a shop near here. Later on, well, if I'm able, I'd like to have a position of responsibility in the party. Only the theory part is quite hard,. . .economics, politics, philosophy,. . .since I didn't get very far in school! My parents don't know I belong to the party. They're business people; to them they're just reds; they haven't gotten beyond the knife-between-the-teeth stage.

JEAN LOUIS: *(approaching her)* What do they do?

JOSYANE: They're butchers.

*(He embraces her; she frees herself.)*

JEAN LOUIS: Don't you like me?

JOSYANE: It's not that, but I don't even know you yet. . . . And we have to be vigilant. . . . Roger, the secretary of our cell, is a real stickler about that.

JEAN LOUIS: About what?

JOSYANE: About being vigilant. Right now, agents of Hitlerism and Trotskyism,. . .of the C.I.A., and of Tito are trying to infiltrate the party.

JEAN LOUIS:   And you think I look like an agent of Hitlerism...?

JOSYANE:   *(interrupting him)* No, but you see, the police are everywhere right now.

*(She opens the cupboard to put away the metal box without seeing Roger, motionless and frozen. Jean Louis sees him.)*

They'd be more than happy to pin some nasty provocation on us. You have to keep your eyes open! *(She closes the door to the cupboard.)*

JEAN LOUIS:   Yes....And you see pretty well, do you?

JOSYANE:   As a matter of fact, no; I'm very nearsighted.

JEAN LOUIS:   Right.

JOSYANE:   Is it very obvious?

JEAN LOUIS:   That you don't see well? No, really, I mean....

JOSYANE:   I don't like wearing glasses; it's somewhat out of vanity, and I can never remember where I put them. They say that nearsighted people have a nice look in their eyes.

JEAN LOUIS:   Yes, well, you're very, very nearsighted! *(He walks to the other side of the room.)* Can you see me now?

JOSYANE:   A little.

*(He steps closer.)*

JEAN LOUIS:   And now?

JOSYANE:   Better.

*(He steps closer again.)*

JEAN LOUIS:   What about now?

*(Heloise comes out of her lodge, singing. Josyane steps away from Jean Louis who, about to kiss her, loses his balance, grabs the stove and burns himself.)*

JEAN LOUIS:   *(screaming)* Ow!

JOSYANE:   Did you burn yourself? *(She panics, not knowing what to do.)* Blow on it,...air,...do something!...There's nothing here....You should put a potato on it!...

JEAN LOUIS:   Yeah? I didn't know potatoes....

JOSYANE:   Potatoes are very good for burns!

*(Desiré enters the courtyard with his motor scooter. He goes and listens at the door to the office.)*

JEAN LOUIS:   Do you have any?

JOSYANE:   At my place, yes.

JEAN LOUIS:   Do you think maybe we could go to your place?

*(There is banging from inside the armoire: Roger wants to be let out.)*

JOSYANE:   I think somebody knocked.

*(As Jean Louis points toward the cupboard, she goes toward the office door, opens it and finds herself nose to nose with the concierge.)*

Hello, Monsieur Scartini!

DESIRÉ:   Hello! The match was postponed because of the cold.

JOSYANE:   You wouldn't have any potatoes, would you?

DESIRÉ:   Yes, of course! I'll go ask Heloise.

JOSYANE:   *(to Jean Louis)* I think we're saved!

*(Jean Louis walks over to the cupboard, as Josyane follows Desiré to the concierges' lodge.)*

JEAN LOUIS:   *(opening the cupboard door)* Hello, there! Come in!

ROGER:   Thank you. It doesn't open from the inside. . . . It's not exactly warm in there, either!

JEAN LOUIS:   Well, we've made a little fire.

*(Roger goes to warm himself next to the stove.)*

DESIRÉ:   *(offstage)* Sweetie pie, you wouldn't have any potatoes for the pinkos, would you?

JOSYANE:   *(on the stoop)* Just one; it's for a burn!

JEAN LOUIS:   *(looking at Roger's black uniform)* Are you on duty?

ROGER:   Oh, no! I'm Roger Blot, secretary of the cell. *(He gives Jean Louis' burnt hand a violent squeeze. It's all Jean Louis can do to keep from screaming.)* I work at the city morgue. . . . Before that, I was a furniture mover.

JEAN LOUIS:   You don't say!

ROGER:   I was conducting a vigilance test. . . . It's unbelievable! Did you see how easy it would be to infiltrate this cell without being exposed? They must be having a good laugh at the C.I.A.!

JEAN LOUIS:   She's very nearsighted.

ROGER:   In politics, that's very serious! No, it's a sorry excuse for a cell! Are you a comrade?

JEAN LOUIS:   *(surprised)* Hunh? No, I was getting some information. . . .

ROGER:   You've done well; information doesn't cost much. No, because you can't hear a thing in the cupboard. By the way, don't say anything to Josyane, since I hope to be nominated for the municipal elections; it could start trouble.

JEAN LOUIS:   I understand. Of course.

*(Desiré comes back out into the courtyard with a sack of potatoes. Roger jumps up and motions to Jean Louis to keep quiet.)*

DESIRÉ:   How's this?

JOSYANE:   That's too many!

DESIRÉ:   No, no,. . .wait, I'll help you. . . .

HELOISE:   *(offstage)* Which one of them got burned?

*(Josyane walks back toward the office with Desiré.)*

JOSYANE:   You're very kind, Monsieur Scartini.

DESIRÉ:   We may not share the same opinions, but that's no reason not to help each other out.

*(Hearing the voice of the concierge getting closer, Roger shuts himself back in the cupboard.)*

ROGER:   Damn, the cop's coming back!

JOSYANE:   *(entering the office)* Here we are. . . . I only need one, Monsieur Scartini. . . .

DESIRÉ:   Fine,. . .then I'll just take the rest back. . . .

JOSYANE:   *(to Jean Louis)* Give me your hand.

DESIRÉ:   *(retracing his steps)* Did you find the package?

JOSYANE:   *(tending to Jean Louis)* No,. . .what package?

DESIRÉ:   One of your old comrades came by this morning, old man Grospierre; he said it was the present for Stalin.

JOSYANE:   What was it?

DESIRÉ:   A dismantled model, I think;. . .a rare item, it seems. I didn't really understand. . . . A real masterpiece,. . .a scale model of Notre Dame made out of matchsticks, or something like that. He put it over there.

*(He points to the place where Jean Louis found the bundle that he used to start the fire. Josyane, busy giving first aid, doesn't pay attention.)*

Well, then, I guess I'll be leaving you.

JOSYANE:  Goodbye, Monsieur Scartini!

*(Desiré leaves.)*

Every day in *L'Humanité* they publish the list of presents from cells all over France. Until now, we were the last ones. That's terrific if we've finally found a present!

*(Jean Louis runs to the stove, opens it, tries to take out whatever might be saved of the model and burns himself.)*

What are you doing? You've burned yourself again! It's a mania with you! Let me put the potato back on. . . . On the whole, it's been a pretty good day: a subscription to *Soviet Union*, our first copy of *Son of the People*. . . .

JEAN LOUIS:  I see; and I'm the first again?

JOSYANE:  Yes, just like the gift fund! We're way behind.

JEAN LOUIS:  Good thing I'm here.

JOSYANE:  Ours is one of the worst run cells in this district; they're even talking about dissolving it.

JEAN LOUIS:  No joke!

JOSYANE:  Yes; it would be a real shame, especially for Roger, our secretary. The national federation has named him a party candidate in the next municipal election: it's a promotion. With the cell being so late, he was afraid they'd name somebody else! Now that we've finally found a present for Stalin, we don't have anything to worry about! You might say you've brought us good luck! *(She kisses him as the lights dim.)*

## ACT TWO

*(A few days later. Heloise sings as she sweeps up and Desiré, seated on the stairs, reads his paper. The radio is on. In the cell office, Roger is clearly having a hard time concentrating on his report. Entering the courtyard, a tenant continues into the hallway leading to the upper floors. Heloise watches him.)*

HELOISE: Your feet, Monsieur Jolibois? Are they going to wipe themselves? The mat isn't there just for looks. And I'm here to clean up the crap, of course!

JOLIBOIS: *(offstage)* Ah, clam up!

HELOISE: Go learn some manners! *(She speaks under her breath.)* Jolibois, yeah, Jolijerk! *(She addresses Desiré.)* Do you hear how people talk to me? Oh, the police are great; they provide such protection!

DESIRÉ: Hunh? You talking to me?

HELOISE: Yes, I am, so you can just take off your mask. . . . You're afraid of Jolibois. While he's insulting me, you're acting deaf as Beethoven!

DESIRÉ: I'm late. See you later. *(He leaves, pushing his bicycle.)*

HELOISE: *(watching him leave)* Real men are like seasons: there aren't any anymore!

*(In the office, Roger appears unable to bear the noise coming from the courtyard. The radio plays the theme to "Sur le banc," a popular program of the period. Heloise shouts to the upper floors.)*

HELOISE: Madame Merlu! Yoo-hoo, Madame Merlu!. . . "Sur le banc" is on!. . . Madame Merlu! *(Pause. No answer.)* That one's worse than Beethoven. On the other hand, it's no big deal if she doesn't hear me, because she wouldn't hear the radio either! *(Wearily, Heloise disappears into her lodge.)*

ROGER: *(reading)* "Yes, Comrades, we are not ashamed to say it, Stalin is the man we most admire. . . ." *(He grabs a pamphlet and checks the exact slogan, then corrects himself.)* ". . .we admire most. . . . And, as André Wurmser has said, whoever claims to be anti-Soviet is thereby anti-French. . . . Yes, the struggle against anti-Sovietism is a sacred duty of all communists. . . ."

*(Heloise comes out of her lodge singing and walks toward the office.)*

HELOISE:
> "Hail, hail to you,
> Brave soldiers of the 17th,
> Hail, brave soldier boys,
> You are admired and loved by all."

*(Roger rushes to the door. He tries to keep Heloise from coming in.)*

HELOISE: *(cajoling)* Who is that hiding there on the other side of this door?

ROGER: *(embarrassed)* No, listen,. . . Madame Scartini, listen. . . .

HELOISE: Who is that hiding there on the other side of this door?

ROGER: I didn't give the signal,. . . and I have work to do. . . .

*(She advances on him, greedily.)*

No, stop, Madame Scartini,. . . not now. . . . I'm expecting someone. . . .

HELOISE: But your little paws are frozen, my pet!

ROGER: *(pulling away)* I forbid you to call me a pet! Listen, Heloise, unless I give the signal, we're not playing! And it's not Sunday, either!

*(Hurt, Heloise starts to leave. As a kind of pretext, Roger straightens the portrait of Stalin. Heloise walks back over to him and tickles him. Taken by surprise, he jumps, causing the portrait to fall.)*

ROGER: Now that was clever! Comrade Stalin, no less! Are you happy now?! *(He picks up the portrait.)*

HELOISE:   He didn't feel anything, did he?

ROGER:   No, but. . . I'm expecting someone, . . . a very important comrade, . . . and if he finds you here. . . . It's about my nomination for the municipal elections. . . . Last Sunday, Desiré almost caught me! *(He points to the cupboard.)*

HELOISE:   *(sitting down)* You're all the same. As soon as you try to add a little romance. . . . *(She pouts. Roger sees this and sits down next to her.)*

ROGER:   Another time. . . . Are you mad, Heloise? *(She won't answer. He grows more gentle, and sings.)* "Timéla lamelou panpan timéla. . . ."

*(Just as he goes to unbutton Heloise's blouse, several knocks on the door stop him. Enter Leona Chalière, a woman of about fifty, with a severe manner. She carries a large briefcase. As she enters, Roger and Heloise stand up.)*

LEONA:   You are comrade Blot?

ROGER:   Yes.

LEONA:   Leona Chalière from the national committee, official in charge.

ROGER:   Oh?. . . Yes, . . . come in, . . . come in, comrade! I was explaining to Madame Scartini, . . . she's the concierge, . . . . But I was expecting comrade Mazurski, so I'm a little surprised to see you.

*(Leona looks at Heloise with a certain amount of mistrust.)*

LEONA:   Is she a comrade of the cell?

ROGER:   No, she's the concierge, . . . and in fact, . . . we were talking about *Son of the People*, . . . and she was saying some very. . . . *(He sticks a copy of* Son of the People *in Heloise's hands at the same time Leona turns around to take off her coat.)* She brought the mail.

HELOISE: *(to Roger)* Who is this dame?

ROGER: *(pushing her out)* Good,...another time, Madame Scartini,...we'll pick up this discussion another time.

*(Heloise goes out slowly, at once mysterious and menacing, under Leona's cold eye. Pause.)*

ROGER: *(embarrassed)* She's a sort of sympathizer. Sit down, comrade....It's not exactly hot in here, is it?

*(Without answering, Leona walks over to the impressive pile of unsold newspapers. Embarrassed, Roger joins her.)*

ROGER: It makes quite a nice little pile! The fact is, we've gotten a little behind on the newspapers....The whole Committee for the Defense of Humanity came down with this terrible flu....It's very bad this year....The Italian flu, they call it....

*(Leona walks over to some shelves; Roger follows.)*

As for *Son of the People,* we've set ourselves a goal: fifty copies. *(Pause.)* Maybe it was a little ambitious, and we're a little behind on that, too. *(Pause.)* Mind you, we sold one Sunday,... a big one....I mean, a regular copy....

*(Again Leona moves off toward a list stuck to the wall.)*

And that's the list of contributors to Stalin's gift fund. I can't hide the fact that there, too, we're behind the rest of the quarter, behind the whole district....We've gotten off to a slow start, it's true; maybe we were a little too optimistic, and I'm prepared to give a certain self-criticism about it....

*(Pause.)*

LEONA: You know that your cell is the last?

ROGER: In the whole district? *(Pause.)* In Paris?

LEONA: No, the entire country!

ROGER: Oh, really? I'm a little surprised because not long ago, Mazurski. . . .

LEONA: Sit down, Blot!

ROGER: You startled me, Madame.

LEONA: Is that how we address party comrades now—Madame?

ROGER: Not at all. . . . No, it's just that. . ., you see, I thought it was Elie Mazurski who was coming, so I'm a little. . . .

LEONA: Mazurski is no longer a member of our party.

ROGER: Oh? Since when? But he was an exemplary militant, wasn't he?

LEONA: Do you believe the party has made a mistake?

ROGER: No. . . .

LEONA: Now and then it can make an error, Blot, but it never makes a mistake; don't forget that.

ROGER: Mazurski was a veteran of the Spanish Civil War! The resistance. . . . It's a shame, isn't it?

LEONA: The party has decided to be very strict where the private lives of its permanent members are concerned.

ROGER: Oh? And Mazurski?

LEONA: He was a homosexual.

ROGER: No!

LEONA: Does that surprise you?

ROGER: Yes, it does! *(He catches himself.)* A little. . . .

LEONA: Are you questioning the information gathered by the party?

ROGER:   No, but . . . .

LEONA:   Mazurski continued to foster contacts with former comrades in the resistance.

ROGER:   Were they. . .?

LEONA:   *(cutting him off)* Yugoslavs! Are you aware of our party's position on Yugoslavia?

ROGER:   Of course, comrade Chalière.

LEONA:   Did you know comrade Mazurski well?

ROGER:   Yes and no. I mean, we went out together a couple of times. He was a very likable guy. . . .

LEONA:   Precisely! I believe that the comrades from the federation will have some questions to ask you where he is concerned.

ROGER:   *(upset)* Why me? I wasn't the only one who knew him . . . .

LEONA:   You understand that someone who might have had contacts with an agent of Tito cannot be put forward as a candidate in the elections.

*(Roger grows increasingly upset; Leona, increasingly nervous.)*

ROGER:   But comrade, we went to a dance hall together once!

LEONA:   There is one more thing concerning your cell . . . . Read this. *(She hands him a letter.)*

ROGER:   *(reading)* "One of the members of the Elisa Verlet Cell is in liaison with, or rather, 'having a liaison' with, the wife of a policeman. Comrades, is that revolutionary vigilance? An anonymous cuckold." *(Pause.)* What's this?

LEONA:   That's the signature.

ROGER: Where did this come from?

LEONA: It arrived at the federation. You don't know who it might be about?

ROGER: No! Well, I'm flabbergasted!....An anonymous cuckold. ...No, I really don't know!

LEONA: And Mazurski—you're sure you never noticed anything about him either?

ROGER: And the Yugoslavs?

LEONA: No, about his morals!

*(Roger shakes his head no. Leona picks up her briefcase and walks toward the door.)*

ROGER: *(stopping her)* Well, now that you tell me this,...wait, wait....Yes, it seems to me that one time..., oh, yes, I'm sure of it....Once while I was at the federal school, he asked me if I was married....I told him no....And then, I'm sure he had this...this sort of smile in his eyes....And then he was always a little too....No, when it comes right down to it, what you're telling me doesn't surprise me at all! *(Pause.)* Do you think my nomination to the municipal elections is in jeopardy?

*(Before Leona can respond, Heloise comes out of her lodge singing. "Timela lamelou...." Roger plasters himself up against the door. Heloise hangs out her underwear.)*

LEONA: What does your concierge's husband do?

ROGER: *(panic-stricken)* I don't know....I think he changes jobs a lot,...but even if he were a policeman, Monsieur Scartini would look phoney....What I mean to say is, he wouldn't look like a policeman...even with a uniform, I'm sure....

*(Heloise goes back into her lodge.)*

LEONA:   Listen to me, comrade. The struggle is planetary in scale, but it takes place on our simple local level. Everything conspires to try and make us falter, like Tito, into the warmongers' camp led by imperialism. But the one who consorts with the concierge is most certainly an agent paid by the Intelligence Service to infiltrate first your cell and then the entire party!

ROGER:   Do you . . . have any suspicions?

LEONA:   Do you?

ROGER:   There aren't many of us; they're almost all old militants, faithful, devoted, quiet . . . .

LEONA:   Listen carefully, Blot. You haven't sold one copy of *Son of the People* since it was published. Haven't added a single new member in three years. You sell two newspapers in a week and what's more, now your cell threatens the security of the entire party! *(Her voice rises.)*

ROGER:   Mazurski had told me . . . .

LEONA:   *(shouting)* Mazurski is no longer one of us!

ROGER:   I forgot . . . .

LEONA:   And what about Stalin's present, hunh? For months now, from all over France, gifts have come to us for the seventieth birthday of our inspired leader. And you, where is yours?

ROGER:   We had a model, made out of matchsticks, . . . but it disappeared . . . .

LEONA:   And you don't find that strange? Comrade Blot, the train taking the presents from the people of France is leaving in a few days for Moscow. We must have results, new members, presents and a name! Otherwise your nomination and your rise through the ranks of the party will go up in smoke!

ROGER:   Mazurski assured me . . . .

LEONA:   We must fight, Blot! Do not forget that we are the great party of the workers, . . .the heirs of the revolutionaries of '89, of the Commune, of the Uprising in Beziers, of the revolutionaries of the 17th! "Hail, hail to you. . . ." Come, sing with me, Blot. *(She sings.)*
". . .Brave soldiers of the 17th,
Hail, hail to you,
To your great deeds. . . ."

*(Roger begins to sing, then starts to run helter skelter, gesturing to Leona to be quiet. Shooting out of her lodge like a cannonball, Heloise responds to what she believes is the signal, and bursts into the cell office singing, "Timela lamelou panpan timela." Roger has just enough time to push her outside. Leona, at the height of exaltation, takes a bag of candy out of her pocket and swallows one or two pieces.)*

LEONA:   *(collecting herself)* I read in your biography that you work at the city morgue?

ROGER:   Hunh? Yes, it's not as strenuous; I was a mover before.

LEONA:   And you wouldn't like to become a party official?

ROGER:   Yes, of course!

LEONA:   Very well, then, . . .you know what you must do!

ROGER:   You don't know who wrote the anonymous letter? No, of course you don't, how stupid of me!. . .

LEONA:   You're having a meeting in a little while?

ROGER:   A meeting? Yes. . . .Won't you stay?

LEONA:   Do you have any objections?

ROGER:   No, not at all, . . .since it's a small meeting. . . .

LEONA:   Don't worry, I won't intervene. You see, I enjoy being an observer. *(She takes another piece of candy.)*

ROGER: Are those aspirin you're taking?

LEONA: No, "gummy bears.". . . I also have some strawberry chews. Every now and then, it's difficult to fight for the party. The nerves take a beating. Would you like a "gummy bear"?

ROGER: No, thank you. . . . Don't you want. . .wouldn't you rather go home and rest?

*(There is knocking at the door. Roger goes to open it. Jean Louis enters, arms loaded with logs.)*

JEAN LOUIS: Hello! I'm a little early. We cleaned out a cellar this afternoon and I salvaged a little wood for you.

ROGER: I'd like you to meet Leona Chalière, a party official, . . .important. . . .

JEAN LOUIS: Nice to meet you! *(He introduces himself.)* Jean Louis Sélavy.

*(They shake hands.)*

ROGER: Our friend here is one of the cell's sympathizers. He's interested in our politics.

JEAN LOUIS: Josyane's not here yet?

ROGER: Not yet.

*(Pause.)*

JEAN LOUIS: I'm going to get a little fire started for you.

ROGER: It's not exactly hot in here!

JEAN LOUIS: Hey, make sure I don't burn anything important now! Let's see here. . . . *(He grabs a poster and reads it.)* "Men, Women All! To the Union Hall for the seventieth birthday of Comrade Stalin!". . .Is this okay?

*(Roger rushes over and tears the poster out of his hands.)*

ROGER: No....Yes....We were going to put them up on Sunday and then something came up and I couldn't make it,...and Josyane wasn't able....

JEAN LOUIS: She was at the movies. That's where we met. We saw *The Happy Peasants*..., no,...*The Joyous Collective Farm*....

ROGER: *(to Leona)* As for the posters, don't worry; we'll get them up. *(He puts down the poster under the disapproving gaze of Leona. He points to Jean Louis.)* He bought a copy of *Son of the People* from us!

JEAN LOUIS: Yes, I even started reading it.

ROGER: *(overjoyed)* And?

JEAN LOUIS: It's not exactly light reading....

*(He laughs under Leona's chilly gaze. She nervously swallows a "gummy bear.")*

ROGER: He pitched in for the present, too!

JEAN LOUIS: By the way, there was a guy at the flea market who talked to me about this thing for Stalin....

*(Marcel Feuillard, a scrawny little man about thirty years old, enters. He stutters and speaks with the accent from the Midi.)*

MARCEL: Greetings, gentlemen...and others! *(He laughs, then, belatedly, notices Leona Chalière.)* Oh, there *are* others! My mistake!

ROGER: *(forcing a laugh)* Marcel, you old devil! Comrade Chalière from the federation, whom you must know.... Monsieur Sélavy,...sympathizer.

MARCEL: *(to Jean Louis)* Ah, yes, bravo!... *(He addresses Leona.)* Isn't it Mazurski who usually represents the federation?

ROGER: *(embarrassed)* Yes. . . . No,. . . he's not anymore. . . . Now it's comrade Chalière.

MARCEL: Great fun, Mazurski, especially with the ladies! I knew him during the war; you had to fight them off!

ROGER: *(nervous, walking over to Marcel)* Right, that's just fine,. . . since we told you he's not here. . . . Naturally the others are late, as usual!

MARCEL: *(to Leona)* Mazurski's not sick, is he?

LEONA: No.

JEAN LOUIS: *(to Roger)* Are you sure Josyane's coming?

ROGER: How am I supposed to know!

MARCEL: *(upset, to Jean Louis)* Oh! You know Josyane?

JEAN LOUIS: Yes, a little. . . . She's the one who invited me to your meeting.

MARCEL: Oh, good, you know her a little. . . . I've known Josyane for a long time. . . . She's a very good friend of mine.

ROGER: *(to Leona)* Marcel is okay,. . . a good egg!

MARCEL: *(to Jean Louis)* I'll help you with the fire! *(He grabs up the poster announcing the meeting marking Stalin's seventieth birthday.)*

ROGER: *(to Leona)* You'd never believe it to hear him like this, but he really is very capable.

*(Marcel tears up the poster. Leona glowers at him.)*

ROGER: *(exploding)* What the hell are they doing, damn it!

MARCEL: Hey, Roger! Take it easy. . . . Usually *you're* the one who's always late. *(He addresses Jean Louis.)* It's a nice little cell we've got here,. . . cushy.

ROGER: Precisely, and maybe that will have to change! Do you think our class enemies are soft? The stakes of our struggle are world peace, pure and simple. . . . Did you remember to bring my bike clips?

MARCEL: Damn! I even put a string on my finger!

ROGER: Bravo, and thank you very much. That'll be nice when I show up at work with clothespins on my pants.

MARCEL: Well, your clients aren't going to complain! Roger works with stiffs!

*(He laughs. Josyane enters.)*

JOSYANE: Hi, everybody!

MARCEL: *(singing)* "Hail, hail to you . . . ."

ROGER: Enough!

MARCEL: ". . . brave soldiers of the 17th . . . ."

*(Heloise ventures a few steps out of her lodge, but, definitely more cautious this time, stops. Roger, frightened, explodes again.)*

ROGER: Enough!

MARCEL: This is something new. . . . The party doesn't allow singing anymore?

ROGER: Yes. . . . No. . . . Yes. . . . I mean, not now.

JOSYANE: Has anyone seen my glasses?

*(Suzanne Lalande, a schoolteacher of about forty, enters. She's carrying several sacks.)*

SUZANNE: Hi!

JEAN LOUIS: *(to Josyane)* Hello.

JOSYANE: Oh, so you came.

JEAN LOUIS:   Are you glad?

JOSYANE:   Yes!

SUZANNE:   It's as disgusting as ever in here!

MARCEL:   Am I imagining it, or does it smell funny?

SUZANNE:   *(picking up an ashtray, which she empties out the window)* It's your cigarette butts!

JOSYANE:   No, it's a different smell.

ROGER:   Comrades....

*(No one listens to him.)*

JEAN LOUIS:   I brought some wood.

JOSYANE:   That's terribly nice of you.

ROGER:   Comrades,...today we have the pleasure of welcoming....

*(Suzanne, who has come back with a broom, begins cleaning house.)*

That's enough now, Suzanne!

SUZANNE:   You may not mind filth, but I....

MARCEL:   Don't I get a kiss, Josyane?

JOSYANE:   Yes, of course.

*(They kiss each other on the cheek. No one pays attention to Leona, who remains sitting off to the side.)*

ROGER:   Comrades,...I would like you to meet Leona Chalière from the federation, who has come to observe our cell,.... *(He catches himself.)* No, I mean, who has come to pay us a visit....

*(Pause. Handshakes all around.)*

Well, now, I believe we can start the meeting.

JOSYANE: Jean Louis, give me a hand.

*(They set about getting the table top on the trestles and arranging the chairs.)*

MARCEL: Suzanne, you still haven't given me a kiss!

SUZANNE: Listen, Marcel, I told you that in the party, if we're less formal with each other out of a sense of fraternity, we're not here to be slobbering on each other's face all the time, right?

MARCEL: At Bissos, in my old cell, everybody kissed everybody. Bissos is in the South, near Bordeaux.

JEAN LOUIS: While we're on the subject, Josyane, why don't we do like they do in Bissos?

*(He gives her a kiss. Embarrassed, she pulls away. Marcel doesn't appreciate it; Suzanne looks at Marcel and laughs.)*

MARCEL: Suzanne, I find the woman in you a little too strict. I'm not talking about the militant, . . . from my point of view the militant is flawless, . . . but the woman, I'm sorry. . . .

ROGER: *(to Marcel)* Are you finished? You're not going to join us, comrade?·

*(Leona shakes her head no.)*

You're better over there? . . . Fine. . . .

*(Roger sits down, then Josyane. Marcel tries to sit next to her, but Jean Louis, quicker, sits there.)*

ROGER: Comrade Chalière from the federation has come, . . . in part, . . . to see . . . how we're functioning: . . . .our sales, . . . circulation, . . . our political lives, . . . our private. . . .

*(Marcel, who has gone around to the other side of Josyane, seated at the end of the bench, tries to squeeze in next to her. Roger watches.)*

What in the hell are you doing? Are you going to sit down or not, damn it!

MARCEL:   I usually sit next to Josyane.

ROGER:   Josyane. . . .

JOSYANE:   It's better if I'm next to Jean Louis. If there's something he doesn't understand, I can explain. . . .

MARCEL:   But he could sit on one side and I could sit on the other!

SUZANNE:   Poor Feuillard! How old are you? *(She addresses Leona.)* He reminds me of my fourth graders. Marcel, sit down!

MARCEL:   You see how you are, Suzanne! As a militant, flawless, . . . no complaints, . . . but as a person you're hard; I'm telling you this like a brother.

ROGER:   Marcel, sit down right now!

MARCEL:   I'm sorry, Roger. Go ahead.

ROGER:   Comrades, . . .

MARCEL:   *(interrupting)* It's not that I absolutely have to sit next to Josyane, but that's usually my place. . . . *(He finishes by calling Leona to witness.)*

SUZANNE:   Okay, let's get going!

ROGER:   Thank you, Suzanne. Okay, . . .

JOSYANE:   This smell is very strange. . .

SUZANNE:   My *kügelvath* won't be warm anymore if this drags on too long!

*(General restlessness. Pause.)*

MARCEL:   You made a cake?

SUZANNE:  Yes.

 *(Pause.)*

JOSYANE:  Is it the recipe that was in *French-Hungarian Friendship?*

SUZANNE:  Yes.... I thought I'd try it out. They say it should be eaten warm. You can go ahead, Roger.

ROGER:  Comrades, ....

JOSYANE:  *(to Leona)* Suzanne is the queen of cakes!

MARCEL:  *(to Leona)* Especially socialist cakes.... Recipes that come from popular democracies, well,.... *(He turns to Jean Louis.)* they're often peculiar....

JEAN LOUIS:  My mother's specialty is custard tarts with plums!

SUZANNE:  That's exactly what *kügelvath* is, a kind of custard tart, only Hungarian! It has a noodle and yogurt base. But the secret is measuring out the *chiklov*.... That's the cheese they use.... It's sort of like cream cheese,... soft, but pungent.... Oh, what a smell!

JOSYANE:  Oh, so that's what I smell!

SUZANNE:  Yes, it's musky-smelling.

 *(Pause.)*

MARCEL:  What are we waiting for?

ROGER:  May I go on?

SUZANNE:  We're waiting for you, old boy!

ROGER:  Thank you! *(He reads.)* My dear comrades, our cell is sick.... And when one cell is sick....

ROGER, SUZANNE, JOSYANE and MARCEL:    *(finishing the phrase)*
The whole party sneezes!

*(Pause. Roger, taken aback, looks at Leona.)*

ROGER:    *(starting up again)* At this time, as the class struggle
intensifies day by day, we must respond swiftly and vigorously.
It is true, comrades, that for several months now, we have
fallen behind, despite the presence of a sympathizer among
us this evening. . . .

*(Obviously trying to be as discreet as possible, Marcel gets up.)*

ROGER:    *(continuing)* The first indication of a possible renewal
of our cell. . . .

MARCEL:    *(to Roger, softly)* Don't mind me.

SUZANNE:    *(under her breath)* You should have thought about
it before!

ROGER:    We must commit ourselves to a serious self-criticism. . . .

SUZANNE:    *(to Marcel)* Use some old leaflets!

*(Marcel goes out into the courtyard and disappears into the W.C.)*

ROGER:    *(still reading)* The workers, democrats and partisans
of peace in France and throughout the world will soon enthu-
siastically celebrate, on the twenty-first of December, the
seventieth anniversary of the birth of our beloved and great
comrade Stalin. . . .

*(From the W.C. we hear the sound of a toilet flushing; then Marcel
reappears. Heloise comes out of her lodge. Her radio can be heard
playing. An exchange takes place between Heloise and Marcel as Roger's
voice tries to rise above the ruckus.)*

HELOISE: Did you use the little brush?

MARCEL: Didn't need it. . . .

HELOISE: According to you, it never needs it, and that means I'm the one who always gets stuck doing it!

MARCEL: What's Desiré up to?

HELOISE: Blowing his whistle! Did you find your present?

*(At a sign from Josyane, Jean Louis gets up and goes outside.)*

JEAN LOUIS: Shh! Keep it down!

HELOISE: *(to Marcel, pointing to Jean Louis)* Who's that one? He's cute!

MARCEL: A sympathizer, . . . weisenheimer.

HELOISE: Good old Feuillard!

ROGER: *(reading)* All those who suffer, all those who hope, all those who struggle turn with a strong surge of affection and gratitude toward their friend, their educator, their leader, their inspiration: Josef Stalin. . . .

Thousands of French men and women have already written moving letters and sent gifts to Stalin for his seventieth birthday.

What are we waiting for?

*(After whispering something in Suzanne's ear, Josyane gets up next and goes as far as the door.)*

JOSYANE: Shhh!

*(They all walk back to their places on tiptoe. Roger has terminated his speech with a shout. All look at him in silence. Pause.)*

MARCEL: Go on, Roger!

ROGER: *(exhausted)* I'm finished!

MARCEL:   I ran into Madame Scartini. . . .

*(Leona gets up and takes another bag of candy out of her briefcase. She gobbles up a fistful.)*

ROGER:   Right. . . . So we've got to find a gift!

MARCEL:   Am I right that somebody misplaced Old Man Grospierre's model of Notre Dame?

ROGER:   Yes, well. . . it's disappeared. It's strange, isn't it? Bizarre, even, . . . as if someone in this cell wanted to sabotage our action! As if someone wanted to prevent us from participating in the celebration of Stalin's birthday. There's no other explanation!

*(He gives Leona a knowing look.)*

MARCEL:   Why?

ROGER:   Why what?

MARCEL:   Who do you think would be upset by our offering Stalin a matchstick model of Notre Dame?

ROGER:   Don't be naive! Marcel!

SUZANNE:   I was against it in the first place. Offering comrade Stalin a reproduction of Notre Dame. . . . No, no, I'm sorry. . . .

JOSYANE:   We'll find something else.

MARCEL:   Nevertheless, it *was* a masterpiece. . . .

*(Suzanne shrugs her shoulders in exasperation.)*

Made of matchsticks, but a masterpiece. *(He turns to Jean Louis.)* Old Man Grospierre really went all out.

ROGER:   Every day our newspaper publishes the list of gifts given by our people to Stalin. *(He reads.)* "An old man from Cantal gives his cane; a Catholic, the rosary beads on which he prayed during the war for the victory of the Red Army; from the north, a group of women is sending him slippers embroidered with his initials." And us?

*(A pause.)*

JOSYANE: What about one of the raffle prizes?

SUZANNE: We're not going to send him a kilo of sugar!

MARCEL: What about a tie?

SUZANNE: He doesn't wear them. Comrade Stalin always wears a pea coat.

*(A pause. Leona starts to gather her things.)*

JOSYANE: It's not that easy. . . .

JEAN LOUIS: When you don't know a person's tastes. . . .

*(Leona stands up and walks toward the door. Roger stops her.)*

ROGER: Don't worry, comrade, we'll find something. *(He has her sit back down.)*

SUZANNE: We need something useful. Oh, brother,. . .what would someone who lives in a cold country. . .where it's freezing. . .? Don't you see?

MARCEL: Ice skates?

JEAN LOUIS: This guy at the flea market talked to me about something. . . .

*(No one listens to him.)*

SUZANNE: It's a good thing I'm here! *(She stands up and takes from her bag an immense, loud sweater on which, in bright, canary yellow relief, is the inscription "For Joseph Stalin, the Elisa Verlet Cell.")* Voila!

*(There is a moment of stupefaction.)*

JOSYANE:   What is that?

SUZANNE:   It's entirely handmade!

JOSYANE:   Isn't this a design that was in the last issue of *French-Bulgarian Friendship?*

SUZANNE:   Yes,...but I added a few ideas of my own! Do you like it?

*(Pause.)*

ROGER:   *(to Leona)* Do you think it'll fit him?

MARCEL:   I think I'm nearly the same size as Stalin; I read it in one of the papers.

JOSYANE:   He's bigger than you across the shoulders. *(She turns to Jean Louis.)* What do you think?

JEAN LOUIS:   The colors are pretty bright!

ROGER:   Maybe a little too, don't you think?

SUZANNE:   That's what's being done now! It's very fashionable! And for a gift from Paris, it's the least we can do. And it's warm, besides!

ROGER:   *(to Leona)* What do you think of it, comrade?

LEONA:   *(wearily)* I don't know. I don't know anymore!

JEAN LOUIS:   You'd have to see it on him. You can't really tell like this.

ROGER:   Marcel, put it on!

MARCEL:   Okay! I'm almost, I said, almost the same size as the Marshallissimo. *(With help from Suzanne, he puts on the sweater.)*

SUZANNE: Pull it down, here.... Try hard, Marcel. *(The sweater is two times too big for Marcel: his hands are no longer visible; it goes all the way down to his knees.)* Naturally, on Feuillard, it's not going to hang right.

MARCEL: You see how you are, Suzanne:...as a militant, flawless,...but as a woman, sometimes, you're hard....

JEAN LOUIS: It just has to be taken in a little...here and there. And the whole thing needs to be shortened!

JOSYANE: This design is meant to be full, isn't it?

SUZANNE: Yes! This is the indoor style, and I combined it with the sport version. *(She plants a curious-looking baby bonnet on Marcel's head. On it are embroidered a hammer and sickle.)* For skiing!

JOSYANE: That's not the same pattern!

SUZANNE: No; I got the bonnet out of *Your Layette.* This way is better, I think.

ROGER: *(groping)* There's something.... I don't know what it is....

*(With difficulty, Leona stands up. She looks very, very tired.)*

ROGER: *(servile)* With your experience, comrade, I'm sure you can tell us what it is that's not quite right.

SUZANNE: It's pure wool!

LEONA: I don't know what I.... My head is spinning....

JOSYANE: Maybe you're hungry?

ROGER: Of course.... Did you eat before you came?

LEONA: No, but I don't think it's that....

ROGER: Maybe it's the "gummy bears"?

MARCEL: *(still in costume)* Do I look all right?

LEONA: Yes, but for Stalin, I'm not sure. . . .

ROGER: Sit down, comrade. *(He addresses the others.)* I'm sure she'll feel better if she has something to eat.

SUZANNE: My cake! That's what she needs! Don't move!

MARCEL: It's just the pick-me-up she needs!

*(Suzanne takes a strange object out of a tea towel, a cake the colors of which are a little like those of the sweater.)*

ROGER: Did you knit it with the same wool?

SUZANNE: *(cutting her cake)* Go on, laugh it up! Our comrade here is in for a treat!

JOSYANE: *(walking away)* I already ate. . . .

MARCEL: *(to Jean Louis)* Suzanne's cakes are good, but a little peculiar.

SUZANNE: *(to Leona)* Help yourself! *(She offers Leona the plate, but Roger grabs it.)*

ROGER: *(to Jean Louis)* Sympathizers first!

*(Jean Louis, surprised, hesitates to take the first piece.)*

JEAN LOUIS: The lady first!

*(Roger slaps a piece of cake in his hands. Suzanne takes back her plate and walks over to Leona who, visibly hungry, helps herself.)*

SUZANNE: *(to Leona)* Enjoy!

JOSYANE: *(softly, to Jean Louis)* Take little bites; it'll go down easier. . . .

*(All stare at Jean Louis, except Suzanne, who watches with pleasure as Leona eats hungrily.)*

ROGER:   She was hungry!

JOSYANE:   *(to Jean Louis)* Are you all right?

JEAN LOUIS:   Yes. . . . It's very peculiar. . . . It's a little like the sweater; there's just something about it that's not quite right. . . .

*(Suzanne turns toward him. His tone changes to one of flattery.)*

But still, it's not your ordinary taste. . . . I have a feeling it'll be hard to forget!

*(Suzanne, pleased, goes back over to Leona. Josyane takes the opportunity to grab the cake from Jean Louis' hands and hide it behind her back. Suzanne walks back over to Jean Louis and gives him another piece, which he doesn't dare refuse.)*

SUZANNE:   Go ahead; there's plenty more. . . .

MARCEL:   *(aside, to Josyane)* And people wonder why we can't get new members!

JEAN LOUIS:   I think my eyes were bigger than my stomach. I think I'll save some for tomorrow. . . I'm sure it'll be good for breakfast.

SUZANNE:   What in the world do you mean! Will you finish that? I'll wrap some up for you to take home.

JEAN LOUIS:   How nice.

*(Leona is looking strange: pale, wide-eyed and staring.)*

MARCEL:   All this and we still haven't come up with a present for Stalin!

SUZANNE:   *(surprised)* What do you mean, we don't have a present? You don't like my ensemble? *(She seems distressed.)*

ROGER:   It's not that, Suzanne. . . .

MARCEL:   It's not that it isn't nice. . . .

JOSYANE:  It's just that, considering Comrade Stalin's personality. . . .

SUZANNE:  He's being given embroidered slippers!

JEAN LOUIS:  A guy at the flea market offered me a bronze sculpture. *(No one listens.)* He says it was a present to Lenin in 1910. . . .

*(Slowly, everyone turns toward him.)*

. . .when he was in exile in Paris. It's called "The Effort," and on the bottom there's an inscription in Russian.

*(All stare at him in silence except Leona, who seems to be getting worse.)*

That's no good? I mean, I said I wasn't sure you'd be interested.

ROGER:  A bronze sculpture?

JOSYANE:  That belonged to Lenin?

MARCEL:  That's fantastic!

SUZANNE:  It must cost a fortune!

JEAN LOUIS:  No. Sam, that's my friend, seemed so happy when I told him about your trying to find a present for Stalin that he told me he was ready to give it to you.

*(A pause.)*

ROGER:  Now, that's what I call a present!

JOSYANE:  Surely he's a sympathizer.

JEAN LOUIS:  I don't know. His name's Sam. He's this funny guy with a foreign accent.

MARCEL:  Accents don't mean anything. With a coup like that, our cell will be famous!

SUZANNE:   I'm sure Stalin would rather have a sweater.

ROGER:   Now I do believe I've got my nomination for the city elections! Eh, comrade Chalière?

*(Leona is quiet, eyes half-closed.)*

JEAN LOUIS:   It doesn't look like the *kügelvath* went down very well.

ROGER:   Just think of it, comrade! Something that belonged to Lenin! No one can top that!

*(Leona remains quiet. Suzanne consults a notebook.)*

SUZANNE:   *(bursts out laughing)* I made a mistake!

JEAN LOUIS:   We were supposed to eat the sweater!

MARCEL:   You want me to wear the cake, too?!

SUZANNE:   No! The recipe for the cake isn't Hungarian....

ROGER:   That doesn't explain everything!

SUZANNE:   It comes from Bosnia.

MARCEL:   And Bosnia isn't in Hungary?

JEAN LOUIS:   No, Yugoslavia.

*(Leona lets out a little cry, then dashes into the courtyard toward the W.C., into which she disappears. They all watch, stunned.)*

MARCEL:   Overwork, it's what kills party officials!

SUZANNE:   You'll have to be careful, Roger.

*(Leona, quite pale, emerges from the W.C. and leans against the door as Heloise appears at her window.)*

HELOISE:   You too! And who's supposed to clean up in there?

*(Blackout.)*

## ACT THREE

*(Same set. In the office, Roger is seated, busy reading* Paris-Hollywood, *a 1940s girlie magazine, which he hides in a copy of* L'Humanité. *A voice rises, but it is hard to tell where it is coming from.)*

VOICE: *(offstage)*
"Hail, hail to you,
Brave soldiers of the 17th...."

*(Heloise comes out of her lodge singing and walks across the courtyard to the office of the cell.)*

HELOISE:
"Hail, brave soldier boys,
You are admired and loved by all...."

*(At the same time, we see Roger shutting himself in the cupboard after throwing his magazine away, as Heloise is stopped by Desiré, who emerges unexpectedly from the W.C.)*

DESIRÉ: *(mockingly)* "Timela lamelou panpan timela...."

HELOISE: If you think you scare me, Desiré.... In the first place, I know everything! You have no shame! Signing it "an anonymous cuckold" was not too bright, even for a cop! *(She goes back inside.)*

*(Josyane appears in the courtyard carrying a bucket of glue, a brush and rolls of posters under her arm. She is dressed in old, glue-stained clothes.)*

JOSYANE: Hello, Monsieur Scartini! *(She tries to open the door to the office.)*

DESIRÉ: Here, let me help you.

JOSYANE: Thanks.... I still haven't found my glasses....

DESIRÉ: Oh! You've got a little spot...right...here....

*(He tries to scratch at a spot on Josyane's pants up on the buttocks.)*

JOSYANE: It's nothing.... Leave it, Monsieur Scartini!

DESIRÉ: If you rub it a little.... Hold on!

JOSYANE: These pants are old. Leave it....

HELOISE: *(from her window)* Can I give you a hand, Desiré?
*(He splutters out a response.)*

JOSYANE: Hello, Madame Scartini.... I've got a stain....

*(Marcel enters, carrying a rather bulky package. He seems quite cheerful.)*

MARCEL: Ladies, gentlemen!

JOSYANE: Did you get it?

MARCEL: Fantastic!

JOSYANE: *(to Desiré)* We finally found a present for Stalin!

*(They enter the office.)*

DESIRÉ: Lucky Stalin!... *(He leaves.)*

HELOISE: *(closing her window)* Yeah, but not as lucky as you!

MARCEL: *(to Josyane)* What are the posters you were putting up?

JOSYANE: The ones for the meeting at the union hall.

*(She opens the armoire to put away her materials without seeing Roger hidden inside. Marcel picks up the magazine still lying on the floor.)*

MARCEL: *Paris-Hollywood*.... What's this?

*(Roger comes out of the cupboard and snatches the magazine from his hands without Josyane seeing.)*

ROGER: Nothing.... A new weekly,... *French-American Friendship*....

JOSYANE: Were you in there?

ROGER: Yes; I was thinking. . . .

*(Roger surreptitiously throws the magazine into the courtyard, as Marcel begins unwrapping his package. Désiré enters. He is the next to come upon the magazine, hides it under his pea coat and goes back into the lodge. Marcel shows Josyane and Roger the bronze sculpture, which is now unwrapped: It shows a worker pushing against a mass, in the purest turn-of-the-century style.)*

MARCEL: Look at this marvel!

JOSYANE: It's so beautiful!

ROGER: There wasn't any problem?

MARCEL: None! Jean Louis' friend — very nice. He gave it to me — just like that!

ROGER: Suzanne wasn't with you?

MARCEL: Yes! But she went to ask her friend Josette to translate the Russian inscription, right here. . . . She could make out "Lenin," here, . . . but the rest. . . .

ROGER: It's still terrific!

JOSYANE: This is all thanks to Jean Louis!

*(She starts to change her clothes. Roger and Marcel turn around.)*

ROGER: Really a nice guy!

JOSYANE: Yes, I *do* like him!

ROGER: Good! Make the most of it and get him to join.

JOSYANE: We don't know each other that well yet. . . . We're supposed to go out together one of these nights.

MARCEL: Josyane, you haven't forgotten that you promised you'd go dancing with me next Sunday, have you?

JOSYANE: Why, no, Marcel, I haven't forgotten. . . . But weren't you supposed to go on a trip with people from work?

MARCEL: Yes, but I cancelled. Hey, Roger, you know where my fellow workers are going? Actually. . . a small delegation? Guess! Can't you guess?

JOSYANE: No.

ROGER: Go on!

MARCEL: To the U.S.S.R. At the invitation of the Union of Soviet Steelworkers. I was supposed to go with them.

ROGER: And you're not going?

MARCEL: No, it's not for me. I have my dog to look after, . . . and my mother, who can't go downstairs anymore to do her errands. . . .

JOSYANE: We could have done them for her!

MARCEL: You're sweet, Josyane. . . And ever since you promised to go dancing with me. . . . Now that it's almost Sunday, I won't miss out!

JOSYANE: You know, they must dance in Moscow too, don't they, Roger?

ROGER: You bet, . . . and with the birthday celebration!

MARCEL: It's not the same. Besides, I don't know their dances.

ROGER: Fine, forget about it; we have to get our present to the exhibition.

JOSYANE: It could use a little cleaning up.

ROGER: I'll help you.

(*Roger takes the sculpture, Josyane, a basin, out into the courtyard. Marcel follows.*)

MARCEL:   Nah,...and then, I never did like traveling....
You know, even last year, when I went to Dieppe with the
people from work,... I was a little sorry I did,... and disappointed....Compared to photographs,...there isn't that
much to see.

ROGER:   With a present like this, if I'm not nominated for
the elections!.... An official in the French Communist Party!

MARCEL:   You won't miss the old caskets, eh, Roger?

ROGER:   You can say that again!

JOSYANE:   *(to Marcel)* Jean Louis' friend didn't tell you how it
was that he had it?

MARCEL:   Sam? He must have found it in some attic or cellar.

*(Suzanne enters, very upset. She's carrying several bags.)*

SUZANNE:   Some comrades have lost their minds!

ROGER:   What do you mean?

SUZANNE:   They just pasted up a whole wall of posters for the
meeting at the union hall—upside down!

ROGER:   They must be blind!

*(Josyane forces a laugh. Suzanne goes inside to put down her bags.)*

ROGER:   Unless it was intentional! There are provocateurs
everywhere, even in the party!

SUZANNE:   *(going back out into the courtyard)* In a way, it's funny....
From a distance, upside down, it looks as if they're written
in Russian.

JOSYANE:   *(timidly)* So it's not so bad....

SUZANNE:   No one will understand a word! If you have to
stand on your head to read our posters, we're nowhere near
ready for socialism, that's what I say! *(She goes back into the office.)*

MARCEL:   By the way, the inscription....?

SUZANNE:   Oh, here it is! Josette translated it for me. *(She takes a notebook from her purse.)*

ROGER:   Was it really given to Lenin?

SUZANNE:   *(coming into the courtyard)* No question! Let's see here.... Did you know that Lenin lived in this neighborhood?

JOSYANE:   No kidding!

ROGER:   You didn't know that?

MARCEL:   There's a plaque in the Rue Marie Rose. Before that, he lived in the Rue Beaunier,... nearby,... but he had a falling out with his concierge.

SUZANNE:   All the Russian revolutionaries lived in this neighborhood before 1917.... Josette could go on forever about it.

ROGER:   What does the inscription say?

SUZANNE:   Oh, yes.... Let's see.... Oops!... That was a new cake recipe that was in *France-China*.... Josette tried it....

   *(Roger makes a sign to her to stop.)*

   What did I do with that other piece of paper? *(She goes back into the office.)*

ROGER:   Well?

SUZANNE:   *(digging through her purse)* It's here, it's here....

HELOISE:   *(offstage)* Tell me it's not true, Desiré.... That's the last straw! *(*Paris-Hollywood, *thrown by Heloise, flies out the window and lands at Josyane's feet.)*

DESIRÉ:   *(offstage)* I'm telling you, it's not mine!

HELOISE:   *(offstage)* At your age!

*(Josyane picks up the magazine.)*

JOSYANE:   What's this?

*(Roger snatches it from her and sticks it in Marcel's hands, to Marcel's surprise.)*

ROGER:   It's Marcel's. . . . So, do we get the translation today or tomorrow?

*(Suzanne rejoins them in the courtyard.)*

SUZANNE:   Found it! So, it reads, "Long live Comrade Ulianov."
. . . Ulianov was his real name; Lenin was a pseudonym.

ROGER:   We know that!

JOSYANE:   I didn't know that. Did you know that, Marcel?

MARCEL:   No.

SUZANNE:   See! So, "Long live Comrade Ulianov-Lenin on his Fortieth Birthday, Paris 1910." And it's signed, "Apfelbaum, Bronstein and Rosenfeld."

*(Pause.)*

JOSYANE:   Who are they?

SUZANNE:   Apfelbaum, Bronstein and Rosenfeld? I don't know.

*(Pause.)*

MARCEL:   Those aren't Russian names!

ROGER:   No, they're more like German names.

JOSYANE:   Is that bad?

ROGER:   I don't know, . . . but with Germany's present rearmament campaign. . . .

SUZANNE:   Those are Jewish names, typical Jewish names. According to Josette, they were shopkeepers in the neighborhood.

MARCEL:   There's that furrier in the Rue Dareau who's named Rosenfeld; he takes the Sunday edition of *L'Humanité* sometimes.

ROGER:   It can't be him; he was too young in 1910.

JOSYANE:   Maybe it was his father.

SUZANNE:   What does it matter? What we know for sure is that it really was Lenin who received it!

ROGER:   We'll include a letter with it.

*(Roger takes the sculpture and, followed by Suzanne, returns to the office. Josyane walks over to Marcel, who's still holding* Paris-Hollywood.*)*

JOSYANE:   *(shocked)* Are you the one who's reading this, Marcel?

MARCEL:   No; it's a new weekly. . . .

JOSYANE:   Bravo!

*(Josyane and Marcel enter the office in turn.)*

MARCEL:   But, . . . I'm not the one reading it!

*(Suzanne has set a bag next to the sculpture.)*

ROGER:   What's that?

SUZANNE:   A little surprise, . . . a little extra!

ROGER:   What is it?

SUZANNE:   It's my own personal gift.

*(They seem disturbed.)*

Listen, write your letter and don't worry about it!

JOSYANE:   It's not a new sweater design, is it?

SUZANNE:  No. . . .

*(Brief pause. Suzanne unwraps her package.)*

SUZANNE:  It's the same one, which I've improved!

*(It is indeed the same awful pullover, to which she has added a few little tufts of fur around the collar and cuffs. There is a stupefied pause.)*

It has an entirely different look with the fur, doesn't it?

*(Pause.)*

MARCEL:  *(upset)* You didn't make a cake?

SUZANNE:  Yes, I did! You want a taste?

*(Before anyone can answer, Leona Chalière enters the room.)*

LEONA:  Good day, comrades!

ROGER:  Hello! *(He points to the statue.)* Have you seen the marvel?

MARCEL:  It was some shopkeepers in this neighborhood who gave it to Lenin for his fortieth birthday.

JOSYANE:  It's beautiful, isn't it?

SUZANNE:  *(showing her sweater)* And this is personal. . . .Would you like to taste my cake, comrade?

LEONA:  No,. . .thank you. Bravo to all of you! "Gummy bear"?

*(She offers them a bag of candy. All help themselves except Suzanne, who, annoyed, folds her pullover.)*

ROGER:  Not to brag, comrade, but there can't be many gifts at the exhibition as valuable as this.

LEONA:  No, it. . . .

*(Pause. They all seem surprised by her lack of enthusiasm.)*

JOSYANE:   Even the tea service that belonged to Marx. . . .

MARCEL:   In the first place, there's no proof. . . .

ROGER:   We, it's written on it. . .Lenin,. . .right here!

JOSYANE:   A bronze sculpture!

SUZANNE:   Plus an article of high fashion and a confection!

ROGER:   Honestly, there can't be many cells giving presents like these, can there?

*(Pause.)*

LEONA:   No! But what they all have over yours is that their gifts, however small they may be, will in fact arrive in Moscow!

*(Pause.)*

MARCEL:   And ours, why wouldn't it arrive?

LEONA:   Because the last truck in the convoy taking the presents for comrade Stalin's birthday celebration left yesterday. *(She swallows a "gummy bear." Pause.)*

ROGER:   Damn!

LEONA:   And they're not going to charter another truck just for you. Understandably, don't you think?

*(Dejection sets in.)*

ROGER:   They could have given some notice. . .

LEONA:   People have been talking about Stalin's birthday for six months!

JOSYANE:   Even so, it's not our fault if no one found anything. . . .

LEONA:   I'm not criticizing; I'm informing.

SUZANNE: If we had agreed to send my sweater in the first place. . . .

ROGER: It still stinks! We have the best present, the one likely to please Stalin most, and we're going to be left holding it?

MARCEL: No! It's got to be sent!

ROGER: Why?

MARCEL: Yes, well, . . . the guy insisted. He gave it to us on condition that it be given to Stalin. If not, . . . hunh, Suzanne?

SUZANNE: Absolutely! I'm going to fix up a package and send the pullover and the cake through the mail; the bronze is too heavy. . . . It'll be better than nothing! *(She starts to ready her package.)*

JOSYANE: You don't have the address.

MARCEL: You put "Stalin, The Kremlin, U.S.S.R."; I'm sure it'll get there. . . .

JOSYANE: Jean Louis will be disappointed.

LEONA: There might be a solution.

*(Everyone looks at her.)*

It's not very orthodox, if I can put it that way, but I could take it myself, if I try, with the help of the federation, to go to Moscow.

*(They regain their confidence. Only Roger seems mistrustful.)*

ROGER: This present is from our cell!

LEONA: You don't trust me?

ROGER: *(hesitant)* It's not that. . . .

LEONA: Would you rather it never get there?

ROGER: *(stubborn)* No, but....

LEONA: The party is not in the habit....

ROGER: I agree about the party,...but our cell is the one offering Stalin this museum piece....That has to be made clear!

MARCEL: It would be most unfortunate if you weren't nominated for the city elections.

*(Brief pause.)*

ROGER: *(embarrassed)* I don't give a damn about that! That has nothing to do with it....As if I was absolutely fixed on that!...No, it's a question of fairness, that's all!

*(Pause.)*

JOSYANE: What about Marcel?

ROGER: That's right, your delegation....

MARCEL: I said no.

SUZANNE: Where are they going?

MARCEL: Russia.

SUZANNE: You refused to go to the U.S.S.R.?

MARCEL: *(embarrassed)* Not really,...but my mother has to be helped downstairs....I have the dog to take care of....

ROGER: But we'll help your mother get downstairs, won't we, comrades?

*(All agree.)*

JOSYANE: *(cajoling)* It would be so wonderful if you went, Marcel.

MARCEL: Listen, I've never liked traveling....

ROGER: *(appealing to the others)* Moscow is nothing like Dieppe, is it?

SUZANNE: Not at all!

ROGER: It's farther!

JOSYANE: First of all, there's no ocean!

LEONA: I don't see the connection.

JOSYANE: We'll explain it to you.

ROGER: You realize you might be able to put our present in his very own hands?!

SUZANNE: You would be so fortunate, Feuillard,...to be near comrade Stalin! And right then, you must ask him to try on the sweater.... It'd only take a couple of seconds....

MARCEL: And why not have him taste the cake while you're at it!

ROGER: No, no!

SUZANNE: Why not?

ROGER: Suzanne, that's enough now! *(He turns to Marcel.)* Imagine it,...you yourself offering Stalin, in the name of our cell, an object that once belonged to Lenin! I mean,... for the party,...and for you....What a memory! *(He gives time for Marcel to think.)*

LEONA: I find it rather strange, to say the least, that a party comrade would refuse to go to the country of true socialism.

ROGER: Right;...it certainly is odd, Marcel.

JOSYANE: Afterwards, at work, when you start singing the praises of the U.S.S.R. to everybody, they'll be the first one to throw your attitude now in your face!

SUZANNE:   If it was me, I can tell you, I'd have jumped at the chance!

*(Marcel stands up and walks slowly toward the door, then stops and walks back over to the others.)*

MARCEL:   Okay, I'll go! I have until tomorrow to give my answer. . . .

ROGER:   Terrific!

*(They surround him, slap him on the back and congratulate him.)*

SUZANNE:   You are so lucky, Feuillard!

MARCEL:   Josyane. . .

JOSYANE:   Don't worry, I swear I won't dance with anyone else until you get back.

*(She gives him a kiss; he blushes.)*

MARCEL:   It won't be long! Two weeks, no more. . . .We're only going to Moscow and Leningrad.

JOSYANE:   In that case, I won't have long to wait!

MARCEL:   No. . . . *(He turns to Leona.)* We've been invited to factories and collective farms,. . .everything. . . .It certainly is going to be an interesting trip!

LEONA:   What isn't certain is that you'll be able to get into the Kremlin to give Stalin the present with your own hands!

ROGER:   You don't know Marcel Feuillard.

MARCEL:   You can have confidence in me. . . .The Russians may have socialism, but we have system D, don't we?

SUZANNE:   Thatta boy, Feuillard!

JOSYANE:   Bravo, Marcel!

ROGER:   Good ol' Marcel!

LEONA:   Bravo, comrade!

*(They laugh. Jean Louis enters.)*

JEAN LOUIS:   Sounds like happiness! Did you get it?

MARCEL:   Look who's here!

*(Jean Louis picks up the bronze.)*

JEAN LOUIS:   It's great!

ROGER:   Thank you! Let's give Jean Louis a hand!

*(They clap their hands rhythmically: "One, two, three, four, five . . .," etc.)*

LEONA:   *(to Jean Louis)* In the name of the party, thank you . . . .
I can't call you comrade yet . . . .

JEAN LOUIS:   No . . . .

JOSYANE:   That may not be so for long, hunh, Jean Louis?

*(Without answering, Jean Louis holds her tenderly to himself. Marcel sees them.)*

MARCEL:   Josyane, remember? You promised . . . .

JOSYANE:   Yes, Marcel. *(She moves away from Jean Louis.)*

JEAN LOUIS:   *(surprised)* What's going on?

SUZANNE:   Marcel is a little jealous.

MARCEL:   *(vexed)* Don't be stupid! That's not it at all! If you can't go out with a friend anymore! You see, Suzanne, as a militant, you're very effective, . . . .

ROGER: *(cutting him off)* Don't get upset, Marcel, she's joking!

SUZANNE: Go on, give me a kiss. *(She turns to Jean Louis.)* Marcel — our cell's special courier!

JEAN LOUIS: Oh, yeah?

ROGER: With a present like this, it's the least we can do. . . .

MARCEL: Awfully nice guy, your friend Sam!

LEONA: To give such a gift, he must be a comrade!

JEAN LOUIS: He told me he was in Russia before 1917 and that he participated in the October revolution.

SUZANNE: Not surprising!

JEAN LOUIS: No, . . .well, . . . I talked about it with him a little . . . . He says he's still a communist, but that in the U.S.S.R. they betrayed Lenin. I don't really know much about it. . . .

*(Prolonged pause.)*

ROGER: That's the best one yet!

SUZANNE: Betrayed Lenin?

JEAN LOUIS: I, you know. . . .

LEONA: Classic anti-Soviet slander!

JOSYANE: And you believed him?

JEAN LOUIS: Yes. . . .I mean, no. . . . I'm hopeless when it comes to politics. . . .

MARCEL: He must have said it as a joke.

LEONA: You think that's funny?

ROGER: *(upset)* Come on, now, the present did belong to Lenin, didn't it?

SUZANNE: Without a doubt; it's written right on it!

ROGER: Stalin can't help but be happy to receive it. That's all that counts, right?

*(All agree.)*

MARCEL: Right, well then, whatever..., but since I'll be leaving in a few days....

LEONA: There must be a letter!

*(They set the table top on the trestles. Jean Louis goes out into the courtyard, followed by Josyane.)*

ROGER: You'll bring us back souvenirs, won't you, Marcel?

SUZANNE: Oh, yes, if you find any cake recipes, or sweater patterns....I'll make you a list.

MARCEL: Are you coming, Josyane?

JOSYANE: Coming!

JEAN LOUIS: *(to Josyane)* What are you doing this evening? They're showing a Bulgarian film at the Palace....

JOSYANE: "Eagle from the Heights."...I've already seen it.

*(Jean Louis appears disappointed. Marcel, in the doorway, watches them.)*

SUZANNE: Well, are you coming, Marcel? *(She pulls him over to the table, around which the others are seated.)*

ROGER: What shall we put for a salutation?

SUZANNE: Dear Stalin,...or Dear Comrade Stalin,....

MARCEL: My dearest Joseph!

ROGER: Cut the jokes, Marcel!

*(Josyane and Jean Louis are still in the courtyard.)*

JOSYANE:  I should go work on the letter.

JEAN LOUIS:  *(holding her back)* Don't you want to come?

JOSYANE:  *(freeing herself)* No. . . . Maybe another time. . . .

JEAN LOUIS:  Is it because of what I said in there just now?

JOSYANE:  No. . . . Well, . . . yes, a little.

LEONA:  To the inspired continuer of the thought of Lenin!

SUZANNE:  It's not direct enough.

MARCEL:  Maybe it's a little too long?

LEONA:  *(reading)* It's in *L'Humanité!*

ROGER:  After all, Stalin is still a comrade. "Dear Joseph Stalin."

*(Heloise appears at her window.)*

JEAN LOUIS:  *(to Josyane)* But I just said it. . . . I don't know anything about politics. . . . And even if you don't agree about everything, it doesn't keep you from. . . .

JOSYANE:  For me it does!

*(Roger gets up and walks to the door.)*

ROGER:  Either come in or go out, but it's not exactly warm. . . .

JOSYANE:  Coming.

*(She goes in. Jean Louis starts to follow her, but Roger shuts the door.)*

ROGER:  Excuse us. . . .

*(Josyane stands still near the door. Suzanne sees her and walks over to her.)*

SUZANNE:  Stop him! *(Seeing the copy of* Paris-Hollywood *dropped by Marcel, she hands it to Josyane.)* Here, Jean Louis forgot this.

*(Josyane hesitates, then rejoins the others around the table.)*

JOSYANE:  You're sweet, Suzanne.

*(Sitting down, she sets the* Paris-Hollywood *down in front of Leona, who leafs through it coldly and contemptuously.)*

LEONA:  It doesn't surprise me that he reads this!

ROGER:  *(hypocritically)* It goes well with his opinions. . . . So, about this letter. . . .

*(Heloise, at her window, watches Jean Louis walk away.)*

HELOISE:  Men — you better think twice before you let them go!. . . I really liked this one. . . . Oh, well!

MARCEL:  Did Jean Louis leave?

JOSYANE:  Yes.

ROGER:  It's insane to be so gullible! Well, it's to be expected.

LEONA:  He's marginal,. . .without any real class consciousness. If he joins someday, he'll get over it.

SUZANNE:  All the same, it *is* thanks to him that we have a present.

JOSYANE:  There, now, shall we finish the letter?

ROGER:  *(reading)* "This magnificent bronze sculpture once belonged to your loyal companion, Lenin,. . .given to him by comrades. . . ." We'll put the names here. . . . Apfel,. . . whatshisname,. . .and Grunstein?. . .

SUZANNE:  Apfelbaum, Bronstein and Rosenfeld! *(She takes the letter from Roger's hands.)*

MARCEL:   Maybe it's not worth the trouble. . . .

SUZANNE:   Of course it is! If we don't put them in, it won't be authentic.

LEONA:   Fine. Let's get on with it, comrades; let's not waste time!

ROGER:   The fire's out. Anyway, it's not every day you celebrate comrade Stalin's seventieth birthday!

*(Suzanne writes as the others watch.)*

LEONA:   *(standing up)* No, but I would like to announce that in three months, the party will celebrate with great joy the fiftieth birthday of the leader of the French Communist Party, Comrade Maurice Thorez. So, . . . .

*(All heads turn slowly toward Leona. They look at her, stupefied. Blackout.)*

## ACT FOUR

*(Same set, but seven years later, a Sunday in December 1956. Stalin has been dead for three years. This same year, at the XXth Congress of the Bolshevik Communist Party of the U.S.S.R., Krushchev has read his famous speech denouncing the crimes of his predecessor. When the action resumes, Jean Louis is talking with Desiré, who seems not to recognize him.)*

DESIRÉ:   Do you understand what I'm telling you? All the cellars have already been emptied out.

JEAN LOUIS:   I'll buy everything,. . . new, old. . . .

DESIRÉ:   You are a persistent one! When the rats were exterminated, they all took the chance to clean out their cellars.

JEAN LOUIS:   So I'm too late?

DESIRÉ:   Affirmative!

JEAN LOUIS:   Well, too bad, I guess.

*(He walks toward the corridor leading upstairs just as Heloise comes out of her lodge, a basket of laundry under her arm.)*

DESIRÉ:   *(stopping him)* Where are you going?

JEAN LOUIS:   I'll buy knickknacks and furniture, too. . . .Well, maybe people have some things they want to get rid of. . . .

DESIRÉ:   There's nobody here today; it's Sunday!

HELOISE:   *(to Jean Louis)* I know you!

JEAN LOUIS:   It's possible; I spent some time in the neighborhood a few years ago.

HELOISE:   *(to Desiré)* Don't you remember the man?

*(Desiré mimes his answer: he doesn't remember.)*

You're not Madame Merlu's nephew?

JEAN LOUIS:   No.

HELOISE: Oh! That's it! *(She points toward the cell office.)* You were with them!

JEAN LOUIS: If you like.

HELOISE: Of course, . . . little Josyane. . . . I remember now! That was a good five years ago, wasn't it?

JEAN LOUIS: Seven. It was 1949.

HELOISE: *(starting to hang her laundry)* You really don't realize how quickly time passes. *(To herself.)* Oh, yes, . . . yes, Desiré was still refereeing then.

JEAN LOUIS: I was passing by, so I said to myself. . . .

HELOISE: And you haven't been back since then?

JEAN LOUIS: No.

HELOISE: What a shame! Josyane was so darling back then. Poor kid!

JEAN LOUIS: She's not around anymore?

HELOISE: Yes! But there are bastards everywhere. . . .Well, I'd rather not say anything.

*(Jean Louis turns to leave; she stops him.)*

So you don't know about Marcel Feuillard?

JEAN LOUIS: No.

HELOISE: You know who Feuillard was? He stuttered. . . .

JEAN LOUIS: Yes, I remember him. What ever became of him?

DESIRÉ: *(uneasy)* That's no concern of ours, Heloise. . . .

HELOISE: He left to take their present to Stalin. . . .Well, he was never seen again. Marcel vanished into thin air!

JEAN LOUIS: They never tried to find out?

DESIRÉ: You think it's easy over there?

HELOISE: When they decide to keep something quiet, it's sealed up tighter than King Tut's tomb!

JEAN LOUIS:   No news at all?

HELOISE:   Nothing! Yet he'd left with the others he worked with. And they were unable to find out anything either, not a word!

DESIRÉ:   Who knows what kind of foolishness Marcel didn't get himself into over there. He was an odd one!

HELOISE:   That's a real cop's reaction!

DESIRÉ:   Where there's smoke, there's fire.

JEAN LOUIS:   Could it have been the present?

HELOISE:   That's what everybody told themselves.

DESIRÉ:   It had to be a stolen item!

JEAN LOUIS:   I don't think so. . . .

DESIRÉ:   Presents!. . .Giving them will always get you into trouble! *(He goes back in his lodge.)*

HELOISE:   Well, at least with you, there's no danger of that happening.

*(Jean Louis starts to leave.)*

You're not staying for their bash?

JEAN LOUIS:   No, I was just passing by. . . .

HELOISE:   Like every year, they have their card renewal day, as they call it. I'm sure they'd be very pleased. Hey, what do you know, here's the poor girl now!

*(Josyane, loaded down with parcels, enters the courtyard. She is pregnant.)*

JOSYANE:   Hello, Madame Scartini! Could you give me a hand here?

HELOISE:   Of course! Roger might have helped you! I don't know about that one. . . .

*(Heloise sets down one parcel in the cell office, then returns to her lodge. Jean Louis finds himself face to face with Josyane.)*

JEAN LOUIS:   Hello!

JOSYANE:   Oh, my gosh!

JEAN LOUIS:   I was passing through the neighborhood. . . . I saw some light. . . .

*(They laugh.)*

JOSYANE:   You haven't changed at all!

JEAN LOUIS:   No. *(Pause.)* Still in politics?

JOSYANE:   Still. And you, still in antiques?

*(Pause. Heloise appears on the stoop. Jean Louis enters the cell office.)*

JOSYANE:   *(calling to Heloise)* Madame Scartini, can we count on you and Desiré in a little while?

HELOISE:   I think so, as always. Well, . . . I can't speak for Desiré; . . . all the goings on in Hungary haven't made him too happy. Between what you say and what you hear on the radio. . . .

JOSYANE:   Don't you trust us?

HELOISE:   All I can say is, . . . I don't understand anything about it. I'm going to go finish doing my dishes!

*(Heloise reenters her lodge. Josyane joins Jean Louis in the cell office. He's flipping through a magazine. Josyane begins putting up decorations.)*

JEAN LOUIS:   *Soviet Studies;* I subscribed to a magazine like this.

JOSYANE:   That's right; I remember. I also sold you a copy of *Son of the People.*

JEAN LOUIS:   And hit me up for Stalin's present.

*(Pause.)*

JOSYANE:   Had you known about Marcel?

JEAN LOUIS:   No; I just found out.

JOSYANE: Our Soviet comrades assured us that they had done everything they could to find him. He could have had an accident. Nobody knows anything. With everything that's going on now, maybe we'll find out more.

*(Jean Louis stares at her in silence.)*

JOSYANE: *(embarrassed)* Have I changed a little? Filled out a little, maybe?

JEAN LOUIS: Yes, a little. . . .

JOSYANE: And you?

JEAN LOUIS: Fine.

JOSYANE: You're not. . . .

JEAN LOUIS: What?

JOSYANE: Well, you know what I mean. . . .

JEAN LOUIS: No! Whenever you stop talking politics, you still have a pretty hard time expressing yourself. . . .

*(Pause. Josyane sets napkins, plates and glasses on the table.)*

JOSYANE: You seem happy!

JEAN LOUIS: And you?

JOSYANE: I'm okay. . . . It's hard right now. People are saying such terrible things. It's not easy for us.

JEAN LOUIS: You wanted the baby?

JOSYANE: Yes. Well, . . . it was mostly Roger.

JEAN LOUIS: Oh, it's Roger! Good ol' Roger!

*(Brief pause.)*

JOSYANE:    There's something of a difference in our ages. Marcel's
disappearance brought us closer together. . . .Yes, it was
mostly him who wanted to keep the baby. You know the
party's stand on abortions, birth control, . . . .

JEAN LOUIS:    Not really, no.

JOSYANE:    It's against it, especially Jeannette!

JEAN LOUIS:    Of course! *(Brief pause.)* Who's Jeannette?

JOSYANE:    Jeannette Vermeersche, Maurice's companion.

JEAN LOUIS:    Maurice. . .?

JOSYANE:    Why, Maurice Thorez, of course!

JEAN LOUIS:    Of course. . . .

JOSYANE:    Roger is a party official now, so. . . .

JEAN LOUIS:    I see! *(Pause.)* Yes, well, it's been very nice. . . .

JOSYANE:    Won't you stay a little? Here's Suzanne.

*(Suzanne enters, carrying several packages and a record player.)*

SUZANNE:    Hello, comrades!

JOSYANE:    Suzanne, do you remember Jean Louis?

SUZANNE:    Do I remember? You bet I do, the birthday present
for Stalin. . . .It was you.

JEAN LOUIS:    If you like. . . .

SUZANNE:    It's been ages since we last saw you! It's nice of
you to come back for card renewal day. You are going to
join, aren't you?

JOSYANE:    That'll be the day!

*(Jean Louis doesn't answer. The two women busy themselves setting out sandwiches, drinks, raffle prizes, records, etc.)*

SUZANNE: Is Leona or Roger going to give the speech?

JOSYANE: Roger, I think.

*(While Jean Louis flips through a book, Josyane talks in a low voice to Suzanne.)*

What did you decide to do with. . . ? *(She points to the portrait of Stalin.)*

SUZANNE: I don't know. We'll have to wait for Leona.

*(Jean Louis is looking at them.)*

JOSYANE: *(embarrassed)* So many things are being said about Stalin now. . . .

SUZANNE: The party is right to be vigilant about it all. And this report that's been attributed to Krushchev; nobody's seen it.

JOSYANE: And that a newspaper like *Le Monde* should publish it. . . . It's pretty fishy!

SUZANNE: You see, the party recognizes that mistakes were made. Who doesn't make mistakes?

JEAN LOUIS: Yes. . . . It's been a pleasure. . . . I think I'll leave you now. . . . *(He goes to leave.)*

SUZANNE: *(stopping him)* Aren't you going to wait for Roger? I'm sure he'd be happy to see you again.

*(Jean Louis gives in. Suzanne puts on a record, a popular waltz.)*

JOSYANE: This reminds me of Marcel all of a sudden. He always wanted to go dancing. . . .

SUZANNE: Well, it might turn out that Marcel has it better

than we do! Maybe he found a pretty little Russian girl! From him, it wouldn't surprise me!

*(Roger appears in the courtyard, a full wine rack in his hand, which he sets down outside the door. He's wearing a suit and tie; he looks as if he has "made it.")*

ROGER:   Hello, everybody!

JOSYANE:   Do you remember Jean Louis?

ROGER:   No. . . .Oh, my gosh! What in the hell are you doing here?

JEAN LOUIS:   You don't come out of closets anymore?

*(Roger forces a laugh.)*

JOSYANE:   What?

ROGER:   Nothing; nonsense, nonsense. It's good to see you again. You're going to join this time, I hope? *(He turns to Josyane.)* Leona's not here?

*(Josyane stops the record player.)*

SUZANNE:   I thought she was coming with you.

ROGER:   I waited for her for an hour!

JOSYANE:   What happened?

*(Roger indicates that he doesn't know.)*

JEAN LOUIS:   Well. . . . *(He looks as if he's about to leave.)*

ROGER:   *(stopping him, leading him over to the table)* You're going to have a drink with us! Today is card renewal day!

*(Suzanne puts the record on again and waltzes with Josyane.)*

SUZANNE:   Forward, waltzers!

ROGER: *(to Jean Louis)* They told you about Marcel? Unbelievable, a thing like that! Mind you, in France too, people disappear like that every year. . . .

*(Suzanne twirls Josyane faster and faster.)*

JOSYANE: *(freeing herself)* You're crazy! And what about the baby? Ask Jean Louis!

JEAN LOUIS: I'm not very talented. . . .

SUZANNE: As soon as I hear the accordion, it's stronger than me!

*(They waltz. The two concierges enter.)*

HELOISE: I somehow managed to convince Desiré.

ROGER: Come in, Monsieur Scartini! What can I offer you?

DESIRÉ: *(walking over to the table)* A little red!

ROGER: *(to Josyane)* The bottles are outside.

*(Josyane goes out. Roger finds himself face to face with Heloise and, embarrassed, joins Josyane outside.)*

DESIRÉ: That jerk's still here?

HELOISE: Which?

DESIRÉ: *(pointing to the portraits on the wall)* The moustache!

HELOISE: What do you care? Waltz with me instead!

*(He complies, as Josyane and Roger come back in with the bottles of wine.)*

JOSYANE: Are you expecting anyone besides Leona?

ROGER: She should be here. Maybe one or two sympathizers, but it's getting late. . . . I think we can start.

*(He stops the record player. Josyane fills the glasses.)*

JOSYANE:   What about the raffle?

ROGER:   Afterwards.

SUZANNE:   *(to Jean Louis)* Did you take a ticket?

JOSYANE:   *(to the concierges)* Here we are, Monsieur Scartini! And what about you, Madame Scartini?

HELOISE:   I'm not very thirsty.

SUZANNE:   *(still to Jean Louis)* It's twenty francs. There are some lovely prizes. We donated them. The Russian doll there is mine; I won it last year. And there are books. . . .

*(While Jean Louis is buying a ticket, Roger takes the portrait of Stalin down from the wall.)*

JOSYANE:   What are you doing?

ROGER:   They've taken it down at the section and at the federation.

SUZANNE:   *(to Jean Louis)* Oh, you won! A little ceramic swan, here. . . . *(She gives him his prize, then notices the empty space left by the portrait of Stalin. She walks over to it.)*

JOSYANE:   *(to Suzanne)* It looks strange, empty like that. . . .

*(The concierges turn and look. To distract them, Suzanne walks over to them.)*

SUZANNE:   You're going to take one little ticket from me!

*(Grudgingly, Desiré takes out his billfold, as Roger finishes tacking up a poster of Mickey Mouse to replace Stalin's portrait.)*

ROGER:   There!

*(Embarrassed pause. Everyone looks at it.)*

It's not ideal, but it'll tide us over. . . . *(He turns to Jean Louis, to break the embarrassed silence that has settled over them.)* Are you having fun?

JEAN LOUIS:  Yeah. . . .

ROGER:  You know, it's partially thanks to you and your present that I became a municipal counsellor.

JEAN LOUIS:  You exaggerate!

SUZANNE:  *(to Roger)* We should get going now. . . .

ROGER:  Too bad about Leona. Fortunately, I thought this might happen. . . .Go on!

SUZANNE:  I now yield the floor to our comrade Roger Blot, member of the federal bureau and municipal counsellor of our district.

*(She initiates applause, meager of course. Roger has taken several sheets of paper from his pocket.)*

ROGER:  Dear comrades and sympathizers, on this day when the Elisa Verlet cell renews its cards, we can't help but be moved by the thought of comrade Marcel Feuillard. . . .

*(Leona enters.)*

LEONA:  He's back!

ROGER:  No!

JOSYANE:  Marcel?

LEONA:  Yes!

SUZANNE:  That's wonderful!

JEAN LOUIS:  Where is he?

HELOISE:  Good ol' Feuillard! I would have been surprised if he never found a way out!

DESIRÉ:  He's going to have some tale to tell!

JOSYANE:  This calls for a toast!

*(Everyone gathers around the table. Leona goes into the courtyard. Roger follows.)*

ROGER:  What is it?

LEONA:  A catastrophe!

ROGER:  Is he sick? Crippled?

LEONA:  I don't know. . . . It was the leadership who informed me of his return. . . .

ROGER:  He really is coming back! With all the rumors running around, . . . at least Marcel will be able to tell us the truth!

LEONA:  I knew it! *(Pause.)* He spent seven years in a camp!

ROGER:  No!. . . A camp. . . . Why? What kind of camp?

LEONA:  A summer camp! You really can be a fool sometimes, Roger! *(She returns to the office while Roger stands in the courtyard, overcome.)*

ROGER:  *(to himself)* Damn!

*(Josyane joins Roger in the courtyard.)*

JOSYANE:  Is Marcel coming? What's the matter?

ROGER:  I'll explain later.

*(They go back inside.)*

SUZANNE:  I propose a toast. . . to Marcel!

ALL:  Marcel! *(They clink glasses.)*

ROGER:  Yes. . . . Just knowing he's alive is cause to be happy. . . .

SUZANNE:  To his return to us!

ALL: *(except Leona)* His return!

*(They raise their glasses. Leona takes Roger aside.)*

LEONA: But you don't realize! Card renewal day.... *(To herself.)* It can't be true.

ROGER: But,...what if it is?

*(Pause. Leona looks at him in surprise.)*

LEONA: You too?

ROGER: Of course not, comrade.

LEONA: Fine; shall we continue?

*(They rejoin the others.)*

SUZANNE: Is he in the neighborhood?

LEONA: No one knows. He's a little tired....I believe he was first received by the party leadership....Well, go on, Roger....

*(With some difficulty, Roger picks up the thread of his speech.)*

ROGER: After this good news,...I believe that as an unprecedented anti-Sovietism is unleashed...with sensational pseudo-revelations which would have us swallow I don't know what crimes of comrade Stalin.... *(He has gotten the pages of his speech mixed up, loses his place, is visibly unnerved.)* Fortunately, the abortive attempt by the forces of fascism to overturn socialism in Hungary has put things back on course....And if certain necessary,...critiques can be based on one error or another,...comrades,...comrades,...the tree must not keep us from seeing the forest....

*(Leona applauds. Carrying a parcel under his arm, Marcel enters. He is dressed in a gabardine overcoat a little too big for him; his hair has turned white; his features are marked by his experience.)*

SUZANNE: Marcel!

ROGER:   Marcel! When did you get back?!

MARCEL:   *(with only a hint of a stutter now)* I'm a little late. . . .

*(In silence, he crosses the room and sets his parcel on the table, where the raffle prizes are.)*

JOSYANE:   Where have you been, Marcel?

MARCEL:   Hello, Josyane. You didn't wait for me to go dancing!

JOSYANE:   Yes. . . .

*(After noticing Josyane's condition, he smiles.)*

SUZANNE:   Aren't you going to give me a kiss, Marcel?

*(They kiss.)*

MARCEL:   As a woman, . . . flawless, . . . .

HELOISE:   I really am pleased, Feuillard!

*(They kiss.)*

DESIRÉ:   *(shaking his hand)* You haven't really changed!

JEAN LOUIS:   Hello, Marcel.

MARCEL:   You're still here? I didn't think you'd stay around.

JEAN LOUIS:   I haven't been back since the day you left with the present. . . .

MARCEL:   Your friend Sam is one hell of a prankster! . . . Really, to have me give Stalin a present engraved with the names of three men Stalin had. . . . *(He runs his finger across his throat.)* That took nerve!

LEONA:   What are you saying, Marcel?

ROGER:   Where were you?

MARCEL: Oh, I got around a little everywhere,...toward the seventh circle....Where they sing, "Here it's winter twelve months a year, the rest of the time is summer."

SUZANNE: We tried to find out where you were, what had happened,...but there was no way.

MARCEL: I took a tour that isn't part of the official Intourist package.

JOSYANE: Tell us, where were you, Marcel?

*(He goes to get his parcel, which he sets on a stool in the middle of the room.)*

MARCEL: It's awfully nice to see you all again. *(He unwraps the parcel, revealing a model of a concentration camp. He points to a place in the camp.)* Usually, there's an inscription here: "Communism will triumph throughout the world." I didn't get a chance to put it on; they freed me before I could finish. *(Pause. He looks at them.)* This is where I've come from. I felt right at home; the place was filled with communists. Some had been there a long time. I met a friend of Sam's who'd been there since 1936, the same time Zinoviev and Kamenev were shot by Stalin. *(Pause.)* Oh yes, "Apfelbaum" and "Rosenfeld," if you prefer! Does that ring a bell? *(Pause.)* They weren't shopkeepers! Revolutionary pseudonyms can play nasty tricks on you!

JEAN LOUIS: Deported? Seven years?

SUZANNE: All this time, because of the sculpture?

MARCEL: Or the names that were on it,...or because of your cake,...or your sweater,...who knows? Or maybe because I stuttered? Parasitism, cake, politically dangerous; a sweater, deviation. A.S.V.Z.: Anti-Soviet military plot. K.R.D.: counterrevolutionary activities....My own initials were K.R.D.T. ...The T was for Trotskyism....Speaking of whom, the third name on the present, "Bronstein": that's who it was, Trotsky....Stalin didn't have much of a sense of humor. *(He turns to Jean Louis.)* You can tell that to Sam.

JEAN LOUIS:   I never saw him again. But he didn't think you'd take the present yourself. If he ever imagined. . . .

MARCEL:   *(interrupting)* Who could have imagined? If he had told me what was happening there, I wouldn't have believed him. We wanted. . . needed so much to believe it was paradise.

*(A deep silence settles over them.)*

MARCEL:   I made the model while I was there. To replace the one Old Man Grospierre made.

ROGER:   You shouldn't have. . . .

MARCEL:   I'll leave it with you. Since I wasn't here for Maurice Thorez's fiftieth, this will make up for it. It's my present. He should be told it's a matchstick model of a Soviet labor camp with Marcel Feuillard's "signature" on it. He'll understand.

*(Leona walks up to him, barely able to control her anger and emotion.)*

LEONA:   Even if everything you say is true, Marcel, you have no right to say it!

SUZANNE:   But if it's true!

LEONA:   *(to Suzanne)* You think our class enemies aren't going to use all this?

JOSYANE:   But if it's true!

LEONA:   All the more reason! We must not carry water to the reaction mill!

*(Unable to master her emotions, she runs into the courtyard and sits on a stair, face in hands. Josyane puts the record player back on; the record starts where it stopped.)*

JOSYANE:   Marcel, wanna dance?

*(They dance for several seconds, then stop. The record is over. Josyane moves away from Marcel. Roger walks up to him.)*

ROGER:  Marcel, for the last seven years, on each card renewal day, we hoped that you would turn up again, that you'd be back with us. We didn't know anything, so, just in case, we kept your card. . . . Are you still with us, Marcel? *(He holds out the card to Marcel.)*

MARCEL:  *(looking at it and smiling)* Thanks, but I think I'll have to think about it. . . a little.

   *(He leaves slowly, in silence. Blackout.)*

∽

*Jean-Michel Ribes*

# THE REST HAVE
# GOT IT WRONG

**Translated from the French
by Donald Watson**

This English translation of *The Rest Have Got It Wrong* was given its first American reading under the title *A Walk in the Wood* on September 22, 1986 at Ubu Repertory Theater, with the following cast:

| | |
|---|---|
| BLINKA VALLARD | Margaret Harrington |
| ZACRA THE PAINTER | William Ha'o |
| FLIGHT-LIEUTENANT PETER CROOKS | John Talbot |
| MADELEINE/CINTA | Grace Woodard |

Directed by **Lilah Kan**

**JEAN-MICHEL RIBES** was born in Paris in 1946. An actor and director as well as a playwright, he co-founded the Compagnie du Pallium in 1965 and the Compagnie Berto-Ribes in 1974. He has written fifteen plays since 1970 that have all been produced in Paris and abroad. Titles include *Les Fraises musclées* (1970); *Il faut que le sycomore coule* (1971); *Par-delà les marronniers* (1972); *L'Odyssée pour une tasse de thé* (1973); *On loge la nuit café à l'eau* (1975); *Omphalos Hôtel* (1975), which received the Prix des Jeunes Auteurs; *Jacky Parady* (1983); *Batailles*, written with artist-writer Roland Topor; and *Venise zigouillée* (1986). *The Rest Have Got It Wrong (Tout contre un petit bois)* was produced at the Théâtre Récamier in 1976 and received the Prix des "U" and the Prix Plaisir du Théâtre. Ribes also received critical acclaim in Paris for adapting and directing the plays of Arnold Wesker, Sam Shepard (*True West*) and Offenbach. He has written and directed two feature films, *Rien ne va plus* (1980) and *La Galette du Roi* (1985), as well as a number of television films, including a weekly series co-authored with Jean Bouchaud and Roland Topor.

**DONALD WATSON** is one of the most distinguished translators from the French. He is best known for his translations of most of the plays of Eugene Ionesco, but he has also translated Robert Pinget's *The Inquisitory* and two novels by Yves Navarre. Among the playwrights whose work he has translated are Marivaux, René de Obaldia, Michel Vinaver, Hélène Cixous and Jean-Claude Carrière. His translation of Yves Navarre's *Swimming Pools at War* was published by Ubu Repertory Theater Publications. For many years Special Lecturer in French Drama at the University of Bristol, Watson is a Chevalier de l'Ordre des Palmes Académiques and an Officier de l'Ordre des Arts et des Lettres.

## CHARACTERS

BLINKA VALLARD, between 45 and 50, pale and thin.
MADELEINE, a chambermaid or nurse.
ZACRA THE PAINTER, about 40, rather hirsute.
FLIGHT-LIEUTENANT PETER CROOKS, British, tall, about the same age as BLINKA, though from his face he looks 35.
CINTA, beautiful, glowing with health, the same age as BLINKA.

*The parts of MADELEINE and CINTA should be played by the same actress.*

## SET

*A hotel (or hospital?) room in provincial France. The play is written without an intermission.*

*(The set is a bedroom in a hotel in provincial France, just barely comfortable, or the bedroom of a hospital in need of renovation. There is indifferent lighting. The daylight enters through a window of small glass panes in the right-hand wall. On either side are two plain curtains of faded material. An electric light bulb in a bowl of opaque glass is connected to the ceiling by a length of braided electric cord, giving the rest of the lighting a yellow tinge. The walls are white — neither grubby nor antiseptic, just not noticeably white. The room looks clean. There is very little furniture: two wooden chairs, a low table, and a cheap armchair downstage; a table with a bedside lamp and a bed swollen by a bulky eiderdown. Over the bed is a photograph of an English fighter plane from World War II in a frame of varnished wood. To the left, in one corner of the room, a screen conceals a dressing room. A small hallway to the rear contains the entrance door, with a wardrobe opposite. This little hall is lit by light from the corridor, which glimmers through a pane of none-too-clean glass that fills the space between the top of the door and the ceiling. The bedroom is small and characterless, the objects within it being just* there, *standing without shadow or relief; it is a room evoking or recalling nothing in particular. After a brief moment, a woman's voice is heard coming from the dressing room behind the screen. The voice mechanically mouths the following two stanzas, with a barely distinguishable tune.)*

BLINKA'S VOICE:
> Toto's hat is black as night.
> Winnie's hat is far from white
> And not as light as Jerry's.
> Long live caps, hurrah for berets!

*(Pause.)*

> Toto's hat is much too tight.
> Winnie's hat is not quite right
> But not a sight like Terry's.
> Long live caps, hurrah for berets!

*(Someone knocks twice at the door, and without waiting for an answer, turns a key in the lock. It turns, the door opens, and a woman enters. She is holding a tray in one hand; on it is a metal thermos, a cup and saucer, two pieces of toast, and a pot of jam. Her gestures have the precision of a nurse, the politeness of a chambermaid.)*

MADELEINE:  It's me, Madame.

BLINKA'S VOICE:  *(from behind the screen)* What time is it?...
Madeleine? It is you, isn't it?

MADELEINE:  Yes, Madame....A quarter to eleven.

BLINKA'S VOICE:  Already! And I thought I was up early, so
very early....I must have slept...thirteen hours! It's impossible...thirteen hours!

MADELEINE:  The climate 'round here is well known for being
...specially now we're into July....

BLINKA'S VOICE:  No.

MADELEINE:  I expect you were very tired after your journey
yesterday.

BLINKA'S VOICE:  No. Yesterday? Why? No.

MADELEINE:  Sometimes it happens that....

BLINKA'S VOICE:  I've stopped dreaming, Madeleine. I've
stopped dreaming, that's all! It was always my dreams that
woke me up. A dreamless night is an endless night!...*(She
speaks in a worried voice.)* Madeleine, are you still there?

MADELEINE:  Yes, Madame.

BLINKA'S VOICE:  Good....My dreams were my daylight,
knocking at my eyelids until they opened up...yes, rather
like that....No dreams, no more daylight....Perhaps it's
still nighttime and I'm not really awake now? *(She bursts out
laughing.)* You're right; I must have been tired, just very, very
tired....But that's me all over, always choosing the most com-
plex of reasons to explain the simplest of things. *(She pushes
one wing of the screen aside and appears. She is between forty-five and
fifty, of slight build, with short hair. Her face is soft but bony, animated
by two black eyes, glowing but gentle. Her silhouette has the fragility of
ivory, her voice an ashen warmth. A silk dressing-gown falls in generous*

*folds around her body. As her delicate white hands snap the ends of her belt together, the material molds her hips. She looks at Madeleine.)* Does it happen to you too?

MADELEINE:   Madame?

BLINKA:   Not to dream.

MADELEINE:   I don't know.

BLINKA:   *(looking at the breakfast tray)* Oh! Today's it's strawberry. Never the same little pot of jam in the mornings...here, just like everywhere else,...have you noticed?

MADELEINE:   I suppose it's to make a change....

BLINKA:   You come from the South...don't you, Mademoiselle?

MADELEINE:   Yes.

BLINKA:   I was sure you did....*(She laughs.)* That surprises you, doesn't it? I must tell you a secret: I'm so good at guessing, I know everything—absolutely everything. The Southeast, isn't it?

MADELEINE:   Yes.

BLINKA:   You see! I wasn't lying: everything. *(She sits down on the bed. She pours into a cup some of the liquid from the thermos Madeleine has just brought in exchange for the empty one. It is an unidentifiable liquid: some special beverage, an infusion, tea, medicine? As she goes on talking, without looking at Madeleine, Blinka sips her drink.)* No, my dear, it's quite simple, really, nothing mysterious at all.... You have something of Cinta about you, Cinta's hair and *(now she stares at Madeleine)* almost Cinta's look in your eyes. *(She picks up her pot of jam.)* "Cinta the strawberry".... "Cinta with the red cheeks!" *(She laughs.)* We never saw each other again—since she went away, I mean....*(She takes a sip from the cup.)* Pooh, that's not at all nice!...It must be, let's see, now...twenty years?... Twenty years ago since she left? You're smiling.

MADELEINE:   I really can't help you there.

BLINKA:   Of course not!....Anyhow, it was a very long time ago when she went away. To Canada. *To Canada!* To go and join an engineer, a rich engineer.

*(Madeleine takes a step towards the door. Blinka raises her voice in order to detain her.)*

And Cinta was from the South....My best friend came from the South....That was how I was able to guess....Just a coincidence, that's all.

MADELEINE:   *(moving off with her tray)* Well, Madame, I think I'd better....

BLINKA:   *(suddenly decisive)* Does anyone ever come back from Canada? Would *you* have come back from Canada?

MADELEINE:   But, Madame....

BLINKA:   *(insisting)* If you had promised your sister or your best friend, if you had sworn you'd do it, would you have come back from Canada?

MADELEINE:   *(troubled)* But I....

BLINKA:   Give me an answer!

MADELEINE:   Yes,...yes, I think so....

BLINKA:   *(her face lighting up, as if this were a great relief)* I was sure you would....You're a nice, kind girl....Thank you....

MADELEINE:   *(going out)* Madame, I must get on with my work....

BLINKA:   Madeleine! I nearly forgot. *(She takes a note from her dressing-gown pocket.)* Would you be good enough to hand this in downstairs?

*(She holds it out to Madeleine, who takes it, reads what is written, and then gazes at Blinka with a look that is almost hard and clearly interrogative.)*

Vallard, Tommy Vallard, that's my son. . . .

*(Madeleine does not change her expression and remains still.)*

He should be coming about midday. . . .You know, to help me get my things together. . . .You've forgotten, Madeleine, I'm leaving this evening. . . .You're so strange all of a sudden! *(Her voice resumes a natural tone of authority.)* You'll give that in downstairs, then. . . . *(She speaks as though to reassure Madeleine.)* It's my son's name, with the floor and my room number. . .so he doesn't get lost. . . .It's such a vast place!

MADELEINE: *(tensely)* He *has* been here before!

BLINKA: Three days ago, when he brought me. But how do you expect him to remember where. . .?

MADELEINE: *(in a curt voice, handing her note back to her)* All the names and the room and floor numbers are posted in the entrance hall downstairs.

BLINKA: Not mine. . . .I've only been here a little while, I'm sure you. . . .

MADELEINE: All of them.

BLINKA: *(dreamily)* My name's there? Blinka Vallard? They've put my name up. . .for such a short stay. . . . *(She smiles, astonished.)* All right, then. *(She takes the note from Madeleine.)*

MADELEINE: *(kind and polite again before she leaves)* Don't worry, Madame. It's impossible to get lost; he'll find his way easily enough. . . .Goodbye, Madame. *(She goes out. Blinka finishes her cup, pulls a wry face, and murmurs.)*

BLINKA: I can't think what they put into it. . . .

*(She opens her wardrobe, exposing articles of clothing on hangers, towels, and various woolens on the shelves. For a moment she inspects herself in the mirror inside the wardrobe door, holding the dress she has chosen tight against her. Then she closes the wardrobe and goes behind the screen. Regular footsteps can be heard approaching, as if the person were walking from the end of an immensely long corridor. They resound strongly as they reach the door.)*

BLINKA: *(changing in her dressing room)* Tommy?. . . Is that you?. . . Tommy? *(The footsteps have stopped behind the door. Blinka raises her voice.)* Wait a minute, darling,. . . I'm nearly ready!. . . *(then singing out)* I'm co — ming! *(After a brief pause behind the door, the footsteps continue, moving away. Blinka pops her head over the screen.)* Tommy!. . . Tommy, I'm in here. . . . *(She shouts.)* Tommy!. . . I knew he'd get lost! *(She rushes out of the dressing room, still hooking up her dress and trying with one finger to get her right shoe on. Then she runs to the door.)* Tommy darling!

*(She opens the door, screams, and leaps back, clearly twisting her leg as she does so. Framed in the doorway, motionless, is a rather corpulent man of about 40 with abundantly thick hair, almost hirsute, who has not shaved properly. He is wearing blue overalls and a rather grubby white coat with old rags spilling out of its pockets. With his left hand he is steadying a ladder over his shoulder, and in his right hand he carries two paint tins with large paintbrushes and rollers sticking out. There is a brief pause, during which Blinka attempts to recover her wits and compose herself.)*

ZACRA: *(managing to liberate his right hand and read from his notebook)* Madame. . . Madame Vallard, Blinka Vallard?

BLINKA: *(pulling herself together)* I beg your pardon. I'm so sorry, yes.

ZACRA: Madame Blinka Vallard, Room 212.

BLINKA: Yes.

ZACRA: Sorry to repeat myself; I'm making doubly sure. *(He puts a mark in his notebook.)* If there's one thing I can't abide, it's a blunder. . .above all, a professional blunder. *(He comes in and puts his gear down.)* That's great. . . . *(He walks up to the wall and touches it.)* Good thing for you, Zacra! It's grained and varnished, you just glide over it. . . . First glance, I said to myself: "Watch out, Zacra, it's floral embossed, you may have to scrape, fill and rub down, you know, the whole caboodle. . . ." Good thing for me. . . .That's the surface I like best, grained and varnished; it's all done in one coat, and when I say *one* coat, I mean *one* coat and not two. . . .

BLINKA: I'm terribly sorry. . . .I'm expecting my son, and I thought. . . .

ZACRA: You thought I was him. But no, you see, I was me, . . . Zacra the painter.

BLINKA: I'm really so sorry, it was ridiculous, my reaction, . . . .

ZACRA: Never you mind; . . .think nothing of it. Zacra's used to it. . . .Water off a duck's back. . . .Take the day before yesterday, the lady in 72. You know the lady in 72?

BLINKA: No.

ZACRA: *(while he sets up his equipment)* Well, soon as I appeared, this lady in 72, she says. . .now what was it she said? Oh, yes! She said, "Morning, Mr. Chuckler." *(He laughs.)* Can't help laughing, can you? "Mr. Chuckler"! Then she asked if her husband had phoned, when we were changing her bedside table, and a whole load of drivel like that. I let her go babbling on and got down to the job. . . ."Chuckler"! Can you beat it? Some mothers do have 'em, I can tell you! As if they're expecting Santa Claus, and when you tell 'em they've made a mistake, they up and complain to the powers that be. You know the old codger in 49?

BLINKA: No.

ZACRA: You don't know the lady in 72, or the old codger in 49! You must be a new girl!

BLINKA: Yes, yes, I've only been here since...let me see, I've just gone blank...three days ago, that's right,...and I'm leaving again this evening....

ZACRA: Leaving this evening?

BLINKA: Yes, my son's coming to fetch me.

ZACRA: Christ, that's a blunder! What did I say? *(He searches for the notebook in his pocket.)* Don't blame me! It's a different room every day and in the end you don't know where you are; you get them all muddled up. *(He runs through his notebook and stops at one particular page.)* Ah! No, no...,no..., today, it's you, all right....

BLINKA: Me? What for?

ZACRA: You're due for a fresh coat....They might have waited till tomorrow....

BLINKA: But....

ZACRA: Cross my heart. March 7th; that's today?

BLINKA: Yes.

ZACRA: *(showing his notebook)* Vallard, Blinka, Room 212, 7th of March....Cross my heart! *(He looks at the walls.)* Mind you, can't pretend it's a real posh job....

BLINKA: You mean you're going to....

ZACRA: Give it a going-over....Oh, it won't take me long; don't you worry.

BLINKA: They could have let me know.

ZACRA: Just now they're up to their ears; mustn't hold it against them.

BLINKA: Does it smell?

ZACRA: I beg your pardon?

BLINKA:   Your paint, does it smell?

ZACRA:   *(taking out a brush and spreading his dark paint over the wall)*
No, no, it's the matte enamel. . . . Don't let it fret you; it'll soon
be over.

BLINKA:   I'm going away, as you know; so just between ourselves, it's all the same to me. But I think it's the least they
could have done. . . .

ZACRA:   . . . to keep you in the picture, . . . I know! . . . But you're
not the first. It's always happening. . . . What can you expect
when they're up to their ears? Run off their feet, they are!

*(Blinka is about to remove some of her things from the side of the room
next to the wall.)*

Don't bother, you can leave all that! I'll see to it.

BLINKA:   Right.

*(Zacra starts painting. Blinka finishes her meal.)*

No smell, but it doesn't look very cheerful.

ZACRA:   Can't help that; it's the fashion!

BLINKA:   Oh?

ZACRA:   Yes; dark colors are "in" this year. So here goes with the
dark matte enamel! . . . It's not my fault, you know. I don't
start fashions. Not even the manager does that. . . . Do you
know who creates fashion?

BLINKA:   No.

ZACRA:   Neither do I. A mystery. And intelligence?! Who
creates intelligence? And what about frogs? A frog is bloated
and flabby and slimy, but it can leap into the dry air as high
as a fly. *(With his brush he describes the leap of the frog on the wall.)*
Who creates frogs? No, it's not other little froggies or toadies.
So who? And what about disease? Where does that come from?
Do you know where disease comes from?

BLINKA:   No, I don't know.

ZACRA:   Neither do I. A mystery,...everything's a mystery.

*(Blinka moves towards the door.)*

Right, then, Madame, bye-bye! See you again sometime.

BLINKA:   No, I'm not going....I'm looking for my belt.

ZACRA:   *(pointing to the lower shelf of the bedside table, without hesitation)* It's over there.

BLINKA:   Oh, thanks.

ZACRA:   You here on a holiday, Ma'am?

BLINKA:   No, I'm in transit.

ZACRA:   Transit? Isn't that a teeny-weeny holiday? Bit like a weekend? A mini-mini-holiday, isn't that what transit means?

BLINKA:   Not quite a holiday. A brief respite. It's more like a halt. Not too long, not too short.

ZACRA:   Oh, a halt!...I see....Like a little wait or a rest?

BLINKA:   A pause,...a pause between courses, a wait between planes, like the distance between two coastlines, two stages of life, two sorts of existence, two pavements, two countries,... a halt.

ZACRA:   Yes....Do you smoke?

BLINKA:   Yes, but only American cigarettes.

ZACRA:   Me too.

BLINKA:   Unusual for a man....Thank you....My wretched son smokes nothing but Gauloises. Filthy black tobacco that takes the skin off your teeth....And it would never cross his mind when he pays me a visit to bring a pack of Lucky Strikes with him.

ZACRA: And you, what are you between? Two...what?

BLINKA: You're not curious, are you?

ZACRA: No; I like talking, that's all. Once I liked singing while I worked. But now I'm older; I get too tired. So I talk. And since I started on the inside jobs, I soon noticed it wasn't the paint that upset people, so much as my singing. They don't usually seem to mind me talking. Do you like to hear me talk?

BLINKA: I can't honestly say it bothers me.

ZACRA: No; I'm sure it doesn't. Zacra's never any bother. That's no news to me. A soundless dab of paint. A discreet bit of brushwork here, an invisible stroke or two there. And while it's all going on, time's passing, life's slipping by, till my three little walls are done. Then I'm off and away.... *(He laughs loudly.)* That's Zacra for you all over!...But do you like me talking to you?

BLINKA: Why, yes; I don't find it disagreeable.

ZACRA: Is that all?

BLINKA: *(irritated)* It's...well, I mean, it takes your mind off things....After all, I'm talking back, so I suppose I must quite enjoy it. Is that what you wanted to know?

ZACRA: No. This transit of yours. You're between two what?

BLINKA: Are you really so interested in where I come from and where I'm going?

ZACRA: No. I told you before, what I enjoy is talking while I work. What else do you expect me to talk about? We got started on this transit business, so we might as well stick to it. No?

BLINKA: Yes....

*(He sits down on the edge of her bed and pours out a cup of the beverage in her thermos.)*

ZACRA:   Well?

BLINKA:   I'm sorry.

ZACRA:   Well?

BLINKA:   Oh, yes. . . .Well, I've just come. . . . I've left Paris and I'm going to live at Tommy's. That's all.

ZACRA:   Tommy. That's not a common name with us; it's a word like "transit". . . .

BLINKA:   It's my son's name.

ZACRA:   Oh, you have a son who's not one of us?

BLINKA:   What's the time?

ZACRA:   Hang on. *(He takes a watch from his pocket.)* Half past twelve.

BLINKA:   That'll be the day when he arrives on time! The day he spares a thought for anything but his car, that old bus of his, whether to put the hood up or down, the greasing jobs and the speeding. The day he gets his feet on the ground, on this *terra firma;* the day the penny drops so by the time you've made thirty, there might be a chance you'll soon reach forty; the day he tucks his shirt in his trousers and remembers my taste for American tobacco,. . .when that day comes. . .he won't be my Tommy anymore, not my own son at all,. . .so I'd just as soon go on waiting for him. . . . *(She drinks.)*

ZACRA:   One of these days I must try and corner the managing director.

BLINKA:   Isn't it a woman?

ZACRA:   No, it's Monsieur, now, what's his name. . .? Well, what they've always said to *me* is: "Zacra, it's the manager, that's what *he's* asked for," "*he* wants you to repaint No. 18 or No. 24. . . ."

BLINKA: It was a woman I saw when I arrived. She told me *she* was the managing director. Have you ever seen this manager of yours?

ZACRA: No.

BLINKA: So how do you know it's not the woman I saw?

ZACRA: Because, I tell you, it's a man! Otherwise, they wouldn't call him "him."

BLINKA: So she must be his wife, I suppose.

ZACRA: In which case she's not a manageress. She's the managing director's wife,...a nice distinction....I must say, when you get an idea in your head you wrap your brain around it. There's no shaking you!...Mind you, I don't know if you've noticed, but I'm just the same.... *(He laughs loudly.)* Don't you worry, we're the right ones, you know. *(He starts singing.)*

> The right is on our side,
> The rest have got it wrong.
> It's a fact they cannot hide
> As they listen to my song.

A hundred times a day I used to sing that when I was young and could still stretch my lungs and my paintbrush at one and the same time....Now I just talk,...but it comes to the same thing, really, my chamber music....Anyhow, when it comes to the old grey matter, I reckon you and I are made of the same stuff.

BLINKA: Not entirely. I've no desire to beard the managing director in his den.

ZACRA: That's true, but I have. Because I really want to know why all the rooms in his blasted guesthouse have different types of wallpaper. *(Suddenly he speaks almost aggressively.)* Is that my shirt you're staring at?

BLINKA: Your shirt?

ZACRA: *(putting his hand to the middle of his chest and clutching a handful of the material)* Yes, here, . . .you're looking at my shirt, here?

BLINKA: No, of course I'm not. Why do you think I should. . .?

ZACRA: I'm positive you were staring at my shirt. . . .

BLINKA: *(laughing)* No, honestly, I. . . .

ZACRA: I could have sworn an oath. . . .

BLINKA: You'd have perjured yourself. . . .

ZACRA: Right, O.K., I believe you. . . . Damned walls! It's never the same thing twice, now it's floral embossed, then it's plaster-backed hessian, . . . and sometimes it's pre-pasted vinyl. Why didn't they do them all the same, grained and varnished like this one, for God's sake! Here all you have to do is let it rip, the job just does itself. . . .

BLINKA: I don't know why. To break the monotony.

ZACRA: Break the monotony! Don't make me laugh! I've been repainting this place till I feel I'm on the permanent staff! I know these pads inside out. They're all the same shape, all the same size, and all furnished in the same way. It would take more than paint to break the monotony here, considering the number of rooms he's got. . . . No, you take my word, there's something else behind it. . . . Maybe it's a question of hard cash. . . . I'm not sure what it is, but I'll find out. . . . I'll corner that manager one of these days. *(He puts his paintbrush down, takes out his fob-watch and looks at it.)* Three o'clock. Right; I'll have a small break.

BLINKA: Three o'clock?! How can it be three o'clock?!

ZACRA: It is, you know! It's three p.m.

BLINKA: But only just now you told me it was half-past twelve.

ZACRA: *(sitting down in Blinka's armchair and taking his sandwich out. From a little tumbler he drinks the contents of a thermos identical to Blinka's, which he produces and then returns to his bag.)* Oh no, it *was* half-past twelve when I told you it was half-past twelve. When you asked me the time, I mean, two and a half hours ago.

BLINKA: You're joking! Your watch must have gone wrong.

ZACRA: My watch?

BLINKA: *(bursting out laughing)* Yes, it's gone completely berserk. It was hardly five minutes ago when I. . . .

ZACRA: Now, listen, lady. *(He points the wall out to her.)* If you think I could do all that in five minutes! I may be a fast worker, but my brush isn't jet-propelled. . . .

BLINKA: But it had just gone half-past twelve when you started talking about. . . .

ZACRA: Oh no, I stopped talking quite a while ago. *You've* been talking to *me*.

BLINKA: But only this minute, you were telling me about all these rooms being exactly alike.

ZACRA: No.

BLINKA: And your brain, your grey matter, being just like mine.

ZACRA: But I'd only just turned up when I told you that, and that business about the managing director and his wife.

BLINKA: And your shirt. . . .

ZACRA: What's the matter with my shirt?

BLINKA: Now, listen, Mr. . . . .

ZACRA: Zacra.

BLINKA: This is some sort of game, isn't it? A practical joke you often like to try on?

ZACRA: Just call me Zacra. After all, you've been telling me about your son, it's as if we were intimate friends. Aren't we, lady?

BLINKA: About my son!

ZACRA: Yes, Tommy. About his bicycle trip to Asia and the way he eats spaghetti with his hands. *(He gestures.)* Like this! How he managed to pass all his exams without having to revise. How mad he was for exotic dancing and South American rhythms. And, oh yes, about the day you caught him setting light to the curate's cassock. *(He laughs.)* Couldn't help chuckling over that one. . . .

BLINKA: *(dumbfounded)* But. . . .

ZACRA: And that day when he was six, and you realized that, however fair-haired he was then, he'd be dark before he was twenty, . . . and even how you showed him his dark hairs in the mirror, so they wouldn't frighten him, and he came out with something quite bright for his age.

BLINKA: *(as if she were far away)* "My first white hairs, Mommy."

ZACRA: That's it. But do you know what? Out of all you've told me, what I liked best is that song he used to sing when he was small. *(He sings.)*

> Toto's hat is black as night.
> Winnie's hat is far from white
> And not as light as Jerry's.
> Long live caps, hurrah for berets!
> Toto's hat is much too tight. . . .

BLINKA: *(murmuring)* I don't understand.

ZACRA: Tommy learned to sing before he could talk, didn't he?

BLINKA: Yes.

ZACRA: Just like me. That's when I started to talk, when I really couldn't sing anymore.

BLINKA: I'm terribly sorry, going on boring you about my son.

ZACRA: No harm in that.

BLINKA: I got up so late this morning; don't mind me, I don't think I've woken up yet. I guess I lose all notion of time when I'm talking about him. . . . I turn into a sort of speaking clock, ticking away oblivious of the passing of time. . . .

ZACRA: Well, that's fair enough, lady, isn't it? Not everyone has a son like Tommy. You're right, you have to talk about him. . . . Likeable young rascal, he sounds.

BLINKA: Oh, we mustn't make too much of him. Someone else who's pig-headed, obstinate as a mule. You know what the time is now. Three hours late! There are moments when I really get the feeling I'm the last of his worries.

ZACRA: Go on! I don't know many thirty-year-olds who, for their mother's sake, would. . . .

BLINKA: Who would what?

ZACRA: Well, after all, it's not a bad place he's taking you.

BLINKA: And where's that?

ZACRA: The castle.

BLINKA: The castle??

ZACRA: Yes.

BLINKA: I told you about the castle?

ZACRA: Of course you did.

BLINKA: Oh yes, now it comes back to me.

ZACRA: You'll be all right there. With that lake and the little woods and the mountains behind.

BLINKA: No, there isn't a lake.

ZACRA:  Yes, you told me there was . . . .

BLINKA:  It's not there, the lake; it's further away.

ZACRA:  But at least there *is* a lake; I didn't dream it?

BLINKA:  No, but it's a long way off.

ZACRA:  Right. I knew you'd told me about a lake. I love lakes . . . because of the frogs all hopping about on the banks. *(Again he paints the leap of a frog on the walls.)*

BLINKA:  He never goes to the lake.

ZACRA:  That's his affair. With a keep and dungeons, a drawbridge and all, . . . your castle?

BLINKA:  No, no! It's a ruin, an old ruin, that's all. It's true it's in a lovely spot, very isolated, but not to be compared with . . . . Just a dilapidated old stone house in a little wood . . . . Tommy can't bear city life . . . .

ZACRA:  Yes, I know. You told me that.

BLINKA:  But, you know, I never asked him for anything. Not a thing. It was Tom who wanted me to go and live with him. He can't stand being alone. He needs a maid or a housekeeper. A mother's ideal for him, and what's more, she's free of charge.

ZACRA:  I thought you were rather pleased about it . . . .

BLINKA:  Oh, I am! I'm delighted; I'm out of my mind! So many people of my age have only themselves to think about. And that's the truth, isn't it? . . . Isn't it?

ZACRA:  Yes.

BLINKA:  It's perfect . . . . I still have a son and that's really something. A son who keeps me kicking my heels for three long hours. But even that's better than nothing . . . .

ZACRA:  *(Having finished his sandwich, he puts his mess kit away and stands up.)* Right . . . .

BLINKA: I've stopped; I've said enough; I've really stopped now. I won't say another word. And if I do, you yell at me. I must start getting my things together without him, or we'll still be here this time tomorrow.

ZACRA: I must get back to work too.

BLINKA: (*pouring a little more from the thermos and having a drink before she goes to the wardrobe*) And you'll see the face he has when he does get here. Puce with apology.

ZACRA: (*climbing his ladder*) Like when he came back from school on your birthday, and he'd forgotten to bring you a present.

BLINKA: Did I tell you that too, Mr. . . .?

ZACRA: Zacra.

BLINKA: (*laughing*) Then I really have told you everything. Zacra!

ZACRA: Yes.

*(He starts painting, while Blinka puts a chair in front of her wardrobe and climbs up to take her cases down. She catches hold of one and puts it on the floor. Just as she is about to take the second, she slips and falls heavily to the ground. In a half-sitting position, she stays motionless. She doesn't appear to be hurt, just a bit stunned. Zacra speaks without turning around.)*

Did you hurt yourself? . . . Have you hurt yourself?

*(The door suddenly flies open, as if blown by a hurricane. A violent wind can be heard. A man stumbles into the room and immediately forces the door shut, as if he wanted to prevent the tornado from following him into the room as well. The roar of the wind ceases. He is fairly tall, and all one can see of him at first is his silhouette: a long greyish overcoat, rather shabby, with a curly black fur collar. A dark broad-brimmed hat casts a shadow over his face. The bottom of his trousers and his cracked patent leather shoes are splotched with fresh mud; there are also patches of dry mud on his hat and caking his shoulders.)*

*He moves quickly, and his gestures are sharp and rapid. Zacra has not moved. He goes on painting his wall as though nothing had happened. Throughout the following scene he will go on quietly painting, never turning aside from his work or paying any attention to the conversation. Blinka rises and stares at the man, amazed.)*

PETER:   Stinking weather! In that wind I've got filthy dirty. . . . *(He moves a few paces into the room.)* Apart from Cell 140 in the military prison at Alschewood, I've never seen anything so cozy,. . .though this is a polished floor. . .and the one at Alschewood wasn't. . . .

BLINKA:   Monsieur. . . .

PETER:   Hello. You don't recognize me?

BLINKA:   I. . . .

PETER:   Usually people aren't recognized because they've changed too much. It's because I have *not* changed that I don't get recognized. *(He takes off his hat.)* At all. *(His face appears. Firmly topping a crinkled neck, it seems to have been fossilized at about the age of thirty-five.)* I don't recognize you either, but I know it's you! I saw your name downstairs.

BLINKA:   My name. . . .

PETER:   Blinka Vallard. Age has transformed you, disfigured you completely, but it still hasn't affected your name. You are still Blinka Vallard.

BLINKA:   Yes; Blinka Vallard.

PETER:   Thank God for that! I haven't made this long, hateful journey for nothing. *(He looks at her.)* It doesn't honestly shock me to find you've grown old and quite lost your looks. I was expecting that. But I'm amazed there's not even a withered trace of that plump body of yours, the round behind and the heavy bosom and the smooth, velvety neck. . . .Big breasts hang differently with time and can spread all over the place, but they don't usually evaporate. Who's been nibbling your flesh away?

BLINKA:  I wonder if you'd mind telling me. . . .

PETER:  Disease or diet? I should think it's probably disease. Diets consume the fat, but it's disease that breaks down the meat. And it's the meat that's missing. . . .To think I nearly missed that ghastly train! I wouldn't have arrived till tomorrow. Maybe all I'd have found was bones!

BLINKA:  Bones. . . !

PETER:  Yes, at this stage, it doesn't take long. You stop getting thinner, you dry up, and everything goes. . .except your bones. . . .*They* survive. . .as evidence, some proof that you were "once alive"!

BLINKA:  Are you trying to say that if you'd got here tomorrow. . . ?

PETER:  I've no doubt I'd have found you dead, or not far off it. Yes, it's a stroke of luck I arrived today. . . . At least, the main thing is that you're still here now.

BLINKA:  Who are you?

PETER:  Excellent question. *(He takes a pack of cigarettes from his pocket.)* Cigarette? You only smoke Lucky Strikes, don't you?

*(Blinka shakes her head.)*

These are Lucky Strikes. Unlike you, my name is the only thing that *has* changed. And very often, too. But the name you know is the real one: Peter Crooks. Now, I guess that's clarified things for you.

BLINKA:  No.

PETER:  Lost your memory, as well as your figure?

BLINKA:  Maybe we did know each other once, but it must have been a long time ago. Wasn't it?

PETER:  Thirty years.

BLINKA:   Ah, well! Then it's perfectly understandable.

PETER:   Thirty-one, to be precise. . .since the last time we met.

BLINKA:   Yes, yes; it's only natural.

PETER:   Natural?

BLINKA:   That you have no real existence.

PETER:   Clever Blinka! Shrewd as ever. It's true; I'm a ghost from the past.

BLINKA:   I meant that you've never had any real existence for me. . .until this moment.

PETER:   Don't you think you're going a little too far?

BLINKA:   I don't know you, Monsieur. I have never seen you before.

PETER:   So, . . .you let anyone into your room. You invite any stranger who happens to be passing by to pop through the door, make himself at home, and start a conversation. You don't even call for help; you just welcome him in, just like me. . . .

BLINKA:   It might be someone who knows me perfectly well. . . .

PETER:   You rotten tart, with your oily lies, slippery as ever!. . . That's one thing about you you've still kept intact. It's probably rot-proof, resistant to putrefaction. It's not for your gold teeth they'll rifle your tomb, but your dissimulation, your eternal evasiveness. . . . But you won't get away with it this time. I didn't set out on a long trip like this to go back empty-handed.

BLINKA:   I understand your impatience, Monsieur. But if we have met before, after what you've told me, it must have been before my son was born. Thirty, thirty-one years ago. So there's nothing I can do about it.

PETER:   Really!

BLINKA: Yes. There's no mystery, Monsieur. No dissimulation, as you call it. Just something very natural, even commonplace. . . .

PETER: Commonplace?

BLINKA: Yes. I was born the same time as my son. How shall I put it? When I brought him into the world, I came into it too. (*She smiles.*) Out walking in the park, it was with him, at the very same moment as he did, that I first discovered the trees and the birds and listened to their singing. The tiniest dog would frighten me just as much as him. I completely forgot the names and faces of the grocer and the concierge I'd been chatting with every day for five years. . . . I know it must seem stupid to you, but if you were a woman, none of this would surprise you. It's a very common happening to women, to be born again when they give birth, the same moment as their own child. It's like a surfeit of joy gushing through us, forcing us to unite more closely with the world about us. Especially when that child is a son.

PETER: (*arrogantly*) Yes.

BLINKA: Don't be too hard on me. You're not the only one, you know. Many of the old friends I've met in the last thirty years I've been quite unable to recognize. . . and they all understood perfectly.

PETER: Of course.

BLINKA: How can I help it? It's what happens to a mother. A real mother. (*She motions to him, as though ready to accompany him to the door.*) It's a shame you've had such a long journey. . . .

PETER: His name is Tom, I hope.

BLINKA: I'm sorry?

PETER: Your son, his name *is* Tom!

BLINKA: Please understand that it's not my fault. Besides, I have things to do, I must. . . .

*(Peter removes his coat and throws it on the bed. Now he is seen to be wearing the shabby uniform, discolored by time, of a flight lieutenant in the Royal Air Force. The uniform is stained with splotches of caked mud.)*

PETER: *(going up to Blinka and smiling)* In wartime, it seems, the only beautiful people are its heroes. In the last two years, since the Germans, clean and tidy as ever, started sending their rubbish by plane to tip it over London town, it's been breaking my heart, Mademoiselle, that the only people I meet, especially in this bar, all look so hideously ugly. . . . So don't be surprised that I'm amazed to see you here. . . . You're so beautiful. . . . You must surely be German? They have all the heroes now. . . . French?! Good God! So they haven't wiped you all out? Do you mind if I sit down?. . . Thank you. Harry, two whiskies. . . . Wait! Perhaps you don't drink Scotch. . . . You do? Fine, two whiskies, then, Harry. I'm sorry, you are. . . ? Oh, a civilian refugee. . . . That's a brave thing to be, in a war: you eat bad food, it's hard to find anything reasonable to wear, and it's such a business making a phone call. . . . Thanks, Harry. . . . Just a minute, he doesn't understand French. . . . The lady would like a glass of plain water, Harry. . . . In this part of the world they only speak the local dialect: English. It's a pretty awful language. Three-quarters of the human race have mastered it. . . . *(His tone changes.)* Blinka, I know you're there.

BLINKA: But what is all this, Monsieur?

PETER: *(tensely)* I'm talking to you. . . the Blinka that's there behind you.

BLINKA: I'm listening.

PETER: I've seen you, Blinka, so I know you're there.

BLINKA: What can I do to help you?

PETER: That's fine. Just answer. I can see you. You're there. Here. And you can see me too.

BLINKA: I think it would be more sensible if you went back where you came from. . . .

PETER:  Very well. As you like.... *(His tone changes.)* A civilian
....Yes....Mind you, I can see the advantage....I hesitated
quite a while before *I* got into uniform....But when it came
to the point, I couldn't face strolling through the streets without
a cap. Too much of a coward. And I rather dislike not being
decently dressed. Of course, the color's not ideal....I suggested
grey flannel with a chalk stripe,...but the War Ministry was
positively opposed to the idea.

BLINKA:  *(troubled)* Monsieur....

PETER:  Oh, I completely forgot to present myself: Flight-
Lieutenant Peter Crooks, Royal Air Force. *(He bursts out laughing.)*
No, no, I've never been up in an aeroplane! What an idea!
No, as far as the Royal Air Force is concerned, I stick to the
"Royal" part of it, and leave others to deal with the flying.
And there are plenty of them.... *(He takes a pack of Lucky Strikes
from one of his jacket pockets.)* You want one? I warn you, they're
American. Virginian tobacco. Once you've tried them, you
won't smoke anything else....

   *(Blinka takes a cigarette.)*

Brava! You're sticking your neck out....Quite an occupation
in that....Yes, every now and again I spend an afternoon
transmitting messages. Trying desperately to persuade the
Germans to bomb my bank. I've one hell of an overdraft.
But it's still outstanding, cocking snooks. *(He thumbs his nose.)*
Either they're inefficient or they wrote the address down wrong.
...Still, I can't blame them too much; they've managed to
hit London all right.... *(His tone changes.)* Well?...Still no
reaction? Wriggly as an eel....I'll get you yet....Well?
Right, I'll go on. *(His tone changes.)* I'm sorry, what was that
you just said?

BLINKA:  Nothing.

PETER:  You're expecting a friend? Oh, I see....Another
French girl....Cinta? No, I don't know her.

BLINKA:  *(curtly)* What do you want?

PETER:  Mademoiselle...? Blinka! Oh, what a pretty name! You're beautiful, and you have a pretty name! This is beginning to feel like my nightmare. For ten years I've been having the same terrible nightmare. I meet a beautiful girl with a pretty name, I invite her to dinner, and just as she refuses I wake up screaming. Suppose we went out to dinner, what do you say? You said yes!!

BLINKA:  What do you want? Come on, out with it. It's all right, say it!

PETER:  This is the first time that I've not woken up at that precise moment.

BLINKA:  I've had enough. Enough, you hear me?

PETER:  That's it. Dropped in the drink. Caught napping in your birthday suit. Now you remember, don't you? Remember perfectly. . . .Oh yes, the uniform, that helps! You can't forget the uniform . . . .

BLINKA:  I've forgotten everything. Everything, you hear me? Everything that happened before, now it's gone. But it's that voice. That lousy voice came back to me. That sick-making tone of voice, sour and festering like the plague. I thought my son had wiped out that black virus with everything else. I thought it was dead, but it was only dormant.

PETER:  That quite took it out of me. Though I've used it hundreds of times, my little line in seduction, I've got to admit it's left me quite played out. . . .You know I nearly dried? What *was* the name of that barman? Was it Harry? I'm not quite sure. I think perhaps. . .wasn't it Bill?

BLINKA:  It was Sam.

PETER:  Sam, that's it! By the way, haven't you anything to drink?

BLINKA:  No.

PETER:   The big, fat blonde, that was Cinta, wasn't it?

BLINKA:   Yes.

PETER:   Cinta the inseparable, the bosom friend. . . .You know, Cinta had quite a yen for me,. . .the classic situation. I don't suppose she ever mentioned it to you?. . . No, it's of no interest.

BLINKA:   Is that all?

PETER:   No. Your son, his name *is* Tom?. . .That was what we decided, that we should split them up, the first name English and the surname French. So we'd each have a share.

BLINKA:   You had your share.

PETER:   Good. . . .Tom Vallard! Not bad. . . .Do you call him Tom or Tommy?

BLINKA:   I've no time for all this!

PETER:   I bet you call him Tommy.

BLINKA:   Listen, I'm in a hurry. I haven't the time, you can see I've no time for all this.

PETER:   Neither have I.

BLINKA:   But what are you doing here? Why am I talking to you? Who are you? If you think that for thirty years I've been. . . .

PETER:   Not the story of your life! You either made a success or a hash of it. And as there are no historical records as yet of any successful life — except for that doctor from the Middle West, who suddenly started whinnying, took to his heels and galloped off over his neighbor's land, and two snails who one rainy afternoon acquired a taste for whisky — there's no point in you telling me yours. I know it already. It's the same as everyone else's.

BLINKA:   What is it you want? The address of a publisher who specializes in the British sense of humor? Or one of my party frocks? A pair of dancing shoes or a lipstick?

PETER:   I want Tom.

BLINKA:   What?

PETER:   I want Tommy.

BLINKA:   You came back to ask me that!?

PETER:   Where is Tom?

BLINKA:   Why?

PETER:   Because I'm lonely, Blinka; I'm absolutely alone. Like a cockbird that's had his head chopped off but is still running around. Alone in this world and the next. Absolutely, absolutely alone.

BLINKA:   I don't care about that.

PETER:   Where is he?

BLINKA:   Don't shout!. . .Go away; you won't find anything here.

PETER:   Apart from my capital. That small capital of love I'd completely forgotten about. . . .

BLINKA:   Love?

PETER:   Spunk. That sperm you begged me to deposit inside you thirty years ago.

BLINKA:   If you go on, I'll call down for help. . . .

PETER:   One large pearl of white jelly, which must have grown and matured by now. Which I have come to find,. . .and which you owe me.

BLINKA:   I owe you nothing.

PETER: Tom. You simply owe me Tom.

BLINKA: No. You paid me off and that was that. "Frenchy! Frenchy! This is my little Frenchy!" For four years you went round with your smiling little French girl hanging round your neck, flaunting me next to your tie pin, like a carnation in your buttonhole. Then it was: "Sorry, goodbye. See you!". . . And you were off. Weren't you? Off and away? Only before you went, I asked you to settle your account. Wasn't that only natural?

PETER: You slut!. . . I never paid you off, you robbed me!. . . I left you because you robbed me,. . .you slut!

BLINKA: Rob you! Who could ever rob you?

PETER: You robbed me like a true professional. You waited for the one moment when I stopped thinking about myself. . . .

BLINKA: There never was such a moment.

PETER: You robbed me when I was in love with you.

*(Controlling her embarrassment and misgivings, Blinka bursts out laughing.)*

Sooner or later, you see, stolen property has to be returned. There is such a thing as justice. And if it's late in coming, I don't think I mind that at all. Its value must have increased with time. You stole a few drops of blood from me, and I've come to claim back a human being that weighs eleven stone. . . . Where is he? I hope you don't think I've come all this distance to leave again all by myself. Where is he?. . .Did you ever tell him of my existence?

BLINKA: But you have no existence!

PETER: Right,. . .all right! He never asked any questions about me?

BLINKA: No.

PETER: You told him he was someone else's son?

BLINKA: No.

PETER: Where is he living?

BLINKA: In a castle.

PETER: A castle. . . . He's rich; I was sure he would be. . . . Where is this castle?

BLINKA: Next to a little wood.

PETER: The address! I don't care if it's next to a wood or squatting on top of a cliff; I want that address!

BLINKA: I don't know it.

PETER: Right.

BLINKA: What are you doing?

PETER: Sitting down.

BLINKA: But what do you want of me?. . .What are you waiting for?

PETER: Tom!

BLINKA: Tom? How do you expect him to turn up here, when he doesn't even know that *I'm* here?

PETER: You're lying.

BLINKA: I tell you, he's not coming!

PETER: You know perfectly well he is.

BLINKA: But why should he? And why today? Because *you're* here, I suppose? Because you attract him like a magnet?

PETER: No. Because he's your son. And wherever he or she may be, a son always pops up when his mother's about to die.

BLINKA: And what about you? Why are you here? Why today? Why did you come here today?

PETER: For me, it's different. . . .I know when our end is near,. . .when things are drawing to a close, when we come to a halt. Don't ask me why; that's the way it is.

BLINKA: Get out!

PETER: I wanted to know where he was living, where to find him, and then take off before he arrived. I do have some sense of. . .delicacy? So as to leave you alone for the very last time, to say goodbye to you both. . . . But as you persist in refusing to give me his address, I shall stay here and wait.

BLINKA: You'll never see him. Never, ,you understand?

PETER: Oh, yes I will. Only a few more minutes and then he'll appear. *(He points towards the door.)* Over there.

BLINKA: Go away! I'm tired.

PETER: It's a lot worse than that. I know.

BLINKA: I promise you he won't come. Go away!

PETER: I'd never really noticed, although you look a brunette, really your hair is grey. Like yellow and blue making green, grey and grey make brown. I'd never noticed before. You ought to sit down.

BLINKA: It's better, Peter, if you never find him again.

PETER: Oh yes, why's that?

BLINKA: He'd kill you.

PETER: That wouldn't worry me unduly, but I'm not sure I believe it.

BLINKA: For him, you've arrived a bit late. Far too late. Like a carrier pigeon bringing good news that one's been waiting for year after year. When it finally turns up, you take a pot shot at it. You're relieved to see it, but by this time you're so convinced the news is bad that you don't even bother to open the envelope....Go away.

PETER: You talk too much, Blinka. You shouldn't. Words are debilitating. Like tobacco....You should husband your strength. Otherwise, you'll have so little life left in you when he comes into this room that you'll find it hard to express yourself.

*(Wringing her hands, Blinka walks around in circles. There is a pause, then a knock at the door. She stands still.)*

BLINKA: No!

PETER: You see, we didn't have long to wait.

*(There is another knock. Blinka recoils, her eyes fixed on the door, and slowly sits down on the floor exactly where she was when Peter came in.)*

All right, open it! Open it, it's him! *(He speaks in a loud voice.)* Come in! *(There is another knock. He shouts.)* Come in! *(There is a short pause and then another knock.)* What's the matter with you, Blinka? If you've locked the door, go and let him in!

*(The door swings slowly open. Madeleine appears, bringing a metal thermos on a tray.)*

MADELEINE: Madame?

BLINKA: Yes.

MADELEINE: Oh, I thought you were asleep. *(She puts the thermos down on the table and picks up the old one.)* Would you like me to help you pack?

BLINKA: No, no, thank you.

MADELEINE: I'm sorry about this morning, Madame. I didn't know it was your turn today.

BLINKA:  My turn?

MADELEINE:  To be repainted. So I couldn't let you know in advance.

BLINKA:  It's of no importance.

MADELEINE:  Well, then, if I don't see you again,. . .well,. . . have a good trip, Madame.

BLINKA:  Thank you.

MADELEINE:  Right; goodbye, then, Madame.

BLINKA:  Yes.

*(Madeleine goes out, closing the door so gently behind her that it would seem to be edged with felt. Blinka springs to her feet, suddenly alarmed.)*

Mademoiselle, Mademoiselle! *(She runs to the door.)* Mademoiselle! *(She suddenly swings around and stares at Peter, who has been following her.)* What are you doing? What are you doing. . .? Where are you going, Peter? Well, answer me! What's the matter with you? Why did you get up?

PETER:  Who was that?

BLINKA:  It doesn't matter; it wasn't him.

PETER:  I couldn't see; who was it?

BLINKA:  Go and sit down.

PETER:  It wasn't Tom, was it?

BLINKA:  No.

PETER:  He *is* coming, isn't he?

BLINKA:  You know very well he isn't!

PETER:  Yes; but I'm asking you, he is going to come?

BLINKA: Yes. He is going to come. He's late; he should have been here at midday. But when you know him better, or should I say when you get to know him, you'll see there's nothing surprising in that.

PETER: What are you doing?

BLINKA: Can't you see?

PETER: Packing your bags?

BLINKA: Bravo!

PETER: Now. . .why? Are you leaving?

BLINKA: I'm leaving.

PETER: But you're mad, in the state you're in! You won't get more than a hundred yards in this weather. All the roads are thick mud. And the hailstones. And what about Tom?

BLINKA: You're here.

PETER: But I don't know him!

BLINKA: He's slim, about six feet tall, with green eyes. One of them, anyway, a bit smaller than the other. And underneath his beard you can tell his jaw is too big. The one thing he has in common with you.

PETER: A jaw that's too big?

BLINKA: Yes. You didn't want him to be born. And in a sense he didn't want it either. So he concentrated on having a jaw, so it would get in the way. But I won. He ripped me open, but I was the stronger. He was born.

PETER: What am I going to say to him?

BLINKA: That we've reached half-time. The first half, thirty years, with his mother. Then the whistle blows and you change sides. The second half with his father.

PETER: Listen, Blinka....

BLINKA: Try and introduce him to some nice girl. He doesn't know any.

PETER: How do you know that?

BLINKA: He tells me everything. He's never been to bed with a woman, though I encouraged him. I even explained to him how it was done, when he was quite young, several times. We've often talked about it, but it never happened....

PETER: That's not what I came for.

BLINKA: *(taking things from her handbag)* His blood group, in case of accidents, and they call you. His christening pendant; he's fond of that.

PETER: But wait.... How can I prove that I'm his father, if you're not here?

BLINKA: Leave it to nature. Nature knows how to handle things like that.

PETER: And you, what about you? He's going to ask me where you are.

BLINKA: Tell him the truth.

PETER: What truth?

BLINKA: What you've been proclaiming with every other word you've said.

PETER: What, me!! *I* don't know.

BLINKA: That I'm ill; that I'm practically dead.

PETER: I was joking.

BLINKA: Ah, yes, I was forgetting....

PETER: I promise I was joking.... Kiss me.

BLINKA: *(Taking a shoebox from the wardrobe, she empties its contents at Peter's feet. Hundreds of envelopes are lying on the floor.)* These are the letters he writes me once or twice a week. Read them. The whole man, they'll tell you all about him. No; the last one's missing, the one I had yesterday. *(She searches in her handbag.)* Yes, here it is. He's thinking of taking a trip. Well, you'll see.

PETER: I only said it to see how you'd react. In fact, as far as I can tell, you're looking very well.

BLINKA: Every now and then he gets the urge to travel. Then there's no more news for two or three months. Up to six months sometimes. But he always comes back,...or they bring him home. Don't try and stop him; that never does any good.

PETER: You can't do this. You can't do this to him!

BLINKA: There. I think that's about everything. *(She puts on her outdoor coat.)*

PETER: Sit down for a minute! Don't be so excited; I've got to talk to you.

BLINKA: No, I must go. He won't be long now. Believe me, he'll be here any minute.

PETER: Stay with me!

BLINKA: Au revoir, Flight Lieutenant Peter Crooks of the Royal Air Force.

PETER: You said he'd kill me if he saw me, shoot me like a carrier pigeon.

BLINKA: *(insidiously)* That was a joke.

PETER: You're leaving me?!

BLINKA: Yes.

PETER: Leaving me alone with him,...all alone.

BLINKA: I'm leaving you with him. But not all alone. With Tom, you'll never be lonely again. Don't worry; I'm only leaving you with your son. It's your turn now. You'll see, the time passes so quickly.

PETER: *(Seizing hold of her just as she is about to turn the doorknob, he snatches her suitcase away, opens it, and empties it in the wardrobe. He is trembling. Now his words rush out. Physically, you can see he is frightened.)* You made a mess of him, is that it? You took him from me in one night of love and you've turned him into some imbecile crab with a shell too soft to protect him. Made a hash of him, have you? A deficient nonentity! And now you want to unload him on me! I can see it all now, you know. The whole thing. When you produce an abortion, you're blind to everything else, everything that's gone before. You're too busy trying to repair your mistake. You should never have let go of Tom; you should have loved him and sheltered him. Now I see it all clearly. You tried to pretend there was nothing wrong, that he was just like everyone else, that you'd managed to patch him up. Maybe you did a good job on yourself, but not him. He's the sort of mistake that can't be put right. I've got it all straight now, you know. But you needn't think *I'm* going to carry the can. *I* never wanted him. Besides, there's not much of me about him. Except his jaw. Which appears to indicate that he didn't want to be born either. I don't see why I should be lumbered with him when he's hardly mine at all. I started fucking girls when I was twelve. That proves he's not like me. I bet he's a half-wit and he stammers. . . . It's no good gawping at me like that. I won't take him. *(He quickly slips his coat on and picks up his hat.)* Not a second time, Blinka. You don't trap me twice. I came to find out what was stowed away in my safe-deposit. Not a cracked vase, thank you. You can keep it. . . . And the castle. I suppose you imagined I would fall for that castle and all that dough! . . . I never believed in that for one moment. You don't catch me as easily as that. . . . *(He opens the door. The wind can be heard blowing in gusts, with snatches of driving rain.)* Hear that? It's belting down. The mud will be thicker than ever. I'll have my work cut out getting back to the station. . . . Be fair, at least give me a little money.

BLINKA: No.

PETER: You get so cold in all that mud. . . .

BLINKA: No.

PETER: I won't come back here again. But I'll be expecting you. . . .See you soon. . . .Tomorrow, perhaps, . . .without fail. *(He goes out, and as the door slams, the noise of the storm stops abruptly.)*

BLINKA: *(sitting down next to her suitcase and whispering, with a smile)* Tommy,. . .that was a narrow escape!

ZACRA: Have you hurt yourself? Have you hurt yourself?

BLINKA: I'm sorry?

ZACRA: You had a nasty fall.

BLINKA: *(getting up)* Oh, Monsieur Zacra, I'd quite forgotten you, with all this going on!

ZACRA: It's natural you should feel a bit shaken.

BLINKA: Because of him? No, not really! He was bound to come back one day. I was just very scared that Tom might arrive while he was here. It would have been too much for him. And he'd have been too much for Tom. Tom always wanted me all to himself. Ever since he was born. That's quite normal in a child. Tom's an angel, you know. So he beat his great wings and swept from my mind everything that cluttered my memory. He took me over completely. If he'd have realized that man was still around, he'd have gone raving mad!

ZACRA: What man?

BLINKA: Well, you know,. . .I've forgotten his name already. My scars heal fast. That's a good sign. His father. I must apologize, inflicting that rather shameful conversation on you. It was almost indecent.

ZACRA: But you haven't opened your mouth.

BLINKA: And then all that noise, coming and going.

ZACRA: You mean the little lady on duty?

BLINKA: Madeleine?

ZACRA: I don't know what she's called, but anyway, she didn't make a sound. I wouldn't even have noticed she was here, if she hadn't had a bit of a chat.

BLINKA: Do you think she saw him? She didn't seem to notice him at all.

ZACRA: Didn't seem to notice *who?*

BLINKA: Tom's father. Yet in that old blue uniform with its officer's stripes all frayed, he ought to have intrigued her, . . . especially all stained and covered in mud. Perhaps she was overawed. Unless she was being discreet, one of the old school. Do you think it was that?

ZACRA: Are you trying to tie me into knots, lady, or what?

BLINKA: Me? Why do you say that? I don't understand.

ZACRA: Neither do I. You go sprawling trying to take one of your cases down, I ask if you've hurt yourself, then that girl comes in, you have a bit of a chat, she says goodbye and off she goes. Again I ask if you've hurt yourself, and you start going on about your kid's father being here, dressed up as some sort of Austrian! I'm ready to go with you all the way, but come off it, I ask you!

BLINKA: He wasn't dressed up as an Austrian.

ZACRA: That's what it sounded like. At least you said he was in blue, with officer's stripes.

BLINKA: You're not very observant, Monsieur Zacra. He was here for nearly an hour and you never even noticed he was wearing a British uniform. Royal Air Force.

ZACRA: *(bursts out laughing)* And here I go, getting taken in again! I don't just fall, I jump at it! What's more, I've had it tried on me before. Less than two months ago, by the client in No. 49. And again I swallowed it like a greenhorn. Same sort of thing. Talk about a sucker! But that time he really took me for a ride!

BLINKA: But what's got into you? Why won't you answer my question?

ZACRA: Yes, yes. I know all about that.

BLINKA: All I'm asking is whether you think Madeleine saw Tom's father or not.

ZACRA: Don't strain yourself, lady. I've been through all this before. Monsieur Riquier in No. 49, the day I did his room up, he started the same little game. I was on the point of moving his wardrobe, when he says, "Be careful how you go, because I'm inside, you know." "Inside"!? "Yes," he goes on, "I'm inside this wardrobe, so be a good chap and take care. I can give you a hand, if you like. I can help you to push it as well." Then, without a second's thought, I found myself asking, "What the hell are you doing inside this wardrobe?" "Reading," he says. "Just reading!" Without the word of a lie! So I says to him, "But Monsieur Riquier, I ask you, how can you be reading inside this wardrobe, when you're standing here in front of it talking to me?" And he comes straight back with, "Ah! That's just it. To read *and* to talk, it's hard to do both at once. So I thought I'd step inside the wardrobe to read, while we go on undisturbed with our little chat." Well, what can you possibly say to that?! So we both moved the wardrobe out of the way, taking every care not to disturb him. Then I went back to my painting. But I could hardly think straight.

BLINKA: That's not surprising.

ZACRA: Whenever his back was turned, I was dying to peep in the wardrobe. But if he *was* there inside, it wouldn't do me much good that he *had* turned his back, 'cos he'd see me just the same. And that's how I went on, lady, right through the day.

BLINKA:    What a funny story!

ZACRA:    I'd like to know what you'd have done. About a week later I told Liliane about it. That's the woman who sees to No. 49. I had to tell someone, because it went spinning round in my mind, night and day. It was like a circus inside, with a nonstop program. She had a good laugh, and then she told me Monsieur Riquier was a . . ., what do you call it?

BLINKA:    A schizophrenic?

ZACRA:    No, . . . a ventriloquist. That's it; a ventriloquist. One of those fellows whose eyes pop out on stalks and who talk from the pit of their stomach. Stupid, wasn't it? But you can imagine how relieved I was: while he was chatting to me with his stomach, his eyes were somewhere else, reading away in the wardrobe. It helps when you understand things. Nothing mysterious about it. Tricks of the trade, that's all. . . . That's why it's no good you going on, lady, about that British pilot of yours, who's meant to have spent an hour with you in here. I've been fumigated. No flies on me.

BLINKA:    I'm not a ventriloquist, Monsieur Zacra.

ZACRA:    Oh, but that doesn't prove a thing. Some people are ventriloquists and don't even know it. Besides, you could be something else.

BLINKA:    *(staggering a little)* Such as what?

ZACRA:    Aren't you feeling well, lady?

BLINKA:    Yes, I'm all right. What, then?

ZACRA:    God, I don't know. You could be a tightrope walker, a fortune-teller, a juggler, a clairvoyant. . . .

BLINKA:    A clairvoyant?

ZACRA:   Yes, that would do just as well in a case like this. You
 don't have to be a ventriloquist. I've made a few inquiries,
 you know.

BLINKA:   You don't think perhaps it's you being a bit . . . blind?

ZACRA:   Because I never saw that fellow of yours?! That's a
 good one, I like that, me blind! Me, Zacra, the painter, blind!
 . . . You've got a nerve!

BLINKA:   *(picking up the pack of Lucky Strikes from the floor)* He even
 left his cigarettes behind. . . . You see, it's the truth I'm telling
 you, . . . Virginian tobacco. . . .

ZACRA:   Now, listen, lady, I promise you I don't believe in this
 sort of thing. . . .

BLINKA:   What sort of thing?

ZACRA:   In folks some people see and some people can't, in
 the tricks ventriloquists get up to. . . .

BLINKA:   You're a strange man, Zacra.

ZACRA:   *I* am?

BLINKA:   For a painter, I find you somewhat unusual. . . . Are
 you sure you're really on the maintenance staff of this place?

ZACRA:   You won't get anywhere that way. We'll call it a day,
 if you don't mind. I'm unflappable, lady.

BLINKA:   So am I, Monsieur Zacra; I warn you.

ZACRA:   I know. I know we've both got our heads screwed
 on. . . . So what's the point, making up all these stories?

BLINKA:   Did you recognize him? Is that why?

ZACRA:   What did you say?

BLINKA:   Crooks, Peter Crooks, you recognized him.

ZACRA: Peter what?

BLINKA: It was you who told him about me. You gave him my address, so he could find me again!

ZACRA: Tell me another!

BLINKA: I bet he wasn't too lavish with his tips.

ZACRA: Got to get this finished by this evening.

BLINKA: He bribed you, didn't he? It could be a lot worse, Monsieur Zacra. The main thing is that he didn't see Tommy. Yes, that's the only thing that matters. . . . It's not worth your trying so hard to make me believe you never saw him and that no one else came except Madeleine, . . . not worth the effort. . . . I'm not going to hold it against you.

ZACRA: Wouldn't you like to sit down, lady?

BLINKA: I've got to get my things together.

ZACRA: You can do that later, when your son's here with you. . . . Sit down. . . . I think you really want to.

BLINKA: Why are you talking to me like this?

ZACRA: Just being nice to you.

BLINKA: Why are you being nice to me?

ZACRA: I'll tell you, if you sit down.

*(Blinka sits down. Zacra goes up to her and talks very quietly.)*

I like you. I don't always understand you, but I really like you. Rest for a bit. . . . You probably hurt yourself. . . . It'll soon pass, . . . but you mustn't get excited. . . .

BLINKA: What's the matter with you?

ZACRA: You just relax. I've got to go on with my work. . . .

It's all got to be finished by seven. . . . It gets dark so quickly, you know.

BLINKA: Monsieur, . . .who are you?

ZACRA: The painter, . . .Zacra the painter, . . .that's all. . . .

BLINKA: Why are you doing this?

ZACRA: We've got to earn our living.

BLINKA: Why are you doing this to me? You know perfectly well he was here.

ZACRA: No one was here. Only Madeleine. For three minutes, then she went away. . . .Three minutes. . . .

BLINKA: Have you got the time?

ZACRA: *(Taking his watch from his pocket, he looks at it and places it against his ear.)* It's stopped.

BLINKA: Three minutes. . . .

ZACRA: Yes. You see, you're feeling better already. *(He climbs back up his ladder.)*

BLINKA: And you painted all that in three minutes? All that wall?

ZACRA: But. . . .

BLINKA: You don't use spray paint?

ZACRA: No.

BLINKA: So it must take at least an hour to paint all that. . . , doesn't it?

ZACRA: I haven't a clue, really. . . .

BLINKA: Yes, it must take an hour, a good hour. Not three minutes. . . .

ZACRA: If that's what you say. . . .

BLINKA: Well, let's suppose you were concentrating, giving it all you've got. . . .

ZACRA: If you like.

BLINKA: So that you weren't aware of him or of our conversation. Is that it?

ZACRA: Could be.

BLINKA: You saw nothing, heard nothing. You were far too absorbed in your work. That's it, isn't it?

ZACRA: I. . . .

BLINKA: Look! Look how much you've done. . . . Half of it's black already.

ZACRA: Yes.

BLINKA: I'm right, aren't I? I am right?

ZACRA: Of course you are.

BLINKA: That's logical, isn't it? Tell me! It's obvious!

ZACRA: *(giving way, without conviction)* I guess so. I was too pre-occupied, painting my walls. I expect that's it. I couldn't really notice anything else. That's right. Please accept my apologies. . . . *(He starts painting again.)*

BLINKA: *(Relieved, she is suddenly gay and light-hearted.)* Oh, what a painter! What a tease my little painter man is! It all seems so funny to me now! *(She is taken with a fit of uncontrollable laughter.)* Nothing makes me happier than people who just rattle on and say the first thing that crosses their minds. People like you.

ZACRA: I told you before, people love to hear me talking.

BLINKA: *(putting her suitcase on the bed and starting to pack it)* You know what you're going to do?

ZACRA:   No.

BLINKA:   Give me your address, then I'll invite you to dinner
one evening at Tommy's.

ZACRA:   In the castle?

BLINKA:   Yes. . . . Do you have a phone?

ZACRA:   No, but my neighbor does. She can pass a message on.

BLINKA:   *(still packing her case)* Good. I'll do the cooking for you
both. I can't wait for Tommy to meet you! . . . He's like me,
crazy about people who are real characters. And you're a
real character, Monsieur Zacra.

ZACRA:   I know. I've been told that before.

BLINKA:   Do you dance the tango?

ZACRA:   Beg pardon?

BLINKA:   The tango, do you dance the tango?

ZACRA:   No.

BLINKA:   No? Not at all?

ZACRA:   Not at all.

BLINKA:   Pity.

ZACRA:   Why?

BLINKA:   Tommy likes people who dance the tango. . .even
badly.

ZACRA:   Oh, good.

BLINKA:   Yes, because of Hong Kong.

ZACRA:   Don't know him.

BLINKA:  In China. . . .Tommy worked in Hong Kong for six months as a barman at the Argentina Club. And there was a competition every Friday night for the best tango dancer of the week. Do you see?

ZACRA:  Must have been very interesting.

BLINKA:  Very. In fact, the only reason he sometimes misses China is the tango.

ZACRA:  I see.

BLINKA:  It's rotten for him, not being able to dance it anymore. He always wants us to do it together. But I'm hopeless at it and God knows, he's tried hard enough to teach me! *(She hums a tango and tries out two or three clumsy steps.)* It's a disaster!

ZACRA:  Just like me. You know, I've never managed to sleep without a pillow. . . . It's not all that difficult, but I just can't, and it's not for want of trying.

BLINKA:  *(taking out of her wardrobe a very elegant dress, a satin evening gown)* Look! He even bought this dress for me, to make me want to try harder. . . . *(She holds it up against her.)* When I'm with him, he likes me to wear it all the time. So I keep it on all day long.

ZACRA:  Just like me. I can't paint if I don't have my knife on me. Under my shirt. It gets hot against the skin and I sweat. But it makes me feel safe, and I have to know it's there. *(He takes out a knife.)* It gives me a sense of stability. Heaven knows why. . . .

BLINKA:  At first I used to get it caught up. So he'd put it on to show me how to pull it in here and let it hang there, and then he'd dance. *(She hums a tango.)* And he moved so beautifully that afterwards I didn't dare. He'd go like this, you see? *(She makes a gesture with her hands.)* And make it stream out like a horse's mane. He's astonishing. Just too incredible!

ZACRA: When I'm at home or in town, it's no problem at all; I can manage without it. It's when I'm working that I have to have it next to my skin. Otherwise, how can I put it, I feel I'm losing my balance. . . . It took me ages to discover the secret. . . . But it's like so many of the things you look for: it stares you in the face, but you just can't see it.

BLINKA: It's not his fault. That's the way he is. He dazzles you, like a prince. People don't like princes; they prefer town clerks. But he couldn't care less about living on his own and seeing no one but me. *(She folds her dress.)* I'll master it one of these days. It seems it doesn't matter how old you are. The older, the better. Still, it's a great pity you can't do it either.

ZACRA: The tango.

BLINKA: Yes. I'd have made you a lovely dinner, spaghetti à l'oeuf, my specialty. And during the meal you'd have come out with your small talk, and then later you and Tommy, the two of you, could have danced the tango to an audience of mountains. *(She hums a tango.)* What a wonderful evening. . . !

ZACRA: I can sing if you like:

Toto's hat is black as night.
Winnie's hat is. . . .

BLINKA: That's not quite the same. . . . *(She closes her suitcase.)* There's one thing done. *(She moves it over near the door, staggering a little, then she goes and sits down on a chair.)*

ZACRA: *(without turning around)* Not feeling so good? A touch of giddiness, perhaps?

BLINKA: It's nothing.

ZACRA: Of course it's nothing. Just feeling rather faint, are you?

BLINKA: Only a little. I hurt myself when you came in just now. I must have pulled a muscle in my leg.

ZACRA: Would you like my belt to put around it? It's made of wool.

BLINKA: No, thank you.

ZACRA: Did I really give you a fright?

BLINKA: Yes, you really did.

ZACRA: People aren't usually frightened of me.... Never, in fact.

BLINKA: I was taken by surprise. It wasn't you I was expecting....

ZACRA: Yes, I know.

BLINKA: Don't they ever say when you're coming?

ZACRA: Hardly ever.

BLINKA: I've lost so much weight these days.

ZACRA: Do you feel weak?

BLINKA: No, but I'm far too thin.

ZACRA: Still proud of your figure, I see!

BLINKA: Yes.

ZACRA: You get pains in your legs?

BLINKA: No.

ZACRA: In the back?

BLINKA: No.

ZACRA: Not yet!

BLINKA: What do you mean, "not yet"?

ZACRA: I thought you might.

BLINKA:   You thought I might??

ZACRA:   Because *I* do, but I'm probably older than you. . . .
No, it's mainly because of my job, . . . that's all. *(He turns around,
smiling, and stares at her.)* Because of my job, you understand,
lady. . . .

   *(Blinka does not answer and makes for the door. Just as she is about
   to open it, Zacra speaks to her.)*

Where are you going?

BLINKA:   Downstairs, to ask the time.

ZACRA:   It's five o'clock.

BLINKA:   I thought your watch had stopped.

ZACRA:   I can tell by the daylight, lady. I'm a local man; I
only have to look out of doors and I can tell you the time
within thirty seconds: five o'clock.

BLINKA:   Five o'clock! That must be wrong.

ZACRA:   Impossible; I never make a mistake. About the time
or the weather. Do you want to know what the weather will
be like tomorrow?

BLINKA:   I'm not interested.

ZACRA:   You're wrong, you know. The future's important.

BLINKA:   Tomorrow, maybe I'll be. . . .

ZACRA:   Yes, yes, I know. You were about to say: "Tomorrow
I may not be here anymore. . . so after me, the deluge." O.K.,
but it would still be nice to know if it's going to be raining
cats and dogs when you're buried. Suppose I can tell you
*now* that tomorrow it's going to be sunny or just a bit cloudy,
then that will stop you from saying: "After me, the deluge. . . ."

BLINKA:   People don't get buried the day after. *(You can hear
yelping and barking.)* What's that?

ZACRA:   Jean-Claude and Pauline.

BLINKA:   Why are they barking?

ZACRA:   They're the new watchman's dogs. They bark when anyone comes in through the garden at the back. They're not used to that yet. . . .

BLINKA:   Through the garden at the back, you said. . . .

ZACRA:   Yes, they're tied to the railings by the red gate, the delivery entrance, the back way, as they call it.

BLINKA:   *(suddenly excited and overjoyed)* It's him, it must be him!

ZACRA:   Your son?

BLINKA:   *(throwing the rest of her things into a second suitcase higgledy-piggledy)* Yes.

ZACRA:   The back way?

BLINKA:   *(going to fetch her toilet articles from behind the screen)* Yes; he's so absent-minded, he comes in the wrong way, at the wrong time, and it's lucky if he doesn't. . . .

ZACRA:   I'm glad he's turned up, your Tommy; I really mean it. I was beginning to get anxious.

BLINKA:   You were?

ZACRA:   Yes, I was. Don't laugh, but I was even beginning to wonder if he really existed, that son of yours, if you see what I mean.

BLINKA:   *(Running from the wardrobe to her suitcase, she takes down the little framed photograph of the British fighter plane hanging over her bed and she packs it in her suitcase.)* That doesn't matter now.

ZACRA:   Oh, but it does! There are stories about people waiting for someone to come, and they wait and wait, but no one arrives. And in the end you realize that the person never existed! So of course, they could have gone on waiting forever. See what I mean?

BLINKA: *(Rapidly closing her suitcase and slipping on her coat, she has obviously not listened to a word Zacra has been saying.)* Sorry? Oh yes, "they could have gone on waiting forever." I see. Well, Monsieur Zacra, thank you for everything. Good luck, see you again soon perhaps.... *(She makes for the door.)* Your address! For our dinner! Oh yes, promise made, promise kept! Here, you can write it down here....

ZACRA: May I ask you something, lady?

BLINKA: Go ahead.

ZACRA: Your son.

BLINKA: Yes.

ZACRA: I'd like to see him.

BLINKA: Now?

ZACRA: Yes, you've talked so much about him....

BLINKA: Come with me.

ZACRA: I can't.

BLINKA: Why not?

ZACRA: If the manager sees me, he'll give me hell.... I'm not allowed to go wandering about downstairs during the day.

BLINKA: Take my luggage down for me.

ZACRA: No. That's forbidden. Even if I'm asked, I'm not allowed to. It's a rule of the house.

BLINKA: That's just too bad, then. You'll see him when you come to dinner.

ZACRA:   Lady,...we've spent the whole day together, and there's nothing I've asked you for, except this....I started waiting for him too.

BLINKA:   But you say you can't leave.

ZACRA:   No, but you can stay....You can wait for him here, with me, in your room.

BLINKA:   No; he'll only get lost in these corridors.

ZACRA:   He'll find his way. Your name's posted downstairs, with the floor and the number of your room....

BLINKA:   Very well. But if he's not here in five minutes, I'll go on down.

ZACRA:   Thanks, thanks very much.

*(Zacra climbs up his ladder again, sits down on one of the rungs, and clears his throat. Blinka sits on one of the suitcases, finger-tapping. There is a pause. She is smiling.)*

BLINKA:   *(as though about to get up)* Right.

ZACRA:   No, lady, not just yet....

*(She sits down again. There is a pause, then a knock at the door.)*

BLINKA:   *(Leaping up, she rushes to stand facing the door, happy and jubilant, opening her arms wide.)* Yes! Yes! Yes! Yes!

ZACRA:   *(standing on the top rung of his ladder and singing at full blast)*
Toto's hat is black as night.
Winnie's hat is far from white
And not as light as Jerry's.
Long live caps, hurrah for berets!

*(The door opens. Zacra stops short. Blinka closes her eyes with happiness and takes a short pace forward.)*

CINTA'S VOICE:   *(heard through the open door)* Thank you, Mademoiselle....

*(Cinta appears. She bears an uncanny resemblance to Madeleine. In traveling clothes, she is dressed for the summer and looks very American, comfortably middle-class. Her clothes are in graded tones of one color, like a ribbon on a chocolate box. She wears butterfly spectacle frames. The North American fashion style, extending from her shoes to her coiffure, cannot conceal her sumptuous beauty; she glows almost insolently with health. Is it Blinka's pallor that makes Cinta look so radiant? Is it Cinta's sudden apparition that throws Blinka's fragile white transparency into relief? Cinta is holding two large bouquets of red and white hothouse flowers, bought at the airport, in her left arm. They are imprisoned in thick cellophane, like high-class whores in a showcase, bereft of perfume. In her free hand she is holding a small air-travel-company bag of tough plastic material. She takes two paces into the room and then stands still. Blinka lets her arms fall quite slowly on either side of her. Zacra does not move. Blinka looks at Cinta, then at Zacra, then again at Cinta. Zacra looks at each woman in turn. No one dares to speak or interrupt with the slightest movement this unexpected general petrification. There is a pause for everyone to think. Then, moving only her lips, Cinta begins to talk. Each word is uttered with care, as she is treading on unknown ground. Her voice is gentle, its tone colored with compassion; and pauses for breath, generated by a certain embarrassment, punctuate her speech with silence.)*

CINTA:  I'm so glad to see you! . . . I've only just arrived, by plane. . . . I came straight here from the airport. . . . You look wonderful! . . . I nearly got eaten alive by two enormous dogs! . . . You know the ones I mean? . . . Simply huge! . . . Down by the gate. . . . Seeing you quite takes my breath away! . . . You're beautiful. . . . You look terribly well. . . . You don't recognize me?

BLINKA:  Oh, yes.

CINTA:  Are you quite sure?

BLINKA:  Oh, yes.

CINTA:  You don't need me to drop you a hint? You know, there's no reason why you *shouldn't* recognize me. It's quite natural that you *should.*

BLINKA: You're Cinta. Cheesecake Cinta, the girl with a passion for orangeade. We were born in the same village, you a few days before me. You are Cinta, Blinka's friend. We were schoolkids together. Kindergarten, prep school, then coed and college. Cinta and Blinka are both very nice, Cinta and Blinka are two little mice, nicicle, micicle, three bags full. Cinta's bursting with health, like a pot of strawberry jam; yes, but Blinka has the ocean in her eyes. Three bags full. You are Cinta, who hired a little yacht for England and was seasick all the way. And when you brought your coffee up, you sprinkled it all over the flowers of my floral dress. And as the bombs fell over England, you once walked along the gutter when your socks had caught on fire. And after that you were always *there:* "Don't worry, I'm here," "I'm here." "He's beautiful. A beautiful boy. A great, big baby. Gurgling away already." And then you weren't *there* anymore. You went away. Whatever happened to Vitamin-Cin? Your inseparable Cinta? She's gone. Gone away? Yes. Gone away without you? Yes, without me. Where to? Canada, I think; yes, that's right, Canada. Have you heard from her? Why, yes, of course, she married an engineer in Canada; postcards from Montreal, and six views of various lakes. That's all right, then. Yes, I think she's still living there, since 1947. Cinta. The only memory allowed by Tom. The cheeks of Cinta's bottom were as rosy as her face.

CINTA: Blinka, the one and only, you're marvelous!...And here I am again, you see, I'm back, still "there," as I used to be....

BLINKA: I see.

CINTA: (showing her flowers) Where can I put these?

BLINKA: Don't move....Monsieur Zacra.

ZACRA: Yes, lady?

BLINKA: Do you see this person?

CINTA: Who, me?

BLINKA: Monsieur Zacra.

ZACRA: Yes.

BLINKA: I am asking you to tell me if you can see this woman.

ZACRA: Are you serious?

BLINKA: Very serious, Monsieur Zacra.

ZACRA: Of course I can; she's right in front of me.

BLINKA: Speak to her.

ZACRA: I've nothing to say.

CINTA: Good morning, Monsieur. . . .Good morning, Monsieur.

ZACRA: Good morning.

BLINKA: Thank you.

CINTA: They're repainting your room. . . .

BLINKA: Yes, the cleaning staff.

ZACRA: Maintenance, lady, the maintenance staff.

CINTA: You don't have a vase? Never mind; I'll go and find one downstairs. . . . *(She puts the flowers down at the foot of the bed.)* My Blinka! *(She goes up to Blinka and kisses her.)* I'm here now, as always; everything's all right. And knowing you as I do, better than anyone else, I really find you in good shape. It was the first thing that hit me, as I came in. . . .

BLINKA: Thank you, I'm well. . . .

CINTA: Brava! You've got the right attitude. Take your coat off, darling. You look uncomfortable like that. *(She takes off Blinka's coat.)* It doesn't matter what they say; it's all in the mind, really. *(She points to her head.)* In Montreal the doctors told three people I knew that there was no hope left. But two of them had a will of iron. They're still alive now and terribly well....Oh, Blinka, I'm so happy to see you!

BLINKA: Did you come specially for me?

CINTA: Well, you see,...they phoned through to me...about urgent business in Europe,...and it's been so long....I felt so guilty!...But you know the way life is,...so one day I just jumped on the first plane.

BLINKA: You should have let me know!

CINTA: I wanted it to be a surprise. Don't go on standing.... You're wasting your energy....

*(Blinka sits down.)*

BLINKA: *(standing up again to fetch a chair for Cinta)* Here.

CINTA: *(anticipating her)* That's O.K., don't worry about me; everything's just fine. *(She sits down next to Blinka.)* Yes....You were saying....

BLINKA: I don't know....I've gone blank....

CINTA: That often happens to me. Mainly when the summer's coming....

BLINKA: You didn't come across Madeleine?

CINTA: Madeleine?

BLINKA: Yes.

CINTA: I don't think I know her,...do I?

BLINKA: The little woman who looks after this floor.

CINTA: Oh, yes. She was the one who showed me up here. Very sweet, yes. Her name is Madeleine?

BLINKA: You didn't notice she was you?

CINTA: She was me?

BLINKA: Yes.

CINTA: What do you mean?

BLINKA: Your twin.

CINTA: Oh, I see. . . .

BLINKA: She's your double.

CINTA: Oh, yes.

BLINKA: Didn't it strike you?

CINTA: No. But it's other people, you know, who decide that you look like someone else. You can never see it yourself. . . .

BLINKA: Oh?

CINTA: Yes; you spend your life peering at the world outside, or inside at yourself. You never see what lies between. Your own face, I mean; you don't know it at all, so how can you tell what or who it looks like?. . .You must tell me if you're tired. . . .

BLINKA: No, I feel fine.

CINTA: *(going to fetch a cushion from the bed and slipping it at the back of Blinka's chair to support her)* Honest?

BLINKA: I just can't believe you're here!

CINTA: *(smiling)* Try asking the painter again.

BLINKA: His name's Zacra. It's a funny name, isn't it?

CINTA: Rumanian, I expect. *(She opens her suitcase and takes out a bottle, together with a wrapped present.)* Here, this is from Robert; he makes it. . . .You mix it with milk in the morning. . . .I don't think you can get it over here. . . .

BLINKA: Thank you.

CINTA: And this is from the children . . . .Wait, I'll open it for you. *(She tears off the paper to reveal a kind of large scrapbook.)*

BLINKA: Oh, isn't that lovely!

CINTA: They made it themselves. As you don't know them, they drew sketches of each other. That's Jacqueline there with me, and Choutou, our dog, . . . and Norman, when he won the log-splitting competition. *(She stands up and, while still talking, fetches the thermos and the cup.)* The drawing isn't always very good, but they've been doing it every evening for a month . . . .You see what they wrote on the fly-leaf? *(She pours some liquid into the cup and puts the thermos down.)*

BLINKA: *(reading)* "For Aunty Blinka from Norman and Jacqueline. Nicicle, micicle, three bags full . . . ." Nicicle, micicle??

CINTA: *(singing)*
Cinta and Blinka
Are both very nice.
Cinta and Blinka
Are two little mice.
They don't like us
Their tails to pull,
Nicicle, micicle, three bags full.

*(She offers the full cup to Blinka.)* You can imagine, they were brought up on that, rocked to sleep with it. *(She hums the tune.)*

BLINKA: How old are they now?

CINTA: Don't mention it! Norman's twenty-two and Jacqueline's twenty-four. In four months' time, that's it! I get my white wig, as they say over there; I'll be a grandma. Jacqueline's . . . . *(She indicates her daughter's pregnancy with a gesture.)* I've never seen anything like it, more than twice the size you were, and God knows you were pretty enormous!

*(The cup slips from Blinka's hands and all the liquid is spilt over her skirt and blouse. Cinta rushes to pick the cup up from the floor.)*

You didn't scald yourself?

BLINKA:  No..., no....

CINTA:  Well, it's nothing, then. Don't move; it's nothing at all.

*(She goes behind the screen, comes back with a towel, and starts to wipe Blinka's clothes. Blinka is motionless, her eyes fixed on some invisible point, and lets Cinta clean her.)*

Oh, dear, it's everywhere; you're soaking!... I'm afraid you'll catch a chill; you'd better go and take it off. I saw a bathrobe somewhere. *(She fetches it.)* Leave it all to me.

*(She takes off Blinka's skirt and blouse and puts the bathrobe on. Blinka, still absent, lets her do it.)*

There..., you'll be better like that.

BLINKA:  You've undressed me?

CINTA:  Yes.... I'm almost your big sister, aren't I? I've every right to.

BLINKA:  Your son, how old is he?

CINTA:  I told you, twenty-two.

BLINKA:  Yes....Tom's eight years older than he is, and after all, *that* counts....He's let his beard grow....A very black beard, and he used to be so fair. Now his cheeks are all covered with licorice....

CINTA:  You'd be much better, Blinka, if you lay down. You're in luck; you've got a good bed there, you might as well use it....Lean on my arm....

*(She helps Blinka to the bed, where Blinka lies down, her head resting on a pillow.)*

BLINKA:  I feel so good when you're here....

CINTA:  *(pouring some more liquid from the thermos into the cup and going to sit down by Blinka's bed)* Me too. *(She offers Blinka the cup.)*

BLINKA: Do you know who came here just now?

CINTA: No.

BLINKA: Tommy's father.

CINTA: Peter Crooks?!!

BLINKA: Yes; I'd forgotten him, couldn't remember him at all. You know, apart from you. . . . And then, thirty years on, he catches up with me. . . . You might have bumped into each other.

CINTA: You're not making a mistake?

BLINKA: No. It was him.

CINTA: But Blinka. . ., you must be joking!. . .

BLINKA: He was still wearing his uniform.

CINTA: Blinka, my darling. . . .

BLINKA: And an old stained greatcoat, and dirty boots. . . .

CINTA: But you must have known. . ., you must have heard. . . .

BLINKA: What?

CINTA: Peter. . ., Peter Crooks. . . . I wrote to you about it, such a long time ago. . . .

BLINKA: No. . . . Well?

CINTA: Blinka, dear, . . . he's not with us anymore. . . . His plane was shot down, flying with the Anglo-Canadian Squadron, over Korea.

*(The painter stops what he is doing and looks at Blinka.)*

BLINKA: You should have seen him, hopping mad: "I want Tom, I want Tom!"

CINTA: It was in all the papers in Montreal, even the names and the photographs.

BLINKA: There he was, tall, rangy as an old root, sweating out the pox and the Black Plague. He'd come in search of his son, begging and pleading like an aging call girl to be allowed a third face-lift,...to carry on a bit longer.

CINTA: Blinka, they were all killed, when they came down over a rice field.

BLINKA: I never gave him a penny. He can keep his blight to himself!

CINTA: They recovered all the bodies. From the mud.

BLINKA: The mud.

CINTA: Yes. The photos were so horrible! All those young bodies, still whole and intact, caked in clay!

BLINKA: If you'd come in by the main door, you'd have met him. He must have gone out that way....He was going to the station.

CINTA: *(realizing that it is no good insisting)* I'll leave you alone now. *(She gets up slowly.)*

BLINKA: It's funny you both came the same day, don't you think?

CINTA: I'll come back this evening.

BLINKA: This evening?

CINTA: Yes; I've booked a room in a small hotel nearby.... There were no more left here....

BLINKA: But I'm going.

CINTA: *(retreating towards the door, where she quietly picks up her case)* Yes, I know.

BLINKA: I'm going any minute now.

CINTA: They'll let me know when, downstairs. . . .You really have beautiful hair, Blinka, dear.

BLINKA: My cases are all ready. . . .

CINTA: *(talking quietly, as though not to wake Blinka up)* Yes. . ., yes. . . .Everything's all right. . . .Yes, yes. . . .Don't worry about a thing. . . .Sleep!

*(Zacra comes down from the ladder and opens the door for her.)*

Au revoir, Monsieur.

*(She whispers two or three words in his ear, then leaves without turning her back, a fixed smile on her lips. She gives a few little waves of the hand, which can be seen until she has disappeared completely into the corridor. Zacra closes the door after her.)*

ZACRA: Very nice. . . .Now we're on our own again.

BLINKA: *(sitting down painfully on her bed)* You only see the people it suits you to see.

ZACRA: That's true. I enjoy looking at women, especially when they're beautiful. . . .

BLINKA: And when they look like Madeleine.

ZACRA: I didn't notice that.

BLINKA: *(standing up)* It's time I got dressed. *(She moves over to her suitcases, but is unable to move them.)* Have you touched my cases?

ZACRA: Me?

BLINKA: Yes; you've put something inside them. I can't lift them anymore.

ZACRA: How could I? I've been. . . .

BLINKA: I don't know. . . . I can't; they're too heavy; what on earth have you done?

ZACRA: Nothing at all. I've been painting; I haven't stopped painting. . . .

BLINKA: Painting everything black. Still that black paint. Do you specialize in black paint?

ZACRA: It's not black; it's navy blue, the fashionable color.

BLINKA: Stop it. . . . Stop painting!

ZACRA: I'm behind, lady.

BLINKA: Stop it. . . . You can start again when I've gone.

ZACRA: It all comes to the same in the end.

BLINKA: No. Do you think I can't see what you're doing to the walls, bringing the black night down? *(She goes to her bedside table and lights the lamp.)* It's so oppressive!

ZACRA: Not much more to do now, lady. Don't upset yourself.

BLINKA: Stop it! I can hardly breathe!

ZACRA: It's almost finished.

BLINKA: *(locked in position, next to the lamp)* What have you done to me? I can't move!

ZACRA: Is it your legs?

BLINKA: *(her eyes shining with fright)* Don't come near me!. . .

ZACRA: *(coming down from his ladder)* Wait!. . .

BLINKA: *(with a harrowing, animal-like cry, which petrifies Zacra on the third rung of the ladder)* Tommy!. . . Tommy!. . . Tommy!

ZACRA: Madame, control yourself!

BLINKA: Tommy, can you hear me?...

ZACRA: He's not here.

BLINKA: *(like a hunted beast)* He's downstairs. They've stopped him from coming up since this morning, so you could kill me in peace. Don't think I haven't realized....

*(Zacra comes down another rung. She screams.)*

Tommy!

*(She makes a rush for the door. Zacra leaps from the ladder and just as Blinka is about to open the door, he throws his arms around her waist. They both roll on the ground. Zacra releases his hold and gazes at Blinka, who is stretched out on the floor and trying slowly to raise her body with her right arm.)*

ZACRA: But, lady, you'd have got paint all over you, it's not dry yet....

BLINKA: *(suddenly perfectly calm and contained)* I'm really very sorry.

ZACRA: It's nothing, it's nothing....It's just it's so hard to get the filthy stuff off. You didn't get any on you?

BLINKA: No. Thank you.

ZACRA: You know I don't mean you any harm, lady....

BLINKA: Yes....

ZACRA: You really think he's downstairs, that son of yours?

BLINKA: It's of no importance.

ZACRA: I'll go and look for him, you'll see....I'll just give my hands a rinse; then I'll go down. But not a word to a soul, promise? It's only because it's you....But you must tell me what he's like, your son! Wouldn't do for me to bring you someone else.

BLINKA: He's got a thick crop of hair..., like mine....And my eyes; yes, the same eyes and nose *(she passes her first finger over her own)*, and then *(she plunges her hand in the paint can and covers her cheeks and her chin in black paint)* there's his beard.... *(She turns around to face Zacra.)* Yes....He must look rather like this.... *(She goes and sits down again on her chair, motionless.)*

ZACRA: I see....Now there's no risk of my making a mistake....Right....I'll just finish this little bit, to match the rest, and then I'll go down....You'll see....The way things go, this is just the moment for him to turn up. Things always happen when you're least expecting them.... *(He paints the last patch of wall which is not yet covered in black.)*

BLINKA: *(after a short pause, in a quiet, deliberate voice, with a vacant stare)* Do you know the lake of Luvalle, Monsieur Zacra?

ZACRA: No.

BLINKA: A beautiful spot in the middle of a forest, not far from Paris....

ZACRA: No....I don't know it.

BLINKA: Every Sunday I used to take Tom there.

ZACRA: To catch frogs?

BLINKA: No, to go swimming. He's very fond of swimming, swift as a trout in water. Are you there, Monsieur Zacra?

ZACRA: Yes, yes; I've almost finished.

BLINKA: Good....On his fifth birthday, the twenty-eighth of June, we both went to Luvalle together.

ZACRA: Lovely name for a lake: Luvalle.

BLINKA: He couldn't stop diving and raced everyone swimming. Have you noticed how children love the water?

ZACRA: Yes, that's true....

BLINKA: He never came back.

ZACRA: Tommy?

BLINKA: Yes; he never came back to the swimming place. I waited. It started raining and I stayed there all night, so he wouldn't get cold coming out of the water. . . . Monsieur Zacra, would you mind putting this light out?. . .Thank you. . . .The next day a fisherman found him at the bottom of the lake. He was still smiling, and his eyes were wide open. He could see everything; he saw me and all the others. I told them he did, but they wouldn't believe me. They took him away and surrounded him with lilies and marguerites. Tom watched them do it. Then Cinta closed his eyes so he wouldn't be upset by the box they were putting him in, . . . and then they took him to the cemetery, a pretty cemetery next to an old ruined castle. . .close to a little wood.

ZACRA: *(visibly moved)* But, lady. . . .

BLINKA: I talked to him all the way there; I talked to him, sitting just beside him, at the back of that long car. I spoke gently to him and he understood what was going on, everything. But he never moved. He was so good, . . . such a good boy, . . .he kept very quiet.

ZACRA: Poor lady.

BLINKA: He only cried out when they lowered him deep down into that hole. He called to me then, so just to make him laugh I sang him "The Song of the Hat." And he laughed. And then he went to sleep under the flowers they threw over him. . . .They promised I could come for him the next morning, . . .but it wasn't true; they wouldn't allow it. . . . You understand, Monsieur Zacra?

ZACRA: Yes.

BLINKA: "Blinka, you must come to terms with it, little sister. You must try and see sense and get over it." . . .What sense!! You can't get over that as you get over an illness! . . . I wasn't going to let them take him away from me. . . .You understand?

ZACRA: Yes.

BLINKA: I know. . . . In this house you all understand me, you just like everyone else. They've understood me here for twenty-five years. It's the only place where I've ever been allowed to bring Tommy back when I wanted to, so long as I agreed to drink three of those thermos bottles a day. . . . That was all. . . . It was Cinta, you know, who found this home for me. You know, that friend of mine.

ZACRA: Yes, the other lady.

BLINKA: He didn't come today. I expect he didn't wake up. . . . In the castle he sleeps late in the mornings, unless he goes for a walk in the wood.

ZACRA: We can't be sure of that yet.

BLINKA: Yes, we can. Go on with your work, Monsieur Zacra; finish it. It's very serious, really. For once I can go there myself. Today *I'm* going to meet *him*. . . . Monsieur Zacra. . . .

ZACRA: Lady?

BLINKA: Will you pass me my dress?

*(Zacra puts down his roller, opens the suitcase, and takes out the evening dress. He hands it to Blinka, who is still sitting in her chair. The paint has run from her cheeks in places, her body seems slightly more relaxed, and her eyes have an opaque stillness, like someone deprived of sight. Silently, Zacra finishes his work. The room is almost entirely black. Blinka remains still, her arms having fallen by her chair.)*

Monsieur Zacra, I can hear something knocking on my eyelids, something like the light of day.

*(Her grip slackens and the dress falls from her hand to the ground. Zacra has just finished; the room is black. He picks up his things and looks at Blinka, whose head has fallen back, resting on the chair, her mouth slightly open. He opens the door and a ray of light falls on her. He casts a last look at Blinka and then goes out. The door closes. The glimmer of light that remains in the room slowly fades to a total blackout.)*

∽

*Jean Tardieu*

# THE SLEEPLESS CITY

Translated from the French
by **Rosette C. Lamont**

The translator would like to thank Catherine Temerson
and Danielle Brunon for their assistance.

The world premiere of *The Sleepless City* was given by La Mama E.T.C. and Ubu Repertory Theater at La Mama E.T.C. during its silver anniversary season, on April 9, 1987, with the following cast:

**James L. King, Philippe Ambrosini, Miguel Braganza, Alexi Mylonas, Ralph Denzer, Cedering Fox, Waguih Takla, Lilah Kan, Jesse Devine, Kazuki Takase, Nina Zuckerman, René Houtrides, Terrell Robinson, Laurence Gleason, Jennifer Rohn, Margarita Mandaka and Chris Odo.**

Directed by **Françoise Kourilsky**
Music by **Genji Ito**
Environment by **Jun Maeda**
Lighting by **Watoku Ueno**

**JEAN TARDIEU,** whom Martin Esslin called a "Playwright's playwright, a dedicated pioneer bent on enlarging the vocabulary of his art," was born into an artistic family in the Jura region of France in 1903. He studied law and literature in Paris and, during the 1920s, became a good friend of André Gide and Roger Martin du Gard. His first poems appeared in the *Nouvelle Revue Française* in 1927 and his first volume of poetry, *Accents,* in 1939. During World War II, he was involved in the clandestine publishing of the Resistance and became friends with a group of writers that included Paul Eluard and Raymond Queneau. After the Liberation he was appointed Director of the Dramatic Service at the French radio, where he initiated literary broadcasts and began experimenting in applying techniques of sound recording and editing to language. In 1960 he became head of the radio station France-Musique. Painting and music have greatly influenced Tardieu's writings. He has published many volumes of poetry and prose poems, most recently *Margeries* in 1986. His plays, collected into the volumes *Théâtre de Chambre* (1955), *Poèmes à jouer* (1960), *Une Soirée en Provence* (1975) and *La Cité sans sommeil* (1984), have been performed all over the world. His works are published in France by Gallimard and many are available in paperback. A volume of his plays entitled *The Underground Lovers* was published in England by George Allen and Unwin in 1968.

**ROSETTE C. LAMONT** was born in Paris and has lived in the U.S. since 1941. She is a professor of French and Comparative Literature at the Graduate Center of the City University of New York and author of *The Life and Works of Boris Pasternak* (1964), *De Vive Voix* (1971), *Ionesco* (1973) and *The Two Faces of Ionesco* (1978). She writes frequently for the *New York Times* and the *Performing Arts Journal.*

## CHARACTERS

SLEEPING MAN, middle-aged; talks in his sleep.

TWO GUARDS, in uniform.

THE "PROMOTER," the head of an imaginary state. A tyrant in his fifties, an athletic, sanguinary type. The violence of his demeanor and voice, his rapid gestures, his whole person convey the impression of boundless authority, marked by both cruelty and hypocrisy. This does not prevent him from being cowardly and shaky in his wife's presence.

IDA, the Promoter's wife. She is beautiful, coquettish, and shrewd. If she appears to tend towards greater clemency than her husband, it is no doubt out of self-interest. Yet there is an inkling (and this will prove to be so at the end of the play) that her practical common sense makes her more human and lucid.

HEAD OF THE G.S.C., the awesome and highly feared leader of the "General Surveillance Corps," a plain-clothes police force, ubiquitous and ruthless.

THE NURSE of the Promoter's nephew, a fat peasant woman who reared a number of children belonging to the tyrant's family and who, as a result, allows herself to be outspoken with her masters.

THE NEPHEW of the Promoter. A ten-year-old boy, self-assured and arrogant.

G.S.C. POLICEMEN, plain-clothes although militarily organized. There is diversity in their apparel: blue jeans, black leather jackets, overalls, faded business suits. The only two items they all have in common are a grey felt hat and a weighted walking stick. Depending on the capabilities of each theater, they could vary in number from five to twenty.

FIRST STROLLER, who wanders to and fro.

SECOND STROLLER, who follows the first.

FEMALE STROLLER, wife of the latter.

A LITTLE GIRL, their daughter.

REPORTER FOR A RADIO STATION, a corpulent, jovial little man, racing against time. He wears a loud plaid blazer.

MARIO, Paola's love. A very handsome, touchingly sensitive young man. His appearance is athletic and virile. He has a natural kind of elegance and an engaging sincerity, which make him very attractive. His mood varies from enthusiastic gaiety to dreamy pensiveness. When required, he can be decisive, full of a bold bravery. Each of his words and gestures betrays his passionate attachment to Paola.

PAOLA, Mario's love. She is the personification of feminine beauty, youth, and refinement. She goes through the whole gamut of emotions: from love to terror, faith to despair. The sovereign grace of the two lovers suggests a pas-de-deux.

SILENT SUPERNUMERARIES, guards, passers-by, waiters, etc.


*The play takes place in an imaginary country.*
*Time: The present or future.*

*Note: The director has the choice of either letting the audience visualize the nightmare figures on the basis of the characters' lines (those of the radio reporter, for example) or of giving suggestions of the monsters through various means (light and shade, projections, music, sound effects, etc.), as long as the "apparitions" remain mysterious, ambiguous, and impressive.*

# Prologue

*(As the curtain rises, the stage is plunged in semi-darkness. Yet you feel that you are facing a promontory, which looks over a vast remote plain on the left, where scattered lights are blinking. There is a moment of silence. Then one hears vague moanings coming from a man whose prostrate form emerges gradually from the shadows. He seems to have collapsed upon the slope of the promontory (or upon steps carved into the crag). One can make out certain disconnected words. The man's eyes are closed. It is difficult to make out whether he is wounded or dying, or whether he might simply be a drunk sleeping himself sober. He might also be asleep, dreaming out loud.)*

SLEEPING MAN: *(grumbling, his tongue coated)* Oh, no! It can't be! No, no! A head,...a horse,...a headless man,...a dead head....It rolls,...keeps rolling,...in the water,...the sand....Two dead heads,...twenty,...thirty,...fifty,...a hundred thousand dead heads....The river,...the water,...hair flowing,...blue hair....The river,...the noise,...the river....A troop...on horseback,...a herd of horses,... manes,...flowing hair....

*(During the dreamer's soliloquy, two men in uniform appear. They have climbed the sharp slope of the promontory, stopping before the prostrate form of the dreamer.)*

FIRST GUARD: *(to his colleague)* Stop! Quiet! Listen!

*(The dreamer continues his fragmented monologue.)*

SECOND GUARD: What is the matter with you? I don't see anything!

FIRST GUARD: Don't you hear it?

SECOND GUARD: Come on, he's loaded!

*(The first guard switches on a flashlight. He directs the beam of light onto the dreamer's face.)*

FIRST GUARD: No! That's not it! Look!

SECOND GUARD: *(lurching forward, as though ready to pick up the man)* Is he dying? Quick, we've got to. . . .

FIRST GUARD: Stop, you idiot!

SECOND GUARD: What?

*(A spotlight is on the three men. The rest of the stage remains in semi-darkness.)*

FIRST GUARD: You don't get it? You're not too bright, eh!

SECOND GUARD: *(shrugging his shoulders)* And you're a "know-it-all"!

FIRST GUARD: Can't you tell? It's just what we're looking for! A man actually asleep, dreaming out loud! He's breaking the law!

SECOND GUARD: O.K., O.K.! He's talking to himself; so what?

FIRST GUARD: You crazy? He's asleep. We've got to give him a fine.

SLEEPING MAN: *(continuing his drowsy monologue)* Good day, Sir. . . .What feathers! The Noble Savage! Rubies, pearls, a beak of steel! Wings. . .folded! *(He imitates in a dying voice the sound of a muffled trumpet.)* The curfew,. . .night bells,. . . wow!. . .A museum of bright feathers!. . .Snake-women. . . serving drinks! *(He chuckles as though to stifle a laugh.)*

FIRST GUARD: Did you hear that? He's sleeping, the bastard! The nerve! Right in the center of town! And he's dreaming, too! They think they can get away with anything! Let's catch him in the act! You're a witness.

SECOND GUARD: No. Saw nothing.

FIRST GUARD: But you can hear, right? The guy is sleeping, and he's dreaming! The asshole!. . .Come on, let's take him in and book him! *(He pulls his friend in the direction of the dreamer.)*

FIRST GUARD: *(getting ready to grab the dreamer by his collar)* Wake up! What do you think you're doing?

SECOND GUARD: *(helping his buddy to stand the man up)* Get up, d'you hear, bum!

*(The dreamer, heavy with sleep, collapses again.)*

FIRST GUARD: You'd better keep your eyes open, you bastard! *(He strikes the man.)* Take that! And that! Again! That'll teach you to sleep in the middle of the street! *(He hits the man brutally with the back of his right hand.)*

SLEEPING MAN: *(crying out in pain)* Me? No, never! Not asleep! Not sleepy!

SECOND GUARD: So what the hell were you doing?

FIRST GUARD: Don't play dumb! We heard you! Talking in your sleep!

SLEEPING MAN: *(terrified, shielding his face with his arm)* No, no, I swear! Not sleeping! Never sleep!

SECOND GUARD: Oh, no? Reading a book?

SLEEPING MAN: *(in a plaintive voice)* Sick! Sick, I tell you! . . .

*(He falls asleep again, slipping slowly to the ground.)*

FIRST GUARD: Forget it! Let's take him in! You grab his feet; I'll get his shoulders! Oop! You'll see, buddy, we'll get you to wake up.

*(They carry the sleeping man off to the left, going down the slope slowly. The dreamer keeps on muttering in his sleep. All three disappear. The curtain comes down, then rises again almost at once.)*

*(Same set. The glow of a lavender and rose dawn is spreading through the sky. From the shadows, a very lofty portico is emerging (downstage right). It is the peristyle of a royal palace, which we can only guess, since it remains out of sight. It also becomes clear that the promontory hangs over an immense plain in which scattered lights are blinking. It is in this plain that the city is located, presently hidden by the almost total obscurity. Downstage, the portico begins to emerge from darkness. The Promoter enters, striding from his palace. He is a tall man, whose hobnailed boots make a loud sound upon the flagstones. Having reached the edge of the terrace, which extends from the peristyle, he peers for a moment at the horizon, then calls out in his imperious voice.)*

THE PROMOTER:   Guards! *(No one responds.)* Somebody!... *(He grows impatient.)* Hey! Anyone?

*(A soldier comes running up the stairs that lead to the terrace. He stands at attention, a few steps from the Promoter. He is out of breath from having raced up to the promontory.)*

THE SOLDIER:   *(visibly shaking with fear)* Your Excellency!... At your command!

THE PROMOTER:   *(bluntly, then with mounting rage, pointing in the direction of the plain at his feet)* What's happening here? Or, rather, what's *not* happening? The city is in darkness! Only a few lights here and there! I demand an explanation.

THE SOLDIER:   *(stammering)* But, your Excellency,...I...I....

THE PROMOTER:   *(interrupting him angrily)* You know nothing?

THE SOLDIER:   Nothing, your Excellency! Maybe....

THE PROMOTER:   *(cutting him short)* What do you mean, "maybe"? I want an answer. Immediately! Call the secretary's office, the power station, the officer on duty, anyone, right away!

THE SOLDIER:   Right away, your Excellency!

*(He turns around and exits running. In the pale light of dawn, a brighter glow comes from the palace. The steps of a woman walking fast can be heard. She is wearing high-heeled slippers.)*

IDA:   *(carrying a torch)* What is my lord doing? On the terrace, at dawn, in the cold...instead of...?

THE PROMOTER:   *(quieting down, but still gruff)* Instead of..., instead of...? You weren't going to say "instead of sleeping," were you? *(He addresses her tenderly.)* You know that you alone have that right, my dear!

IDA:   *(laughing)* Sleep? Me? When there's so much to be done for the people...and for their beloved leader?

THE PROMOTER:   *(again full of anger, turning towards the horizon and pointing with a sweeping gesture in the direction of the plain)* Look at the city down there! It should be aglow with lights! It should dazzle! As always, night and day! Nothing must interrupt life in my city! Work — I mean, celebration, perpetual celebration! Not a moment's rest! So I can read at midnight as though it were broad daylight. So I can hear the noise of life: train stations, factories, schoolyards....It's daybreak now, and look: Nothing! Nothing! Silence! Darkness! For the first time, after all those years of power and glory, and the total success of my system.... *(He speaks with redoubled rage.)* What the hell is going on?

IDA:   *(coming close to him and taking his hand)* Now, now, don't worry, my dearest Promoter! It could be a temporary breakdown, a power blackout! It can happen, you know.

THE PROMOTER:   *(stamping his foot)* It must not happen! We must stay awake! Wide awake! Not a moment's rest, ever, or else....

IDA:   Or else?

THE PROMOTER:   Or else, our enemy will attack.

IDA:   What enemy? We don't have any! We're the strongest!

THE PROMOTER:   Our worst enemy: inertia! We would be digging our own grave.

*(Two soldiers have climbed the terrace steps. They advance towards the Promoter and stand at attention. At this moment, a third person can be perceived. He stands at a respectful distance, in the shadows.)*

THE PROMOTER:   *(taking some steps in their direction. His voice is threatening.)* So? What is it? I want an explanation. Now!

FIRST SOLDIER:   Your Excellency, . . . an officer would like to see you.

THE PROMOTER:   Who? Let him in! Why the secrecy?

FIRST SOLDIER:   Forgive me, your Excellency. He insists on speaking with you privately.

THE PROMOTER:   All right, then. Go! *(He turns to Ida.)* You too, my tender smile. *(He addresses the third man.)* You, come here!

*(The two soldiers click their heels and step away, as if not to hear the ensuing conversation. But it is obvious that they have been ordered to watch what is going on, to stay on the alert. They stand motionless in the dark. Ida withdraws regretfully, waving to the Promoter. The third man, the head of the G.S.C., steps closer to the Promoter, then stops at a respectful distance. He wears a shabby suit. His face is pale and inexpressive, his gestures slow and deliberate.)*

THE PROMOTER:   We're wasting time! Who are you? Do you have an explanation for this sudden darkness? Life has suddenly stopped. Why?

HEAD OF THE G.S.C.:   *(with embarrassment)* Excellency, if I dared ask for a meeting with you, . . . it's because. . . .

THE PROMOTER:   *(interrupting him with an angry, impatient gesture)* Come to the point! Who are you?

HEAD OF THE G.S.C.:   I'm the Head of the renowned G.S.C., your General Surveillance Corps, Excellency. No one knows my name. Not even you. *(He gives a sinister chuckle.)* Not even me!

THE PROMOTER: *(suddenly kinder in tone)* So, what's going on? Is it serious?

HEAD OF THE G.S.C.: Yes, Excellency. Something strange, very strange, happened during the night.

THE PROMOTER: A technical problem? A breakdown? A power failure? Start an investigation! And keep me informed.

HEAD OF THE G.S.C.: It may be even more serious. . . .

THE PROMOTER: *(barking out)* What?

HEAD OF THE G.S.C.: *(coming closer to the Promoter and addressing him in a low voice)* Excellency, our many undercover agents, our most clever undercover agents, our agents, *your* agents, when they infiltrated the masses, some time ago, began to suspect. . . .

THE PROMOTER: *(increasingly impatient)* To suspect *what?*

HEAD OF THE G.S.C.: *(motioning him to be patient)* We got a lead a few weeks ago. . . .

THE PROMOTER: *(interrupting him)* A few weeks ago? And you didn't do anything about it? And I wasn't even informed?

HEAD OF THE G.S.C.: Forgive me, Excellency, but your Excellency is well aware that in order to develop a lead, one must not interfere. One must know how to listen, wait, prepare the right trap, track down the prey, . . . in short. . . .

THE PROMOTER: *(bursting out)* In short! In short! Will you get to the point?

HEAD OF THE G.S.C.: *(hesitantly, as though struggling to say the words)* We have just. . . received incriminating evidence. . . that points to. . .*(mysteriously, in a low voice, almost inaudible)* something. . . .

THE PROMOTER: *(astonished)* Something! But that's insane! It's *impossible!*

HEAD OF THE G.S.C.: *(with conviction)* And yet, it's true, your Excellency. In any case, we think it is. *(He turns in the direction of the city, which is still plunged in darkness, and makes a sweeping gesture.)* And *this* would be the first visible manifestation of. . . shall we say. . .of this "something."

THE PROMOTER: *(bitterly)* No small something! Our capital, dark, silent, inactive,. . .a necropolis!

HEAD OF THE G.S.C.: Moreover, our agents believe this to be a trial balloon. . .*(catching himself)*, a first attempt. A criminal warning!

THE PROMOTER: *(roaring)* A "warning"! What a word! They'll see what I do with their warnings. Identify the leaders. Bring them to trial. Declare a state of emergency. But, first of all, the city must go back to work immediately. I want to hear its heart beating again, in time to my heart!

*(No sooner has he spoken than a remote grinding noise, interrupted by howling sirens, rises from the city. At the same time, but gradually, neighborhood by neighborhood, the lights of the city go on again: streetlights, skyscraper windows, blinking, moving neon signs.)*

THE PROMOTER: *(drunk with happiness, grabbing the policeman by the arm and swinging him around to make him face the city)* Look, you fool! Look! There's your "warning"! It was nothing more than a simple accident, a power failure. You see, one order — even mentally — from me, and everything starts up again.

HEAD OF THE G.S.C.: With all due respect, Excellency, I beg you not to judge by appearances! We know, I can assure you, *we know* that "something" is going on.

THE PROMOTER: *(blind with rage)* Then give me proof! Hard evidence! Facts, confessions, culprits!

HEAD OF THE G.S.C.: It is not that simple, Excellency! Thousands of devoted spies are only just beginning to detect something, so it's unlikely that one man alone — forgive me, Excellency — even if he were the leader, would be able to control the situation with a word, a gesture,. . .or a thought!

THE PROMOTER: *(his interest stirred)* What do you suggest?

HEAD OF THE G.S.C.: First, if your Excellency were willing, for one day, to be as humble as the humblest of your subjects, to melt into the crowd, to listen and watch....

THE PROMOTER: *(with a mixture of irony and scorn)* I'm not one of your spies!

HEAD OF THE G.S.C.: *(with bitterness)* And yet, Excellency, we — your spies — we are indispensable. No spies, no State, no surveillance, no obedience!

THE PROMOTER: I know, I know, you're as essential as jackals in a charnelhouse! *(He laughs briefly, insolently.)* Don't take it personally!

HEAD OF THE G.S.C.: *(shrugging his shoulders)* We're accustomed to insults!... But take my advice into consideration, Excellency. Follow our procedure: dress casually, inconspicuously; come out of your palace and mix with the crowd. Engage in conversation with people; flirt a bit with the girls. Have a drink — one too many — and bully someone around. Get into a fight. People take sides and things come to the surface. You find out who sleeps and who stays awake. But it takes time; you can't expect to discover in one day what your jackals *(smirking)* — I mean, your spies — were able to discover only over a period of months.

THE PROMOTER: *(disdainfully)* That's all you can come up with? No proof? No solution?

HEAD OF THE G.S.C.: I don't have a remedy yet, just a way of diagnosing trouble. But, believe me, for a leader, there's nothing like blending into the masses.

THE PROMOTER: *(gruffly)* I'll consider it. But first, the city must stay awake around the clock, indefinitely! Sleep has been outlawed. This is my personal creation, my own masterpiece, feared and admired by all. Our people's productivity has tripled. As long as I live, this decree will never be rescinded:

sleep is outdated. It is a monstrous obstacle to the development of society. It is a crime. All those who indulge in it must be punished.

HEAD OF THE G.S.C.: *(harshly)* Including the scientist who discovered the insomnia serum.

THE PROMOTER: His discovery no longer belongs to him alone.

HEAD OF THE G.S.C.: *(with cynical humor)* Excellency, if you wish to experience the insomnia serum's true effect, don't fall asleep on your laurels! It's now or never! Get close to your people! Watch and listen!

THE PROMOTER: *(as though speaking to himself in a state of ecstatic reverie)* General insomnia! A major step for human progress! May no one ever again sink into wretched sleep! Neither young nor old, rich nor poor!...Lights, noise, rumbling, shouts, stadiums, arenas, dance halls, markets and prisons, cafés and courtrooms! Fanfares, fireworks, weddings, funerals, parades, military marches, religious processions, trains pulling into stations, jets breaking the sound barrier, rockets blasting off into space, ships sailing out to sea, screaming crowds, shootouts — I'll accept anything so long as nothing stops and no one sleeps, so long as gold piles up in the coffers and money flows, so long as the bidding is frantic on the exchange floor, making some rich overnight and driving others to despair and suicide, so long as the nurseries are as crowded as cemeteries! *(He is momentarily silent, as though struck by a vision.)*

HEAD OF THE G.S.C.: *(a while later)* Well, all these things, Excellency, will become apparent to you, just by walking around the streets. *(He speaks in a strange, disquieting tone.)* Then you will get to know who threatens your order: those who stay awake, or those who sleep.

THE PROMOTER: I repeat — and you know it well — it is forbidden to sleep!

HEAD OF THE G.S.C.:    Excellency, beware of the poisons distilled by insomnia!

THE PROMOTER:    As for the sick, we know how to take care of them....Enough time wasted! Get out!

HEAD OF THE G.S.C.:    *(bowing with icy irony)* As you wish, Excellency. Your undercover agent presents his respects! *(He takes a couple of steps towards the edge of the terrace; then, before exiting, he turns around to speak pointedly.)* With your permission, I will retire and get some *sleep!*

THE PROMOTER:    *(his arm raised as though to hit the policeman)* Don't provoke me! Enough!

*(The head of the G.S.C. disappears. During the latter part of the confrontation, the two soldiers on duty move in the direction of the terrace, ready to shoot.)*

THE PROMOTER:    *(addressing the soldiers)* You may go now! I need time to think.

*(The soldiers click their heels and disappear. The Promoter remains alone. He paces the stage back and forth, arms crossed behind his back, deep in thought. As the sun rises, the lights of the city begin to go out. City sounds are growing louder: street noises, factory sirens, cars honking their horns, trains chugging in and out of stations, planes taking off and landing. These sounds continue as the curtain is going down and while it is down during the change of set.)*

*(Curtain.)*

*(The curtain rises, revealing the inside of the palace: a high room, adjacent to the covered terrace of the preceding scene. The outside noises have faded. The palace furnishings are discreet, quietly luxurious. This is the Promoter's study. On the left is a large desk covered with papers, files, telephones — the kind of paraphernalia associated with a business office. There are five or six chairs around the desk. To the right is a large sofa-bed, upon which Ida is languidly reclining. She is wearing a négligée. Behind her, two very high French windows reveal trees; another set of French windows opens onto the terrace, which is presently bathed in morning sunlight. The Promoter, whose whole demeanor reveals an anxious frame of mind, strides in from the terrace. Ida, half-rising from the sofa, smiles beguilingly.)*

IDA: What troubles my sweet lord? What dark secrets have been imparted to him? The life of the city seems to have started up again. The sound of activity must delight your ears! I told you it was nothing but a power failure. *(She hesitates.)* A strike, perhaps?

THE PROMOTER: Don't tempt fate! A power failure is bad enough, but a strike!...No, what I heard was far more serious. My secret police warn me that "something" is brewing....A plot! In our country, under my regime — it's impossible! *(He snickers coarsely.)* But we've got to be vigilant. At any rate, I've made up my mind: I'll forestall them.

IDA: *(vaguely worried)* What d'you mean?

THE PROMOTER: *(with a secret, cruel smile, as though he were playing a joke at someone's expense)* I mean, I'll summon the so-called State officials.

*(He walks to the table and touches a bell, whose insistent ring can be heard throughout the palace. After a while, a loud knock on the back door is heard.)*

THE PROMOTER: *(in a strong voice)* Come in!

*(One of the two leaves of the double door swings open. An aging woman is silhouetted in the frame.)*

THE NURSE: *(in a slightly jeering tone)* What's the matter, "my" Excellency?

THE PROMOTER: *(surprised, sneering)* I wasn't calling you! I was calling the guard on duty.

IDA: *(laughing)* Our dear nurse may know more than you think.

THE PROMOTER: *(pressed for time)* All right, then! Tell the guard to summon the President of the Chamber at once.

THE NURSE: This early, "my" Excellency!

THE PROMOTER: There are no hours here! No morning, no evening! This is an extremely urgent matter! That's an order, you hear! The President of the Chamber must meet me here at once. . . .Oh! And tell him to bring me the complete text of our Constitution! Don't forget!

*(The Nurse does not move.)*

THE PROMOTER: *(stamping his foot)* Well? I'm waiting.

THE NURSE: *(beginning to move grumblingly)* All right, all right, "my" Excellency, . . . I'm on my way! *(She pulls the door closed as she exits.)*

THE PROMOTER: *(annoyed)* Who does the old hag think she is? Just because she raises the *(ironically)* "President," your good-for-nothing brother?

IDA: *(with a smile, as though to plead the Nurse's cause)* She's completely devoted to us. We are her pride and joy, the "First Family."

THE PROMOTER: *(with emphasis)* All that matters is the affairs of the State! *(There is a silence.)*

IDA: May I stay while you speak to my brother? Or must I retire again?

THE PROMOTER: *(still with emphasis)* Stay, Madame! *(He changes his tone.)* It's good to refresh your memory. You have no political sense, no inkling of the present danger. I've often noticed it.

IDA: *(Her feelings are visibly hurt, but she decides to ignore it.)* Perhaps, but haven't I dispelled your fears on countless occasions, in the face of nonexistent, imaginary dangers? *(She rises from the couch with feline grace, sure of her charm and power over her husband.)*

THE PROMOTER: *(visibly shaken and a bit ridiculous)* My panther! I beg you, don't distract me! Grave trouble is brewing.

IDA: *(coming closer)* So very grave, my leopard? *(She prowls around him provocatively, tossing her flowing mane of hair.)*

THE PROMOTER: *(catching himself and suddenly very serious)* This is no laughing matter! The President will be arriving at any moment. He's your brother, and completely incompetent; I know it and you know it. But he's President of the Chamber of Representatives, and we must act as though. . . .

*(He does not bother to complete his sentence. Three little knocks are heard at the door.)*

THE PROMOTER: There he is! *(He responds loudly.)* Come in!

*(The large double door at the back of the stage opens wide. A little boy, nine or ten years old, enters. He is dressed in a black suit with a schoolboy kind of jacket with a wide white collar, a wide pink tie, short pants, knee socks, and patent-leather shoes. He is full of self-importance. He carries under his arm a voluminous book bound in green leather. The Nurse is walking behind him, pushing him forward. Ida walks up to the boy, kissing him tenderly on both cheeks.)*

IDA: *(sweetly)* Up so early, my little nephew? What are you doing here?

THE NURSE:   *(anticipating the child's answer)* The President, his daddy, is not feeling well. The doctor ordered rest. He begs to be excused, "my" Excellency. He sent his son instead, bearing the Great Book,. . .the Great Book of Complication: this is what you wanted, isn't it?

THE PROMOTER:   *(grumbling)* The Con-sti-tu-tion, Nurse, not the "complication"! Do you think I'm a fool? The damned President has no right to rest, none whatsoever!

IDA:   *(pleading with him)* Have mercy: my dear brother's health has always been precarious; you know that. He thought you would like it if he sent the boy with the book. *(She kisses the child.)* Isn't that so, my little angel?

THE PROMOTER:   This is absurd! A child in this capacity!

THE BOY:   *(proudly, in a high, clear voice)* Why not, Uncle? I can read.

THE PROMOTER:   *(disarmed and laughing)* You may be right, after all, nephew. Go ahead and read the first few pages. Do you know what it is?

THE BOY:   *(with an air of comic haughtiness)* Sure, Uncle! It's the Contestation of the State, as proclaimed by you before the Chamber two years ago!

THE PROMOTER:   *(stamping his foot)* Wrong on two counts: First, this is the Constitution, not the Contestation. Second, these laws were promulgated four years ago. We live without sleep; hence, our time is double compared to others. I thought you knew that!

THE BOY:   *(with a naive kind of pleasure)* I do know it, Uncle! Under your. . .reign, since I'm nine years old, I'm actually eighteen!

THE PROMOTER:   *(with satisfaction)* Very good. Come over here!

*(He walks over to one of the chairs around the desk, pointing to another for the boy and to a third for Ida. They sit down. The child places the thick ledger on the desk, touching it with reverence as though it were some sacred object. During this time, the Nurse has been standing with a grumbling expression on her face. Suddenly, she shrugs her shoulders with indignation.)*

THE NURSE: Isn't this a sad sight! A child. Engaging in politics at his age!

THE BOY: I'm eighteen years old! In other countries, people get to vote at eighteen!

IDA: *(laughing)* Never mind, Nurse! You can leave us now!

*(The Nurse exits, grumbling.)*

THE PROMOTER: All right! Now, read the first page of the Constitution out loud. Enunciate clearly!

*(The boy proceeds to read in a piping child's voice. His elocution is fine, but his voice remains expressionless. From time to time, he stumbles over a word or stops to catch his breath.)*

THE BOY: *(reading syllable by syllable)* "The Constitution of the New State. Article One. The New State is founded upon the National Science Institute landmark discovery which permits the abolition of sleep."

THE PROMOTER: Perfect. Read carefully. We're listening.

THE BOY: *(still syllable by syllable)* "Article Two. In accordance with the present constitution, every citizen, whether male or female, upon attaining one year of age, shall report to the State laboratory for an innoculation — free of charge — against the inconvenience of sleep."

THE PROMOTER: *(interrupting him and taking the book)* Fine! Nothing to change here! Go on! There, starting with Article Six.

*(During this exchange, Ida has taken some knitting out of a basket and proceeded to knit. Gradually, her head sinks upon her chest and she stops knitting. Suddenly, she utters a small cry while keeping her eyes closed.)*

IDA: *(pointing to something invisible in the distance)* Shhh! Look, I just saw a wild boar running....There!...Under the table!

THE PROMOTER: *(rising suddenly and rushing over to her solicitously)* What? What are you saying? A wild boar under the table? *(He takes her hand.)* Are you all right, dear heart?

IDA: *(as though emerging from a dream, a constrained smile upon her lips)* It's nothing, dear! I thought I saw..., that's all!

THE PROMOTER: Good God, you were sound asleep! Dreaming! *(mezzo voce)* Don't worry! I won't tell! *(to her nephew)* Speak louder. There's nothing like a legal text to put you to sleep.... *(to Ida)* Do you feel better? *(She nods and picks up her knitting once again.)* Good. *(to the boy)* Go on.

THE BOY: *(resuming his reading)* "A total of ten hours shall be exempted from the twenty-four uninterrupted waking hours: two for meals; two for breaks, scheduled at the convenience of the employer; two for romantic endeavors." *(He stops and casts a surreptitious glance in the direction of his uncle.)*

THE PROMOTER: Why'd you stop?

THE BOY: *(slightly embarrassed)* "Romantic endeavors," what does that mean?

IDA: You do have a little girlfriend in school, don't you?

THE BOY: Yes....

IDA: Do you like her?

THE BOY: Yes.

IDA: And from time to time you kiss her, don't you? Well, that's "romantic endeavors."

THE PROMOTER:   Go on.

THE BOY:   "Two hours a day for romantic endeavors, conjugal or otherwise; four hours for commuting, sports, games, shows, general recreation. The normal work day shall consist of fourteen hours...."

THE PROMOTER:   *(interrupting him)* I've been much too generous! I ought to have set the working day at sixteen hours, at the very least.

IDA:   *(simpering)* Don't overdo it, darling!

THE PROMOTER:   Look, if there hadn't been long work days in ancient times, we'd have no pyramids, no cathedrals.

IDA:   *(ironically)* Are you building cathedrals, my dear lord?

THE PROMOTER:   *(with irritation)* Let's drop the subject! *(to the boy)* Continue! Let's skip to Article Ten, the chapter on infractions!

THE BOY:   *(turning the page and reading)* "Article Ten. Any infringement of the Constitution by sleeping during unauthorized hours shall be punishable by a term of imprisonment of not less than six months or more than twenty years."

THE PROMOTER:   *(violently)* There you are! These penalties are too lenient. The consequences — a slackening of discipline and a revolt brewing! Last night, the lights were out; tomorrow, people will sleep through the night! This must be nipped in the bud! At once! We'll go as far as....

IDA:   *(taking his arm, with an expression of terror on her face)* What are you going to say? You frighten me!

THE PROMOTER:   It's the people that we must frighten. So they'll obey! We'll change the law. We'll make surrendering to sleep punishable by *(in a low but forceful voice)* death....Yes, we'll institute a death penalty!

*(Ida cries out with horror, then raises her hands to her mouth as though to stop the sound. A heavy, anxiety-filled silence follows.)*

THE BOY: *(indifferent, as though he had not heard the Promoter)* May I go out to play now?

THE PROMOTER: *(with a mixture of irony and affection)* Of course, Mr. Chamber President.

THE BOY: And may I take the Contestation?

THE PROMOTER: *(absentmindedly)* Go, have fun with it! *(He catches himself.)* What did you say? The Constitution, not the Contestation. On second thought, leave the book here. I need it.

*(The boy gets up, taking a few steps towards the door. The Promoter calls him back by clicking his fingers.)*

THE PROMOTER: Wait; tell your father to recover and come and see me. Within forty-eight hours! This is urgent! Also, tell him to call the Chamber into session next week. For important legislation: a revision of the Constitution! Will you remember?

THE BOY: Yes, Uncle, I will. Good-bye, Uncle, Auntie. *(He runs out.)*

IDA: *(determined to use her influence to bring about a change of mind)* Give the matter a little more thought, my great cougar! If the masses are restless, you might be stirring them up instead of appeasing them.

THE PROMOTER: *(inflexibly)* I know what I've got to do.

IDA: *(stubbornly)* All right, all right, my big wildcat!...But, frankly, I think you're about to make a serious mistake.

THE PROMOTER: I'm sure I'm not.

IDA: I'm sure you are.

THE PROMOTER:  No!

IDA:  Yes!

THE PROMOTER:  No!

IDA:  *(stamping her foot)* And I say "yes"! You'll cause general resentment and give them new reasons to rebel.... *(She reflects.)* Unless....

THE PROMOTER:  *(visibly intrigued)* Unless...what?

IDA:  Unless you compensate for this act of intimidation with an act of kindness.

THE PROMOTER:  *(annoyed)* What do you mean?

IDA:  I mean that your people might more readily accept the death penalty if you'd also extend them some significant advantage....

THE PROMOTER:  The carrot and the stick! That's a bad joke, out of date. What do you have in mind, my love?

IDA:  *(looking for an idea)* Well,...you might restore something you've abolished, like the weekly day of rest?

THE PROMOTER:  Never! That's a relic from the barbaric past! Old-fashioned and completely unworthy of a modern State!

IDA:  *(ironically)* So is capital punishment!

THE PROMOTER:  It's not the same thing. Capital punishment, you see, happens only once.

IDA:  *(scathingly)* Indeed, once in a lifetime.

THE PROMOTER:  *(in a grumbling tone)* You make me say foolish things. I'm certain that rest....

IDA:  *(interrupting him once again)* ...is worse than death, is that it?

THE PROMOTER:  *(stamping his foot)* You're getting on my nerves!

IDA: *(pouting and pretending to leave)* Fine. Forget what I said. I'm going. I'll leave you alone. . .with your conscience. *(She takes a couple of steps towards the door.)*

THE PROMOTER: *(catching up with her)* Wait, my little lamb! Don't leave me! At a time like this!

IDA: *(simpering like a girl)* Then, the great big zebra should listen to his little goat! Let's play proverbs, shall we? Sleep is Death, but on Sundays, the feast follows the fast! "Give them an inch, take a mile."

THE PROMOTER: *(regretfully)* We'll see! You may yet get your weekly day of rest. Maybe! It remains to be seen. . . .

IDA: *(embracing him)* Oh, my little bison is so sweet!

THE PROMOTER: You'll have asked for it. There won't be a moment's peace on Sundays. Noisy streets, cheers, fanfares, fire-crackers!. . . But after all, you may be right. People are so frivolous; they don't care if a few heads get chopped off as long as they can go on drinking and dancing.

IDA: *(horribly)* As long as it's other people's heads, of course!

THE PROMOTER: *(tenderly)* I'll think it over, my little siren! Now you should retire to bed! *(After a moment's hesitation he speaks in a low whisper.)* Go on, go off to sleep!

IDA: *(shivering)* In other words, you want me to die?

THE PROMOTER: *(joking crudely)* Call it a truce! For a few days. Later, we'll see.

IDA: *(making a face)* You are hor-rible, Excellency of my heart!

*(She is about to exit. All of a sudden, the room — which was brightly lit — is plunged into darkness.)*

THE PROMOTER: *(enraged)* Not another damned blackout!. . . Traitors! I'll get them! Careful, my gazelle, don't trip!

*(Silence.)*

THE PROMOTER: *(with anguish disproportionate to the banal incident)* Where are you, dearest? Watch out! This study is so cluttered with furniture!

*(One can hear him groping his way through the room. He knocks down pieces of furniture, which topple with a dull thud. After awhile, Ida's voice can be heard. It is strangely altered. Ida speaks slowly, as though dreaming out loud.)*

IDA'S VOICE: Nothing but seaweed in this river of blood! *(She repeats.)* Seaweed with eyes. *(Crescendo.)* With hands, fingers, pointed nails.... *(She utters a piteous cry.)* Knives! They're strangling me!

*(At that moment the light is turned on again. At first, it flickers weakly; then it becomes as bright as before. Ida can be seen crawling on all fours, in the throes of some dreadful nightmare. The Promoter is standing in the center of the room, a broken lamp in his hand. His clothes are in disarray. Most of the furniture is lying upside down, scattered all over the room. At the sight of Ida, the Promoter lets the lamp drop; he rushes up to her, takes her in his arms, and helps her stand up, calling her back to her senses by gently slapping her face.)*

THE PROMOTER: There, there, my beauty! Another bad dream....It's nothing....Wake up!

IDA: *(touching her face, and slowly opening her eyes)* Ah, here you are! I was...sinking...into a huge marsh...with no shoreline....It was full of terrifying creatures....Ah, hold me tight!

*(Curtain.)*

## THIRD TABLEAU

*(Before the curtain rises, the sounds of the end of the first tableau are heard again, more intensely. These sounds evoke the urban bustle: cars, motorcycles rumbling, trucks, the sharp whistles of traffic police, brakes screeching, the hurried steps of pedestrians, vendors yelling out in outdoor markets, the noises of street fairs, gunshots from shooting galleries, noise-makers, accordion music, street singers playing the guitar, jazz bands, the joyous shouting and laughter of the crowd and of children, etc. Gradually these sounds fade and stop, giving way to the rhythmic beat of a military troupe marching in. Its arrival is accompanied by the muted music of a small military band: two trumpets, a drum, cymbals. The curtain rises as this music also fades and stops. The leader of the troupe shouts: "Attention! Stop!" The troupe comes to a sharp stop. When the curtain has risen, we are before a semicircular public square, from which a number of streets radiate out into the city. In the square are a few frail trees and, to the left, downstage, empty tables and chairs on the terrace of a large café. It is soon revealed that the so-called troupe, marking time in the deserted public square, is composed of only a few characters (at least four, and not more than ten). Some are tall, some short; they are dressed in varied civilian attire with the exception of matching hats and walking sticks. It is the G.S.C. Some of these policemen, who are still holding the musical instruments, set them down carelessly on the ground. We recognize in their midst a character from the First Tableau, the Leader of the G.S.C. He is pushing a streetcleaner's cart containing a shovel and broom.)*

HEAD OF THE G.S.C.: *(in a whisper, after making an exaggerated gesture to indicate silence and secrecy with a finger on his lips)* Shhhh!... Shhh!...Now, spread out....There..., there..., and there....Shhh! Silence!

*(He points to the streets that lead away from the square. The policemen casually start walking to the various assigned destinations and disappear. The leader picks up the instruments and puts them in his cart, then exits. Four strollers enter from stage left: two men, a woman, and a little girl, engaged in conversation yet looking worried and frequently glancing around.)*

FIRST STROLLER:  *(pointing to the café)* Shall we sit here and have a drink?

THE WOMAN:  Drink or no drink, why not? It's nice here.

*(They sit down at one of the tables.)*

SECOND STROLLER:  No one here. D'you know why?

THE WOMAN:  No idea!

SECOND STROLLER:  *(leaning closer and speaking in a confidential tone, after glancing around)* It's because the ceremony will take place in the main square, over there. There'll be crowds, and flags and a choir. The police is stationed all around, in case something happens.

THE WOMAN:  So, it's dangerous here?

SECOND STROLLER:  Not yet. . . . As soon as I see suspicious-looking people, I'll signal and we'll leave!

THE LITTLE GIRL:  *(to the woman)* What's going to happen, Mummy?

THE WOMAN:  A celebration, darling.

THE LITTLE GIRL:  *(applauding)* Great!

THE WOMAN:  *(with tender irony, full of double meaning)* Yes, darling, it'll be a lot of fun. *(She looks at her companions, who seem preoccupied.)*

FIRST STROLLER:  *(snapping his fingers)* Waiter!

*(No one responds to this call, but all four customers act as though a waiter had come to take their orders.)*

FIRST STROLLER:  *(laughing, and turning to his companions)* So, my friends, what will it be? For me, a large one, plain.

SECOND STROLLER:  *(in the same vein)* For me, a small one, very full. *(to the woman)* And you?

THE WOMAN:    *(laughing also)* For me, a hot one. For my
daughter, a sweet one.

*(After a moment's silence, they grow serious again and bring their
chairs closer together. They talk to one another mezzo voce.)*

FIRST STROLLER:    No one yet. Nothing to fear for the time
being.

SECOND STROLLER:    He's going to switch on his charisma,
don't you think?

THE WOMAN:    Sure. He'll go on and on about letting us have
Sunday again. Everyone will cheer! They'll be delirious!

FIRST STROLLER:    I bet the special brigades are already posi-
tioned throughout the crowd, leading the shouts and applause.

*(They act as though the waiter had just brought in their orders.)*

THE FOUR STROLLERS:    *(to the imaginary waiter)* Thank you!...
Thank you..., thank you!...Many thanks!

*(They go through the motions of clinking their imaginary glasses.)*

THE FOUR STROLLERS:    *(laughing)* Cheers! Here's to your health,
little one!... *(addressing the imaginary waiter)* How much?...
Here, keep the change.

*(They pretend that they are drinking, setting down imaginary glasses,
and paying. A heavy silence follows.)*

THE WOMAN:    *(mezzo voce)* What about the other...the other
news?

SECOND STROLLER:    Ah, yes, the amendment to Article Ten.
It's insane! The death penalty for anyone caught sleeping!
Insane! He won't dare mention it!

THE WOMAN:    He's much too cowardly!

FIRST STROLLER:    But he's got to warn the people. They have
to know what to expect! He'll call a referendum. They'll make

us vote simultaneously on the Sunday and the death penalty—fun and torment! And the trick will work. Once again, the people will put a noose around their own necks.

*(Another heavy silence.)*

FIRST STROLLER: *(with a deep sigh)* That's the way it is, and there's nothing we can do about it...for the time being, at least!

*(From a distance one can hear music, at first muffled but very melodious, then identifiable as the strains of dance music. The music seems to move closer and closer as Mario and Paola come in, walking lightly and gracefully, like dancers. They reach the center of the stage when, all of a sudden, Paola seems about to faint. The music grows faint.)*

MARIO: *(holding up the young woman in his arms, strongly and tenderly)* Paola! Paola! Please!

PAOLA: *(emerging from her malaise, and with a smile, touching her forehead)* Oh, Mario! My darling Mario! I was about to faint! Was it from your sweet embrace?

MARIO: *(bitterly)* No, light of my life, you were falling asleep.

PAOLA: *(incredulous)* Asleep? In your arms?

MARIO: Yes; in this mad city, sleep is a crime. It's like impending death, hidden everywhere and always pursuing us.

PAOLA: *(looking about with bewilderment)* What is this place?

MARIO: Perhaps a space from which to take flight. Perhaps a trap. But, you see, walls open up before us.

PAOLA: *(insistently)* Nothing looks familiar. Where are we?

*(At this moment, the four strollers rise discreetly and slip away, stage right.)*

MARIO: Time is suspended. A moment of peace, stolen. See how people leave the moment we arrive!

*(Suddenly, Paola tears herself away, out of Mario's embrace. A cry of terror escapes from her lips as she looks around with horror.)*

PAOLA: What is that? Look! I'm afraid! *(She points to a corner of the square where nothing unusual can be seen, then hides her face in her hands.)*

MARIO: *(seeking to reassure her)* Don't be afraid, my love! Alone together, nothing can hurt us.

PAOLA: *(with mounting anguish)* I swear...I saw....

MARIO: What did you see?

PAOLA: *(moving away and taking some faltering steps, as though to flee)* There! Two eyes, without a face, without a body! They blazed like twin fires!

MARIO: *(catching up with her and taking her back into his arms)* It was the reflection of the sun in a window pane! You were dazzled by it!

PAOLA: *(in a state of hallucination)* They're following us. Eyes full of blood! No face, just a mane of hair.

MARIO: *(in a low but forceful voice)* Please, Paola, don't fall asleep! Stop dreaming! Run with me! Look into the eyes of the one who loves you.

*(The music starts again. Mario sweeps the girl away. They circle the square.)*

PAOLA: *Quick! Take me far away!*

MARIO: I'll carry you off, my love, away from the monsters which people our dreams, our wretched waking dreams!

*(They exit as they entered, on the left side of the square. As they depart, a youngish, roly-poly, hyperactive man comes in from upstage. He looks even tubbier in a loud plaid jacket. He is carrying a heavy radio technician's case in one hand and propelling a transparent plexiglas booth mounted on wheels. The doorless booth is open on one side;*

*it looks much like a public telephone. The man is out of breath from
rushing around. Having reached his destination (upstage right), he
sets down his mobile booth, anchoring it to one spot, then whips
out a mike from his case. The microphone is connected by a cable
to a set of earphones. The man puts on the helmet with the earphones
and, mike in hand, enters the booth.)*

RADIO REPORTER: *(his voice amplified by the speaker)* Testing,
testing! One, two, three! Studio 135? Can you hear me? This
is the reporter on duty!. . . .Can you hear me?. . .Yes, me too!
I just got here. Where am I speaking from?. . .Well, from
where I am. Yes, the small square. . . . No, the ceremony
will be in the main square. . . nearby. . . . I'll go there later. . . .
Hello, hello?. . .We got cut off? Too bad, I'm one of a kind.
Right! Now, get me the sound effects: "Metropolis number
B 17"! *(We hear the same sonorization as the one used during the break,
only fainter.)* What's that? You call this "Metropolis"! You've
got to be kidding! Sounds like a hick town! Come on, turn
up the volume. Raise the decibel level! *(The sound level goes
all the way up.)* O.K., O.K., now turn it down! Easy! That's
too loud, you're bursting my ear drums! *(The sound goes down
to normal.)* All right, that's fine! Leave it there, except when
I'm speaking. . . .Wait a minute. *(He clears his throat.)* O.K.,
I'll start my coverage. Bring it down. *(The background sound
effects fade out.)* Ladies and gentlemen, here I am posted within
walking distance of the main square, the Square of the New
Regime, where in a short time, today's ceremony will be
taking place. The joyous sounds you hear are those of your
capital, where life never stops!. . .Momentarily, our beloved
Promoter is scheduled to deliver his long-awaited speech
announcing Parliament's new legislation. Out of magnanimi-
tarian — I mean, magnanimous and humanitarian — con-
siderations, our distinguished leader will be taking the stand
himself to announce the exciting and welcome news. For
the time being, let us say no more. Allow me to tune into
the sounds of our great city. Listen to the different modulations
of her voice — to the sound of her pedestrians and her bike-
riders, her young girls and her expectant mothers, her children
and her elderly, her civilians and her soldiers, her aircraft
and her shooting galleries. . . . *(The reporter's voice is muffled*

*by the sound effects. He is standing in his booth, seemingly waiting for something. From time to time he looks at his wrist watch. Members of the G.S.C. are walking by on the nearby streets. They are wearing their grey fedoras.)*

FIRST POLICEMAN: *(running and blowing his whistle)* Nothing to report?

SECOND POLICEMAN: *(running from the opposite direction)* Nothing yet.

*(They exit. A third policeman comes from the wings and stops in front of the reporter's booth.)*

THIRD POLICEMAN: *(in a hoarse voice)* What the hell are you doing here?

THE REPORTER: *(with indignation)* Can't you see? I'm on duty; I'm the reporter for the State Radio. I'm covering the ceremony.

THIRD POLICEMAN: *(scornfully)* I beg your pardon! I mistook your booth for a public toilet!

THE REPORTER: *(slightly hurt but laughing)* Always nice and friendly, our police force! Go ahead! You think you can get away with anything!

THIRD POLICEMAN: We do our best. . . . Is this contraption of yours bullet-proof?

THE REPORTER: Why do you ask? You're not planning to hide in it, are you? I'm on duty, just like you. As soon as I hear the signal, I've got to describe the ceremony. True, I won't see it. But I'll pretend. I'm used to that. Anyway, I've got the complete schedule of events.

THIRD POLICEMAN: Then you know it's taking place close by, on the main square?

THE REPORTER: Of course!

THIRD POLICEMAN: . . . And that the Promoter isn't going to appear in the flesh?

THE REPORTER: Sure, that's the gimmick! The crowd will be told he's unwell. But so as not to disappoint them, they've prepared a film in advance, which they'll project onto a large screen outside. It will be almost like seeing him live.

THIRD POLICEMAN: Yes; he'll seem to be addressing the crowd.

THE REPORTER: Do you realize, I've got to explain all that to the people at home, to people who don't have television, to the blind. . .and God knows who else?

THIRD POLICEMAN: I'm sure you'll be able to handle it! Well, I'd better get back to my beat! So long! No hard feelings, His Master's Voice!

THE REPORTER: See you later, Eagle Eyes!

*(The Third Policeman disappears into the wings. Two others enter, running in from opposite directions. They exchange a couple of brief remarks on the run.)*

FOURTH POLICEMAN: *(running and blowing his whistle)* Nothing to report?

FIFTH POLICEMAN: *(meeting him on the run)* No, nothing!

FOURTH POLICEMAN: Okay!

*(Both exit. The reporter looks nervously at his watch. The telephone rings in his booth. He picks up the receiver.)*

THE REPORTER: No, no! Everything's under control!. . . What? Any moment now?. . .Good, it's about time! Just give me the cue and I'll start, okay?

*(The reporter hangs up. At this moment, three characters appear from the wings on the left: a tall, fat man with a black beard and mustache; a veiled woman, hanging on to his arm with sinuous grace; and behind them, a man wearing dark sunglasses. Their clothes are worn and faded. They sit down silently at one of the café tables. Their surreptitious gestures denote their desire to go unnoticed. One must*

*not identify them readily as the Promoter, Ida, and the head of the G.S.C. in disguise. The reporter, still in his booth, has noticed them. He eyes them suspiciously, then picks up the telephone.)*

THE REPORTER: *(in a low voice, not losing sight of the intruders)* Hello!. . .Yes, it's me. I thought the small square was supposed to be off limits in case of emergency. Three weird characters have just appeared. . . .What are you saying?. . . *(He sounds surprised.)* Incognito? So it's a trap? What's he trying to find out? How popular he is?. . .That's dangerous, isn't it?. . .All right, I didn't say anything! I'll act as though they weren't there!. . .Thanks. . . . *(He hangs up.)*

THE PROMOTER: *(leaning toward Ida)* This is certainly the first time I'm mixing with the crowd!

IDA: *(ironically, pointing to the empty square)* Some crowd!

THE PROMOTER: Even if there's no one here, you can sense that there's a huge crowd not far off. *(He makes a sweeping gesture in the direction of the horizon.)*

HEAD OF THE G.S.C.: *(ironically)* Be patient. They're about to let a few people in here. You'll be able to listen to them; *(darkly ironic)* take note of the deep affection your people have for their beloved leader. *(He exits on the left.)*

THE PROMOTER: *(controlling his rage and pointing in the direction where the policeman exited)* As soon as things get back into line, I'm having that guy sent to the gallows!

IDA: *(mocking him gently)* You mean, you'll promote him!

*(The telephone rings in the booth. The reporter lifts the receiver and listens.)*

THE REPORTER: So it's all set?. . .In a few minutes? Good!. . . All right, I'll get ready. *(He hangs up.)* Five,. . .four,. . .three,. . . two,. . .one. . .! Here I am, happy to be back on the air on this eventful day—I mean, this eventful evening—for the people of our country and for all the citizens of our capital.

Our Promoter, always concerned with the public welfare, always attentive to your best interests, whose most solemn and important decisions are always presented in a spirit of joy and festivity, so that they will be forever engraved in each and every citizen's memory, has asked us to assemble on the main square to hear, in all happiness and confidence, the news he wishes to share with us. However, however. . . . *(He catches his breath.)* Let's not rush matters. Our distinguished leader isn't scheduled to appear just yet. He won't be long, but meanwhile, he invites you to enjoy the street fair around the main square. Go on! Have a good time! Go to the shooting galleries and shatter some plates and pipes! Ride the merry-go-rounds! Eat the delicious hot waffles! Let your children blow their horns and bang their toy drums! Let everyone. . . .

*(His voice is drowned in the tumult of the street fair. Waiters, wearing white jackets, enter from the wings. They set up more chairs and tables on the café's open terrace. People begin to arrive and settle down at the various tables. The strollers from the previous scene enter. By chance, they choose a table next to the disguised Promoter and his equally disguised wife.)*

FIRST STROLLER: *(after a moment's silence, during which the noise of the fair fades, becoming a mere background sound effect. He speaks to the Woman in a low whisper.)* D'you know what I've just heard?

THE WOMAN: *(also whispering)* No, what?

FIRST STROLLER: It seems that, contrary to what was announced, the bastard will not show up tonight.

THE WOMAN: *(still in a whisper)* Of course, he's too afraid of an assassination attempt.

SECOND STROLLER: *(with bitter irony)* No danger of that. The dissidents are precisely the people who can't stand staying awake around the clock! All they want to do is sleep!

FIRST STROLLER: Good business for those illicit hotels! I hear you pay an arm and a leg for one or two hours' sleep! The price for a night is exorbitant; only millionaires can afford it!

SECOND STROLLER: *(with hidden rage)* How long is this hell going to last? Patience has its limits!

THE LITTLE GIRL: *(to her mother)* Mummy, when's he going to be killed, the Motor?

THE WOMAN: *(terribly frightened)* Shhh! You're crazy! People can hear you!

THE PROMOTER: *(leaning towards the Woman at the next table, and addressing her in a mealy-mouthed tone)* From the mouths of babes..., isn't it so, Madame?

THE WOMAN: *(examining him, with growing suspicion)* Don't mind her, Sir! She doesn't know what she's saying. She's talking about a toy she just got...a toy that's a lot of fun.

IDA: *(breaking in perfidiously)* A toy? What fun! What's it like?

*(The two Strollers gesture to the Woman behind the Promoter's back to let her know that she should stop talking to her neighbors.)*

THE WOMAN: Nothing much! Some kind of jumping-jack, a puppet! When you shoot it with a toy gun, it collapses. Children find it entertaining.

THE PROMOTER: *(with a terrifying kind of false gentleness)* I see; and does this deflatable toy have a name?

*(The Woman's two companions gesture to her to say no.)*

THE WOMAN: *(increasingly concerned)* Not at all, Sir. No, of course not....

THE PROMOTER: *(his tone polite but icy)* Sorry, I thought....

*(The reporter, still calling from his booth, seems to give an order. The street fair sounds increase. Still, one is able to hear the reporter's voice, shouting over the sound effects.)*

THE REPORTER: Attention, ladies and gentlemen, your attention, please! The ceremony is about to begin. Our distinguished leader is about to speak. But first, the national anthem, the work of one of our best poets and musicians!

*(The national anthem follows. The music, catchy and rhythmic, is sung by a soloist.)*

SINGER:
> Children of our land,
> You've slumbered far too long.
> Arise, arouse yourselves!
> Wake up and sing along!
>
> Mother Earth's on the run,
> Never wastes her time
> Spinning 'round the sun,
> And we must do our best.
>
> Lift your heads high!
> A fearless leader, strong,
> Is showing us the way
> And leading with a song.
>
> Life is for the living,
> Slumber for the grave.
> For the grave is slumber.
> We shall stay awake,
> We shall stay awake!

*(While the national anthem is being sung, various occurrences create a tense atmosphere. A policeman appears, blowing his whistle. He urges the Strollers to rise from their seats. The Strollers do so reluctantly. The Promoter and Ida refuse to do so.)*

THE POLICEMAN: *(addressing the Promoter, whom he has failed to recognize because of the latter's disguise)* Listen, you, stand up, this is the national anthem!

THE PROMOTER: *(in a strong voice)* Absolutely not. I refuse!

*(Ida, on the contrary, is about to rise, but the Promoter grabs her arm and forces her back down into her seat. He speaks like a dissident.)*

No, my darling! This anthem is against our principles! Stay seated, please!

THE POLICEMAN: *(addressing the Promoter menacingly)* Your name, your papers!

*(The Promoter whispers something in his ear.)*

THE POLICEMAN: *(in a low voice)* I'm sorry. I didn't recognize you, Sir.

*(The policeman takes his leave, bowing obsequiously. The Strollers look fearfully about them.)*

THE PROMOTER: *(to Ida, in a low voice)* We'd better get out of here!

IDA: *(mockingly)* Too bad! It was becoming interesting!

*(They try to melt into the crowd as they make their way out in the direction of the wings. The background sound effects begin to fade.)*

THE REPORTER: *(raising his voice)* Ladies and gentlemen, you have just heard our new national anthem, "Down with Sleep!" performed by one of our great operatic singers. We are about to have the exceptional pleasure of hearing our Promoter, who will address us, thanks to the gigantic screen set up on the main square. Those who don't have seats in the bleachers will still be able to hear his voice. I wish to remind you that, unfortunately, our revered Promoter is unwell and was unable to appear in person here today. However, he was filmed at home, and he appears before you now as though he were here in the flesh. Our beloved leader!

*(The light changes to a sinister violet glow, a strange sunset spreading through the sky. The city and street-fair sounds, the conversations of those who are sitting down and of the strollers continue, but their tonality is slightly distorted. All conversations slow down, then stop. From a distance, the Promoter's recorded voice can be heard. The bombastic vehemence of his address comes through, although one cannot distinguish a single word. The Promoter's speech lasts only a few minutes. It is followed by thunderous applause and ecstatic cheering.)*

THE REPORTER:   Listen to that! Can you hear the cheering, the shouting, the applause? This is some ovation!

*(A flourish of brasses picks up the music of the national anthem. This time it is not sung.)*

THE REPORTER:   Once again, you can hear the music of our national anthem. Magnificent, isn't it? Let's all sing along!

*(He sings the first lines off key. While he sings, the music shifts to a minor key, becoming a kind of funeral march, accentuated by the muffled beat of drums. The light grows more and more unusual.)*

THE REPORTER:   Strange, what's happening? Something's gone wrong. What the hell is the band up to? *(He runs into the booth and grabs the telephone.)* Hello! Hello! Do you hear what I hear?. . . No? There must have been a mix-up at the studio! You've spliced a funeral march into the national anthem!. . . Yes, I realize the two recordings are filed next to each other. But that's no excuse! You want to wind up in jail? Turn it off at once, do you hear? *(The recording skips, then stops.)* That's better! For the time being, stop everything! Thanks!

*(During this time, a minor accident has occurred among the customers seated at the cafés' terraces. The two Strollers are leaning over their female companion, who has just collapsed. One of the two is trying to revive her by gently slapping her face.)*

FIRST STROLLER:   *(speaking in a low voice to the Second Stroller)* Bad timing! She just fell asleep!

*(At this moment, two policemen enter from the wings.)*

FIRST POLICEMAN:   *(to his companion)* This music will put everyone to sleep! We'll never manage to keep things under control.

SECOND POLICEMAN:   That's for sure, if they all start dropping off to sleep! *(He yawns loudly.)*

FIRST POLICEMAN:   *(half laughing, half threatening)* Not you, too! I'll turn you in!

SECOND POLICEMAN:    *(getting hold of himself)* It's nothing. I'm fine.

FIRST POLICEMAN:    *(looking in the direction of the group of strollers and pointing to them)* You're not the only one! Look!

SECOND POLICEMAN:    *(looking attentively)* You're right! We're in luck! Let's nab them!

FIRST STROLLER:    *(seeing the policemen coming toward them)* Watch out! They're coming this way!

*(The Strollers sit down, trying to keep the young woman awake.)*

SECOND STROLLER:    *(in a loud voice)* What are you looking for? *(He changes to a low whisper.)* Wake up! *(He speaks louder.)* You've lost your watch? A piece of jewelry? Your wallet?

THE LITTLE GIRL:    *(looking frightened)* Mummy! Mummy! Don't fall asleep!

*(The two policemen join in the conversation.)*

FIRST POLICEMAN:    *(with a false sweetness)* Hey, there! Thought you were going to take a little nap, eh? *(His tone becomes menacing.)* You know the new penalty, don't you? Not just a jail sentence! Now, if you're caught in the act, it's curtains, crrr! *(He makes an eloquent gesture of strangulation.)*

THE LITTLE GIRL:    No! No! Mummy isn't sleeping; she's not asleep! My mummy never sleeps!

THE WOMAN:    *(Dreaming out loud, she embraces her child, a tender smile hovering on her lips. She describes her dream, unaware of the two policemen standing over her in amazement.)* See, I'm not leaving you, my baby! You've climbed up into the large cherry tree in the garden! I can see you, way up there, in the sun, in the branches. . . .They're covered with fruit and birds! You look so happy up there! But you're climbing too high! Watch out! Don't fall. . .! *(She cries out in terror.)* Ah! a dreadful beak, a bird of prey! There, there, . . . hiding in the leaves. . .! Watch out, it's a vulture! Climb down, darling, quick! But. . .!

SECOND POLICEMAN:   *(grabbing the woman brutally)* You'll have to account for this!... It's a strange business..., very, very strange! *(He repeats this last sentence four or five times, each time with a different intonation. As he slows down, his speech becomes blurred. He is entering a dream state, although his eyes are wide open.)*

FIRST POLICEMAN:   *(noticing the change)* Hey, pal! What's going on?

*(The Second Policeman stares at his friend with a lost expression on his face. His voice, when he addresses him, is hoarse and fearful. But the pace of his speech betrays the fact that he is no longer wide awake.)*

SECOND POLICEMAN:   You're not going to turn me in, are you? Why the axe? The fencing mask? The huge boxing gloves? Don't laugh like that, you fool! What's so funny? Look at yourself: you're covered with blood, from head to toe!

FIRST POLICEMAN:   I've already had it, with all these dreamers! *(He shakes his head vigorously, as if to keep himself from falling asleep on his feet.)* Brr! What am I supposed to do? Cart the whole bunch of them off to the precinct?

*(As twilight begins to fall, other policemen enter from the right and the left. They move in strange, gliding steps, swaying slightly, as though sleepwalking.)*

FIRST POLICEMAN:   Here are some reinforcements! Just in the nick of time! *(He hails the new arrivals.)* Hey, guys, over here! Plenty of work here!

*(Instead of rushing to the spot, the policemen stop, look at each other peculiarly, and seem to consult with one another. Suddenly, one hears the first strains of the music that always accompanies the entrance of Mario and Paola. Soon the couple appears. They always seem to exist in a world apart and move with infinite grace, like two dancers. The light changes again, veering to a dark blue, then an electric violet. There is something lunar and stormy about it. Mario is still holding Paola close to him, his arms around her shoulders to hold her up. He casts a worried look all around.)*

MARIO: *(in a somber voice)* Before, you suffered from dreams haunting your sleep. Now reality is worse than dreams: these men are real, and they're the tyrant's henchmen.

PAOLA: Is there no place for us on this earth?

MARIO: Soon there will be no place for those who love — for those who choose love over hate, over fear and submission.

PAOLA: When I see the scowling faces that surround me, I feel reality dragging me down to a quagmire.

MARIO: And when you don't see them?

PAOLA: When I come close to beauty — when splendid visions light up my dreams — then, alas, I no longer believe in reality.

MARIO: Yes, because all is sleep: we merely glide from one dream to another.

PAOLA: Then ours is an encounter between two dreamers. May your dreams protect mine! Envelop me in peace and silence.

MARIO: *(tenderly)* Rest, dream of my dreams! But be vigilant: everything threatens us.

PAOLA: Please, tell me that the merging of our dreams will triumph over all!

MARIO: Rest, my beloved, while I keep watch.

*(Mario leads Paola to one of the chairs of the café terrace while all those who have witnessed this scene look on with amazement, hypnotized, including the policemen, who keep on swaying as though asleep on their feet. The light grows increasingly unreal. Some waiters are moving about in slow motion. Occasionally a policeman blows his whistle, but it is a hoarse, muffled sound. Then two rays of lightning streak the sky, followed by the distant rumbling of thunder. The reporter steps out of his booth, mike in hand, and moves downstage.)*

THE REPORTER: *(in a trembling voice)* Am I still coming across? Can you hear the thunder? A dreadful storm is on its way. It was not forecast — even our infallible Weather Service had predicted a beautiful day. Well, there's nothing to be done. If you forgot your umbrella, take shelter! Make your way home as soon as you can. We should be thankful that the storm didn't interrupt the main event of the day — the film of our leader. I wish you.... *(He is interrupted by the ring of the telephone in his booth. He reenters the booth and picks up the receiver, still holding the microphone in his hand.)* Hello, hello!...Yes, I can hear you! Ah! What's up? There's a lot of static on the line!... What's that? Incredible! Impossible! I should warn people?... But what can be done? Just warn them?...All right! *(He keeps on holding the telephone receiver against his ear, the microphone next to his lips. He speaks in a voice full of anguish.)* Ladies and gentlemen, I have a special message for you. There is no cause for panic, but a warning has been issued. A strange assembly of creatures has been spotted at the city gates. Humans, but odd humans, a kind we have never seen before. *(He speaks into the telephone.)* Can you describe them?...I'm listening! *(He speaks into the mike.)* They're moving in the dark, in a kind of dense fog! All kinds of creatures....Some are tall, some are tiny, *(with growing anguish)* or huge, with dreadful faces.... Some have long teeth, like fangs; others have elephant ears that stick out. Or they look like snakes with arms and hands! Or they have bloated faces, gigantic noses, like trunks!... They waddle as they go. *(He shouts into the telephone.)* Are there many of them? *(He addresses the microphone.)* Yes, there are! They're moving forward, side by side, waddling and limping along....They've already invaded the south suburbs. They're slow, but nothing can stop them. They keep marching on.... What is more unnerving is that not a sound escapes from their midst. They tread forward, silently and inexorably, with muffled steps, in utter and complete stillness....The thing is, many of them are carrying ridiculous weapons... antiquated guns, blunderbusses, immense sabres, bayonets... yet, there is no sound of clinking metal. *(He speaks into the telephone.)* Hey, you! You're scaring the hell out of me!...What? I'd better stop, or we'll spread panic through the crowd....

*(He stops, out of breath, at the height of terror. During all this time, the sky has been streaked with lightning, and thunder has been rumbling continuously. The people on the café terraces have risen, horrified. The stage grows dark.)*

FIRST STROLLER: *(pointing to something invisible at the end of one of the streets)* There, there! Do you see?

SECOND STROLLER: What? I don't see anything!

FIRST STROLLER: Yes, yes, to the left! It's moving forward, slowly. . . . It's coming closer. . . .

THE WOMAN: What is it?

THE LITTLE GIRL: Mummy, I'm scared! *(She hides her face in her mother's skirt.)*

FIRST STROLLER: *(with anguish in his voice)* They're like huge beasts. . . . No, I'm not sure; . . . more like pieces of furniture. . . . Yes, tables. . . . No, small moving towers. . . . No, that's ridiculous. They've thick, hairy paws . . . and eyes . . . ; they're beasts, heavy, sluggish beasts . . . but with blazing eyes!

SECOND STROLLER: Yes, I see them now! Their eyes are startling! . . . They seem to know us, to know everything. . . . Still, . . . I'm not a believer — in either gods or demons — but these creatures definitely seem to come . . . from another world . . . !

FIRST STROLLER: Come on, you know there is no other world! Snap out of it! It doesn't make any sense, it's ridiculous! . . . Though I admit. . . .

THE WOMAN: *(with a strident cry of terror, struggling against something invisible that seems to be attacking her)* Help! I just felt one brush by me! . . . An icy hand; . . . a foul, cold breath. . . . Ahhh!

FIRST STROLLER: *(putting his arms around her)* You didn't see anything; there's nothing there! It's the evening winds. . . . Don't worry, they're still far away!

SECOND STROLLER:  I've never set eyes on such creatures! Yet, there's something oddly familiar about them. Like the dread I felt when I was a child alone in bed. . . .

FIRST STROLLER:  If they exist, . . . if they're real, . . . they might invade the city. . . any time now. . . . Monsters, larvae, creatures of the dark! . . . They'll be crawling out of cellars, like rats! . . . Let's run, before they get here!

PAOLA:  *(sitting)* Mario, my love, I'm dying. I can't go on; I'm much too drowsy!

MARIO:  *(sitting by her side and shaking her to keep her awake)* Shhh! Paola, you mustn't fall asleep!

PAOLA:  *(plaintively)* But, for God's sake, why, why?

MARIO:  You know, the new law is inflexible. Anyone caught sleeping will be put to death!

PAOLA:  So be it! I want to sleep; I want to die!

MARIO:  For the sake of our love, I beg you, one last time, don't fall asleep! But, look, they've already come to arrest us!

*(He points to two policemen who have just appeared and are staring at them with flaming eyes, as though ready to pounce.)*

PAOLA:  I can no longer see anything! Or rather, I can see a crowd, gathering and shifting! Clouds gathering in the sky, dense mountains of fog. Fiery cascades with waving arms! Rumbling volcanoes! A tidal wave moving forward! *(She cries out.)* Help! . . . Screech-owls, millions of them, grazing my hair! . . . They have heads of children, dead children, and long caterpillar bodies. . . . Some are crawling on their bellies, their feet like tiny wheels; . . . Some look like winged cabinets, with flapping doors! Some have trunks; others have wolflike bodies and are feathered, like vultures. . . . A sea of glittering, mocking eyes, staring from everywhere! They're mocking us, they'll carry us off, . . . eat us alive! Here they come! . . . Here they come!

*(The policemen, appearing from all sides, are staring with hard, shiny looks in their eyes as they take a step or two, very slowly, coming closer. Yet some invincible force seems to hold them back.)*

FIRST STROLLER: *(to his friends)* Come close to me! They're swarming through the streets, but I'll protect you!

SECOND STROLLER: No, I won't give in to fear! If reason fails me, it's because I have a fever!

THE REPORTER: *(with mike in hand)* What can I do with my mike? I'm no help to you. Words are not weapons! Even if I shout! What I see defies description! Words are lacking. . . . I can't describe this advancing tide, this infernal noise! *(There is a commotion.)*

PAOLA: *(throwing her arms about Mario's neck)* Mario! Mario! Protect me! They're crushing me in half! I can't feel my body anymore! Protect me!

MARIO: *(shaking her)* For the sake of our love, stop dreaming! Look around! If we give in, we're lost! Yes, the nightmares are invading the city, . . . but there's an even greater cause for alarm! Look! Look! There's a troop of mercenaries; they'll move in, surround us, and drag us to prison! There's danger on all sides. Where is reality, where is the dream? They're one and the same, . . . but *we mustn't give in.*

PAOLA: *(shouting)* Yes, the threat is everywhere, . . . within and without, inside and outside!

MARIO: *(shouting also)* The tyrant's police are in collusion with the nightmares of the world! They'll seize power together. But we won't give in!

PAOLA: What can you do to stop them?

MARIO: We must overcome our fear. Of both! *(He rises.)*

PAOLA: What are you going to do?

MARIO:   I'm going to speak out. Cry out to the people! We must raise our voice!

*(He is interrupted by the Reporter. One can hear blasts of wind and see whirling lights, green and violet. From a distance, the crowd's hostile muttering can also be heard. Mario raises his arms in front of his eyes to protect himself.)*

THE REPORTER:   *(mike in hand)* Ladies and gentlemen, something eerie is happening. They're gaining ground!...Unknown creatures are spilling into the city streets,...deformed and terrifying, wreaking havoc like a hurricane, destroying everything along the way, breaking shop windows, trampling people who have fallen!...The army and the police have mobilized to fight them. But they're having difficulty containing them! They're a hundred times stronger than we are! Invulnerable yet transparent. You think you've struck them, but your blows or shots meet with a film of fog, wisps of darkness. They change faces or shapes with incredible speed. They're impossible to trap. They're everywhere and nowhere, light and heavy! Like snow or sand or soot, like water, a flood!...Stop them! Stop them! Save me! Help! Help!

*(The Reporter seems to be struggling with the strange beings he has just described. He puts up his arms, trying to fight them off, to shield his head and face, as he retreats in terror. In the thickening semi-darkness, broken only by streaks of lightning, we suddenly catch sight of someone on the proscenium, on the left. It is the Promoter, still in disguise. He is holding Ida by the arm. She moves slowly, struggling against him.)*

IDA:   Where are you running? Where are you going?

THE PROMOTER:   To our private shelter!

IDA:   So, you, too, are afraid?

THE PROMOTER:   I'm not afraid! I sense the danger. And I don't understand it.

IDA:   It's all perfectly clear. The monsters have come!

THE PROMOTER:   What monsters? It makes no sense!

IDA:   Oh yes, it does! The monsters within us: our nightmares!

THE PROMOTER:   Nightmares don't exist!

IDA:   They people our dreams. Sleep is their hide-out, their sacred realm. And there, they're harmless.

THE PROMOTER:   *(stubbornly)* Sleep is a crime against the State!

IDA:   *(shouting with all her might)* You've committed the crime! By abolishing sleep, you've repressed the monsters: now their power has multiplied and they seek revenge. They're furious, and they're invading the city!

THE PROMOTER:   *(in a low voice, with fear)* That's absurd! Quiet! People will hear you!

IDA:   *(still shouting)* So much the better! It's all your doing! I'll cry out until everyone listens. *(She shouts.)* Woe unto those who've been kept from sleeping! Woe unto those who've been kept from living! Woe! Woe! *(She falls on the ground, writhing and moaning.)*

THE PROMOTER:   *(his rage reaching its peak)* Stop raving! Stop shouting! Come on!

*(He drags Ida by the arm mercilessly while she crawls on her knees, dishevelled, weeping and moaning.)*

IDA:   Woe! Woe! Woe!

*(They disappear into the wings, stage right. Soon after their departure, the crowd's attention is drawn to Mario, who has climbed onto one of the chairs in the café.)*

PAOLA:   Mario, what are you doing? You're insane!

MARIO:   Words are the most powerful weapons!

*(The Strollers rise as one. The policemen, who made a move in their direction, seem frozen.)*

MARIO: *(in a voice penetrated with the deepest emotion, a tone at once lyrical and full of courage and human dignity)* Insomniacs and dreamers, though you be from this world or the murky depths, living or a vision of our fears, victims or torturers, beware of our forthcoming victory! Love will triumph in the end, even in the darkest labyrinths wherein hope and memory dissolve! The day will come when your prisons will capsize into the sea, like sinking vessels! Stay back, nightmares of this world and visions of our dreams!

*(During Mario's harangue, soldiers materialize from all sides. They are pointing guns and bayonets at him and Paola and the group of Strollers. They enter the ranks of the police forces. Together, soldiers and policemen advance slowly, taking measured steps. Mario has come down from his chair and stands next to Paola, who has collapsed in hers. He lifts her in his arms, shouting to the armed men.)*

MARIO: Stay away! She's not asleep! Isn't that so, my beloved?

PAOLA: *(in an ecstatic rapture)* No, I'm not sleeping. . . . I can hear you, I'll always hear you, . . .even beyond death itself!

*(Paola and Mario break through the encircling ranks of the soldiers and reach the center of the square. They move with infinite grace, as their steps become a dance. The steps are accompanied by the musical leitmotiv which has marked their entrances and constitutes their musical symbol. The soldiers and policemen stand, frozen in a stupor, as they watch the dancing couple move through the square with sovereign ease and grace. The Reporter has returned to his booth, and with his microphone in one hand, the telephone in the other, he has once again resumed his running commentary.)*

THE REPORTER: *(joyfully)* Ladies and gentlemen, I'm glad to report some new and extraordinary developments. There's been an unexpected turn of events! The monsters — you know, those terrifying monsters that were invading the city — well, they've stopped dead in their tracks. It's baffling, but it seems their invasion was somehow caused by the military and police operations. Indeed, the soldiers are at a standstill, just when they were intending to arrest the offenders—I mean, the people who were collapsing in midstreet, overcome by sleep. Right here, under my very own eyes, the most astounding thing is happening: the soldiers and policemen have been gripped by torpor! They're reeling and tottering! In fact, this very minute, I just saw one fall to the ground! And there goes another one! They're all falling; their guns are clinking and tumbling to the ground! Meanwhile, a young couple has darted out into the square and is performing an impressive dance. . . . They look ecstatic, all on their own, defying the world! . . . It's as if their dance had bewitched and hypnotized the police, the soldiers, the strollers, the entire city! . . .

*(While the Reporter is speaking, the music begins to fade out, like a record going off its grooves. At the same time, the stage darkens.)*

At this point, not only have the monsters curtailed their advance, they're beating a retreat. They're jostling each other, tumbling over each other, like a disorderly pack of wild animals on the run. In the distance, I can see the grotesque, dark silhouettes of their lumpy backs, horned heads, and flabby shoulders! I can hear their footsteps, their muffled cries, their savage grunts! If these creatures had been less terrifying, believe me, their headlong flight would have been a comic sight! Meanwhile, all around me, the people who were still standing have all collapsed to the ground, one by one. The pavement is littered with bodies, lying about, helter-skelter, in the most improbable positions. Dead? Certainly not! The expression on their faces is serene, languid, almost ecstatic! It's sleep! Sleep has enfolded them after so many wakeful hours, so many days of insomnia and duress, pain and hardship!

*(During the Reporter's tirade, the stage action follows his words. In the growing darkness, one can see the piles of sleepers on the ground. No one is standing any longer except the Reporter and the dancing couple, who keep on with their enchanted walk through the square. The twelve strokes of midnight sound from a bell tower nearby, then echo throughout the city, from all the churches. When the carillon stops, the music that accompanied the two dancers stops as well.)*

THE REPORTER: *(his voice thick with sleep)* I don't know. . .what's happening to me! I find it hard to speak. . . . I feel so. . . so sleepy,. . . sleepy,. . . sleepy. . . !

*(Night has fallen. One can hardly distinguish the square, with its piles of sleeping people. Paola stretches out and instantly falls asleep. Mario still stands for a while. He speaks in a clear voice, but with great gentleness. This voice hovers over the darkness and the ambient silence.)*

MARIO'S VOICE: The earth is herself again as she spins through space, making light and darkness alternate. Sleep and wakefulness have resumed their life-enhancing cycle. The endless day of the wounded city has ended. Now we can wait for the new dawn. Paola, my love, at last you can sleep by my side without fear! Sleep is no longer forbidden! Sleep can follow love; it's no longer a crime. And the nightmarish monsters escaped from our dreams have retreated where they belong, inside the black space, in our mind's eye. Nevermore will these creatures of hell invade our lucid, waking hours and violate our fragile equilibrium!. . . Sleep, Paola, sleep! I will sleep with you. . . . Sleep, the just reward of the living!

*(The curtain goes down, then comes back up almost instantly.)*

# EPILOGUE

*(The curtain rises on the same square, at the end of a beautiful summer night. By the light of the moon and the stars, still shining in the dark blue sky, one can see the city asleep, with, here and there, the glow of a couple of lights. People are stretched out upon the ground, still in the throes of a profound sleep. Some, however, begin to stir and stretch, moving as though to rise. Others follow as the night sky gradually grows light.*
*Finally, the light of dawn effaces that of the stars and moon. Color begins to return to the city. Then one hears in the distance, but coming closer and closer, the call of a bugle and the marching steps of a small troop. A band of soldiers enters, dragging behind them the Promoter and his wife, no longer in disguise, but with tattered clothes, as though after a struggle: both are handcuffed. Behind this couple, bringing up the rear, walks a smirking, brutal man, the head of the G.S.C., who is pushing them to walk faster. All of them stop at the entrance to the square.*
*At the same time, one can catch a glimpse of the retreating backs of some of the nightmarish apparitions fleeing in disarray through the streets that radiate from the square. One cannot make out their faces, but only black shapes, disparate in size, some tiny creatures in long, hanging cloaks, others enormous and obese, walking with a limp. They are moving fast, uttering small, sharp cries or ridiculous grunts. They disappear completely as daylight is reestablished.)*

HEAD OF THE G.S.C.: *(addressing the Promoter with mocking rage)* Look at what you've achieved! The fleeing nightmares! The sleeping soldiers! Your demented scheme is over!

THE PROMOTER: *(enraged)* So, you were one of the traitors! Wait and see what awaits you when I come back to power!

IDA: *(shrugging her shoulders)* Nonsense, my great big ram, we're as good as dead, ready for the slaughterhouse!

HEAD OF THE G.S.C.: *(with the same ferocious irony)* You'll get your fill of sleep first! Then you'll be put on trial. And then you'll go straight to the scaffold!

THE PROMOTER:   Monster! Ungrateful wretch! It was for your own good!

HEAD OF THE G.S.C.:   Is abolishing sleep good? You see what happened: the dreams took revenge. They almost invaded the city. . . .Go on! Move! You know the prison! You've sent your share of innocent people there! Go on! There's a cell waiting for you!

IDA:   *(with a deep sigh of fatigue)* I'm not going to make it! I'm too tired!

*(Both exit, led out by soldiers, one of whom plays a funeral march rhythm on the drum. The people lying on the stage rise slowly, one after the other, rubbing their eyes.)*

FIRST STROLLER:   I feel as though I've had ten years' sleep!

SECOND STROLLER:   And me, a hundred years'!

THE WOMAN:   *(to her little girl)* Get up, darling! Look at the golden dawn rising over the city!

*(The soldiers and policemen get up also, questioning each other.)*

FIRST SOLDIER:   *(slightly bewildered, but smiling)* What's happened?

SECOND SOLDIER:   I don't know, . . .but I feel better.

THIRD SOLDIER:   Let's drink to that! I wouldn't mind a good, hot cup of coffee.

FOURTH SOLDIER:   And a bite to eat!

FIFTH SOLDIER:   But you're on duty!

*(Laughing, they all tell him to keep quiet.)*

THE SOLDIERS:   *(in unison)* On duty? What duty?

THE REPORTER:   *(exiting from his booth, microphone in hand)* All the monsters have taken to their heels!

A SOLDIER:   What monsters? The Promoter and his henchmen?

THE REPORTER:   Yes, those, and also the repressed dreams —
the nightmares in action.

*(Mario and Paola are the last to rise. As they do, one hears their musical leitmotiv.)*

MARIO:   *(to Paola)* Look at the luminous sky! The bright sun!
We share its warmth and its rhythm. Sleep has made us light
and airy. Wake up! Let's live and breath in harmony with all
living things. Come with me! Let's not lose a moment's time!

*(They exit running with their customary grace, accompanied by their music, which reaches a crescendo. A dazzling kind of daylight shines over the whole square. The other characters separate and begin wandering off. Curtain.)*

$\backsim$

*Tilly*

# TRUMPETS OF DEATH

Translated from the French
by **Timothy Johns**

For Michel Hermon

This English translation of *Trumpets of Death* was first given a staged reading on October 17, 1986 as part of Ubu Repertory Theater's Contemporary French Theater program on the occasion of the exhibition "Angles of Vision: French Art Today, 1986 Exxon International Exhibition" at the Solomon R. Guggenheim Museum, with the following cast:

| | |
|---|---|
| ANNICK | Mary Rae |
| HENRIETTE-ALEXANE | Janna Gjesdal |
| JEAN-FRANÇOIS | Marco Maglich |
| WOMAN'S VOICE | Lenore Sherman |

Directed by **Pierre Epstein**
Lighting Design by **Heather Sacco**
Sound Design by **Brian O'Malley**

**TILLY,** who spent his childhood and adolescence in Brittany, was born in 1946. He began his career as an actor in Paris in the late 'sixties, appearing in stage productions and television films and as a member of Michel Hermon's theater company. Hermon directed the productions of Tilly's first two plays, *Charcuterie Fine* and *Spaghetti Bolognese. Charcuterie Fine (Delicatessen)* was given productions in London and Toronto in 1984. That same year, Tilly spent two months in Ivory Coast acting in a film directed by Kitia Touré. Tilly's most recent plays are *La Maison des Jeanne et de la culture* (1986) and *Ya bon bamboula,* which was performed at the 1987 Avignon Festival and at the Théâtre Paris-Villette in Paris in productions directed by the playwright himself. *Trumpets of Death (Les Trompettes de la mort),* which Tilly also directed at the Théâtre Paris-Villette, was one of the most acclaimed plays of the 1986 Paris season.

**TIMOTHY JOHNS**'s translations of Bernard-Marie Koltès's *Night Just Before The Forest,* Denise Bonal's *Family Portrait,* Tchicaya u Tam'si's *The Glorious Destiny of Marshal Nnikon Nniku* and Jean-Paul Wenzel's *Vater Land, The Country of Our Fathers* have all been published by Ubu Repertory Theater Publications.

# CHARACTERS

ANNICK
WOMAN'S VOICE
HENRIETTE-ALEXANE
JEAN-FRANÇOIS

*(The action takes place uninterrupted between around eight-thirty and ten o'clock one October evening in Paris, in a studio apartment on the eighth floor of a modern building near Place d'Italie. It is raining outside, and throughout the play we hear the sound of street traffic.*

*The living room-bedroom is separated from the kitchenette by a plastic curtain with brightly colored fringes, and from the bathroom by a frosted glass door.*

*At first the stage is in half-shadow, lit only by a dim light coming in through the bay window. The sound of light traffic is heard in the distance. Then, after a minute or so, the sound of a key turning a lock, then a second one, and finally a third. The door opens and a light comes on in the small entryway. The sound of bags being set down, of the door closing, then of two locks being turned. A woman around forty enters, carrying a black plastic travel bag which apparently is quite heavy. She flips a switch to her left, and two lamps light up. The first is above a round teak table with four chairs spaced equally about it; the other is a floor-lamp beside a padded sofa for two made out of a rustic-stained wood, with flowery upholstery in beige tones. In front of it is a small rectangular oak-stained coffee table with a satin finish; facing it are two chairs matching the sofa.*

*The woman, Annick, is wearing a thick burgundy overcoat in a standard cut, with a synthetic fur collar; brown boots; a beige scarf; and over the scarf, a clear plastic rain-hood. She puts her bag down on the round table and removes her hood as she goes into the bathroom to put it away. She returns, leaving the bathroom door open and the light on. She drapes her scarf over the back of one of the chairs, her coat over another. She's wearing a brown pleated skirt and a burgundy blouse.*

*Annick goes back to the entrance to get her other bags: another travel bag, even heavier than the first, which she sets down on the table, and a huge plastic sack, very light, which she stands upright on one of the chairs.*

*She disappears into the bathroom. A moment later we hear the toilet flush, then the sound of a running tap. The telephone rings. She comes back in to answer it. The telephone is right next to the entryway, sitting on top of a piece of furniture known as a "telephone seat" in the catalogue of one of Paris' largest department stores, La Redouté. It consists of a little, rustic-style wooden bench with two levels: one with a little flowery red cushion to sit on, and the other for the telephone.)*

ANNICK: Oh, it's you. I thought it was her calling to cancel. Lord no, I just got in, I haven't even unpacked yet. . . . No, Lord, the train was two hours late, I went straight to work from the station. Talk about a day—fighting the Metro with all my bags, plus the one for that weirdo, I tell you I musta looked a sight! If I'd had any idea it was. . . . Huh? How should I know? A strike, a cow on the tracks, who knows! *(She sits down on the little seat, pushes a button on the telephone, hangs up the receiver, and continues talking as she struggles to remove her boots.)* If this keeps up I'm not gonna come anymore, every time I do there's some screw-up.

*(Having pushed the speaker-button on her telephone, she can carry on the conversation from any point in the room. The voice over the phone is that of a woman in her sixties or seventies. Harsh, guttural, and cracked, it has a Breton accent.)*

WOMAN'S VOICE: Weren't you on time last Monday?

ANNICK: Yeah, but that Friday it was past midnight when I got to your place.

WOMAN'S VOICE: Oh, that's right. Did you give my crêpes to your boss?

ANNICK: I don't see how, since he didn't come in today.

WOMAN'S VOICE: Ah, he must be sick.

ANNICK: Oh, sure, sick enough to take a long weekend off with Miss Stuck-up!

WOMAN'S VOICE: Where to?

ANNICK:   How should I know? I'll tell you Wednesday or Thursday when the Master hands me all the hotel and restaurant bills.

WOMAN'S VOICE:   He does it just to bother you?

ANNICK:   It's all part of his tax write-off.

WOMAN'S VOICE:   Ah, well, that's something else.

*(Annick has gone over to the closet in the entrance to put away her boots and put on her slippers.)*

Huh?

ANNICK:   I didn't say anything.

WOMAN'S VOICE:   Hello? Hello?

ANNICK:   You mind if I put away my boots? *(She comes back to the round table and starts unpacking her bags.)* What's wrong?

WOMAN'S VOICE:   Nothing.

ANNICK:   Ah, I see.

WOMAN'S VOICE:   Guess what! Today the boss talked to Fine about his retirement.

ANNICK:   So? He didn't to you.

WOMAN'S VOICE:   Yeah but we're the same age.

ANNICK:   What the hell it's got to happen some day.

WOMAN'S VOICE:   The county won't let me keep on living here. And the thought of moving, at my age....

ANNICK:   So you'll go live with Madeleine.

WOMAN'S VOICE:   Oh sure, and with Henri who can't stand the sight of me and gets drunk every single night.

ANNICK:   So you should feel right at home after Daddy.

WOMAN'S VOICE: That's just it, I've had my fill. You know what he calls me?

ANNICK: Who?

WOMAN'S VOICE: Henri. The "Bummer," he calls me.

ANNICK: If you only wouldn't go over there every single day.

WOMAN'S VOICE: You know what would happen if I didn't. Your sister'd start to get funny ideas. As it is I never go over when you're here.

ANNICK: Just as well. The fat slug thinks she owns the world.

*(During all this time, Annick has been emptying the bags, pulling out sugar, salad oil, vinegar, bread, fruit, etc. She goes into the kitchen, turns on the light, puts away a couple of things, comes back to the table for more, and so on, back and forth, all the while carrying on the conversation.)*

WOMAN'S VOICE: Well, you've always been strongheaded, the both of you.

ANNICK: I didn't start it. It's not my fault she's jealous just 'cause I have nice things. The dingbat never could save a penny.

WOMAN'S VOICE: That's true enough. You should see the way her own children talk to her!

ANNICK: Good for them; it serves her right.

WOMAN'S VOICE: You think I would like Paris?

ANNICK: Why do you ask?

WOMAN'S VOICE: I was thinking that, when you get your new apartment . . . .

ANNICK: Yeah, what?

WOMAN'S VOICE: That you'll have an extra room.

ANNICK:   I'll have two rooms, dammit!

WOMAN'S VOICE:   Madame Le Treux spends every winter with her daughter.

ANNICK:   You kidding? They got a duplex in the suburbs; there's no comparison. Believe me, you're better off where you are.

WOMAN'S VOICE:   But what if the county asks me to move?

ANNICK:   We'll see about it then. *(At the moment, she's beside the round table. She takes a pair of sheets out of a sack and goes over to put them down on the bed, where, propped up against the pillow, sits a big Breton doll in native costume.)* You didn't wash my blue fitted sheet?

WOMAN'S VOICE:   I did, only it's got a tear and with all your sister's wash this week I just didn't have time.

ANNICK:   That woman is such a worthless bum!

WOMAN'S VOICE:   Oh, now, let's not overdo it.

ANNICK:   What do you mean, you don't need a Ph.D. to serve beer to riffraff and the crowd she's got in that bar of hers isn't exactly wearing her out.

WOMAN'S VOICE:   She does have kids you know.

ANNICK:   Worthless deadheads, the whole lot! I would've made 'em toe the line. They'll see, when it comes time to do their stint in the army. All of 'em except Pierrick. He's a nice kid.

WOMAN'S VOICE:   What time is she coming?

ANNICK:   Who?

WOMAN'S VOICE:   The Bothorel girl.

ANNICK:   That woman, I swear she calls me up at work right at noon and says in that Parisian tone of voice: "Good morning, may I speak to Mademoiselle Annick Nédélec, please? Alexane Aurel, here." Alexane! The hell with these Alexanes! No wonder they called her "Miss Priss" in school.

WOMAN'S VOICE:  What did she want?

ANNICK:  Christ, she wants to know did I bring back her stuff and could she come 'round to pick it up tonight around eight-thirty, nine.

WOMAN'S VOICE:  If she's at all like her mother, you've got a wait ahead of you.

ANNICK:  Well, if she's too late, I'll leave it in front of the door.

WOMAN'S VOICE:  You can't do that; the Chinese'll steal it.

ANNICK:  Why shouldn't I? With this envelope pinned to the plastic bag, full of her mushrooms, her "trumpets of death." And guess what's in the envelope!

WOMAN'S VOICE:  Don't tell me you opened it up?

ANNICK:  It was already coming open. A check for fifteen hundred smackers and a little note from her lawyer daddy: "Spend it wisely, my dear little girl." The hell with these little girls! Nearly forty and still living off her parents.

WOMAN'S VOICE:  Have you got anything to serve her?

ANNICK:  I got tap water in case she's thirsty.

WOMAN'S VOICE:  Now really, surely you could offer her some Bartissol or Dubonnet.

ANNICK:  Like bloody hell! Me I've got to work tomorrow.

WOMAN'S VOICE:  Lord, you don't have to work so late!

ANNICK:  You're not the one who has to do the work.

WOMAN'S VOICE: Oh, my God, somebody's coming!...
Hang on!...Sorry, I was afraid it was the boss. What're
you going to wear tonight?

ANNICK: My nightie and my houserobe.

WOMAN'S VOICE: No, I mean for her.

ANNICK: Damn! It's not as if the President of the Republic
is coming over.

WOMAN'S VOICE: Why don't you wear that little burgundy
outfit? You're so cute in that.

ANNICK: Cute! When I'm ugly as hell. O.K., time to get off
now, otherwise I'll still be straightening up when she gets
here. *(She goes into the bathroom to put away a bottle of shampoo.)*

WOMAN'S VOICE: Say hello for me!

ANNICK: Goodbye.

WOMAN'S VOICE: What?

ANNICK: *(still in the bathroom, screams)* GOODBYE! *(She slams
the door.)*

WOMAN'S VOICE: I'll call back when I get off my shift to see
how it went.

*(The sound of a receiver being hung up, followed by a dial tone.
Annick comes out of the bathroom, hangs up the receiver, picks up
her travel bags, and puts them in the closet to the right of the bathroom.
She goes back to the table and starts placing apples and oranges in
a fruit bowl. Then she carefully folds the paper bags and goes into
the kitchen to put them away. As she passes the nightstand, she turns
on the radio. We hear a waltz sung by André Verchuren, accompanying
himself on the accordion. The song follows a long musical introduction.)*

RADIO:

>J'ai de la valse dans ma musette
>Pour la joie d'mon accordéon
>Quand je tricote la chansonnette
>De mes dix doigts je suis champion.
>J'ai de la valse dans ma musette
>Pour vous faire passer le grand frisson
>Vous cassez pas la nénette
>C'est au fond des mirettes
>Qu'on regarde les lampions.
>Et quand la valse s'arrête
>On peut faire en cachette
>Un tour sur le gazon.[1]

*(Meanwhile Annick has been folding and putting away all the paper bags. Then she goes over to the closet in the entryway, looks inside for something to wear, takes down a burgundy dress with a straight skirt and a little round white collar, and hangs it up on her display cabinet between the kitchen and bathroom. She returns to the kitchen, grabs a dustcloth, and starts rapidly dusting the furniture. The song comes to an end.)*

RADIO *(Announcer's voice)*:   Yesssiree, folks, a little waltz down memory lane with "A Waltz in My Musette." Mind you, you'll get none of that Anglo-American stuff here; no, sir, not with us, none of these songs in a foreign language here, nothing but songs sung in good ol' French. And now for Marcel Amont singing "Farewell Ladies, Farewell Love"— Marcel Amont.

*(Annick rushes over to the dial to change stations. We hear Sylvie Vartan singing "Déprime." She takes the dustcloth back to the kitchen, comes back, picks up the doll on the bed and puts it on the sofa. She does likewise with the padded quilt and matching pillow. Then she changes the sheets while Sylvie Vartan sings.)*

RADIO:

>Déprime, à quoi tu rimes
>Avec ton parfum d'aspirine
>Ne perds pas ton temps

Plus rien ne me mine
J'ai le moral et les idées clean
C'est lui ma médecine
Mon antidote le remède à tout
Rien ne me contamine
J'ai le sourire à l'épreuve de tout.

Déprime, à quoi tu rimes
Avec ces joies que tu abîmes
Passe ton chemin, tu as mauvaise mine
Ton image de marque décline
Ça va pas?
Très très bien
Qu'est-ce que t'as?
Tout va bien. *(Bis.)*

C'est lui ma médecine
Son amour, c'est le remède à tout
Déprime je te réprime
Dans ton jeu tu n'as plus un atout
Déprime tu n'as plus la prime
Je te renvoie à ton abîme.[2]

*(Annick has finished making the bed. She gathers up her coat and scarf from the chairs and takes them to the closet. She removes her skirt and blouse, tosses them on the bed, puts on her burgundy dress, then goes into the bathroom to look at herself in the mirror. The doorbell rings.)*

ANNICK: Oh shit! Coming! Coming!

*(She comes back in, turns off the radio, goes over to the entrance, stops, returns to the bathroom for another glance in the mirror, turns off the light, and goes into the kitchen to turn off the light there. The doorbell rings again. She starts back toward the entrance, stops on her way in front of the display case, and flips a switch. A light comes on inside the glass case, illuminating a collection of dolls dressed in various national costumes—from Bretagne, Normandy, Greece, Sicily, etc. There's also a model gondola lit up with tiny colored lights. She goes over to the entrance, turns the two locks, and opens the door. We hear a woman say "hello," then see her walk rapidly into*

*the room, followed by Annick, who has locked the door once.*

*The woman is in her forties, with flaming red hair frizzed and swept back, wearing enormous glasses in white Emmanuel Kahn frames. She's wearing a big, beautiful coat with a grey lambskin belt looped twice around her waist, light-grey pants very tight at the calves, and black suede high heels, and she holds a black-and-white purse and an umbrella, which is closed and slightly damp. It's Henriette-Alexane.)*

HENRIETTE: First thing, I absolutely must ask you, but where is the loo? I'm absolutely dying to go, I've been holding it now for hours!

ANNICK: Through there.

*(Henriette hurries into the bathroom, dropping her purse and umbrella on the round table.)*

ANNICK: Switch is on the right.

*(Henriette closes the door behind her. Annick gathers up her skirt and blouse from off the bed and quickly stashes them in the entryway closet. She removes her slippers and puts on a pair of brown fur-lined walking shoes with reinforced soles of imitation crepe. She draws the flowery curtains over the bay window. The sound of a toilet flushing, then of a running tap. Henriette emerges from the bathroom, turns off the light, and closes the door. She takes off her leather belt and drapes it over the back of a chair.)*

HENRIETTE: There, that's better! I got caught in this traffic jam on the bridge you just wouldn't *believe.* And then I suddenly realized when I got here I didn't even know which building you're in!

ANNICK: "C."

HENRIETTE: And you even *told* me! Listen, could I ask a favor? Would you mind terribly if I used the phone? I've got this friend of mine coming to pick me up and I realize now I didn't even *mention* the building number, and since he doesn't know your name. . . .

ANNICK:   It's over there.

HENRIETTE:   I just hope he's not gone. *(She takes a cigarette out of her purse, lights it, and sits down on the little telephone-seat.)* What a funny little seat, it's *so* uncomfortable! I guess it keeps you from spending hours on the phone. Listen, could I ask one last favor? I'm absolutely dying of thirst; you suppose I could have a glass of water?

ANNICK:   Of course. All I have though is soda water.

HENRIETTE:   No, no, tap water is fine.

ANNICK:   You sure?

HENRIETTE:   Yes, yes, I promise; I much prefer that to soda. *(She dials the number; Annick disappears into the kitchen.)* It's a regular Chinatown around here, isn't it?

ANNICK:   Huh?

HENRIETTE:   It's funny, all these Oriental shops in your neighborhood.

ANNICK:   Yes. *(She returns with a glass of water, which she hands to Henriette.)*

HENRIETTE:   Thanks. Hello? Is that you? I was afraid you'd gone. *(She gestures to Annick for an ashtray. Annick goes back to the kitchen and returns with one, which she places next to the telephone. Henriette thanks her with a nod of the head.)* The usual story, I'll tell you about it later. But I'm not the only one in on it, you know. Had to wait over an hour and the guy doesn't even apologize. The real pushy kind, you know? But you can tell right off he's just another little bourgeois creep— completely straight, right-wing, macho, racist, the whole bit. The real career man, what can I say he's a turd. Wants to make American-style action flicks. Anyway the guy's not gonna hire me, that's for sure; I scared him half to death! We'll talk about it later. You finish your article? Good, good, no, you're absolutely right. Yeah. Jesus, no kidding! Ah.

And how! No, no, absolutely. Right on. Great. O.K. babe. It's number 37, building C, apartment 708, eighth floor. The name's Nédélec. And hurry, will you, it's five minutes away. No, no, it's two-way, I came in a cab. O.K.? So see you in a minute, babe. What's that. . . ? *(With an English accent)* Dah-ling, how you *do* go on. . . . Righto. O.K., babe. Ciao.

*(During the phone conversation, Annick has brought out of the kitchen a bottle of Bartissol, a bottle of Dubonnet, and two glasses, which she sets on the coffee table. Now she's back in the kitchen breaking out ice cubes. Henriette hangs up the phone, stands up, finishes her glass of water, and puts it back down on the round table. She looks at a poster on the wall above the table, which shows a greenhouse full of plants.)*

HENRIETTE:   What a cute apartment!

*(Annick comes out of the kitchen and puts a bowl of ice cubes with a spoon on the table.)*

I was just saying what a darling little apartment you have.

ANNICK:   You think so?

HENRIETTE:   Do you own it?

ANNICK:   No.

HENRIETTE:   Is it expensive?

ANNICK:   Five hundred a month bills included.

HENRIETTE:   That's expensive! Al*though,* I must say, I wouldn't know, since I own mine. My, my. It's been so long! I'm not even sure I would've known you.

ANNICK:   I'd know *you.* I've seen you on TV. And I saw you at your grandmother's funeral.

HENRIETTE:   That was the first time in twenty years I'd been back home.

ANNICK:   Would you care for an aperitif 'til your friend comes?

HENRIETTE: I'm not really much into aperitifs. But I could use a cup of coffee.

ANNICK: All I've got is instant.

HENRIETTE: That's fine, fine.

*(Annick goes into the kitchen to heat some water. Henriette follows her to the doorway and stands there holding open the curtain.)*

HENRIETTE: Cute kitchen! Don't bother, I don't take sugar.

*(She goes over to the round table to get a cigarette. Annick sets a cup, saucer, spoon, and jar of instant coffee on the table.)*

ANNICK: The water's heating up.

HENRIETTE: How 'bout you? Do you go back a lot?

ANNICK: Every Friday night. I come back on Monday mornings.

HENRIETTE: Sounds deadly!

ANNICK: I take a sleeper.

*(Henriette comes over to the sofa and sits down.)*

HENRIETTE: What lovely furniture!

ANNICK: Bought the living room at Redoute.

HENRIETTE: Do you stay with your mother?

ANNICK: Yes.

HENRIETTE: What is *she* up to these days?

ANNICK: She works at the old folks' home.

HENRIETTE: Let's see, you had a sister, too, right?

ANNICK: Right. Madeleine.

HENRIETTE: Big tall skinny girl.

ANNICK: Not anymore. She got fat.

HENRIETTE: Let me think, you guys used to have these nick-names—how'd it go now?

ANNICK: Pork and Bean.

HENRIETTE: Oh my God that's right, how horrible! Mine was "Miss Priss."

ANNICK: I'd forgotten about that.

HENRIETTE: Well not me. What a bunch of hicks!

*(Annick goes into the kitchen to get the kettle.)*

ANNICK: Water's hot now.

HENRIETTE: 'Scuse me. *(She serves herself some instant coffee; Annick pours hot water into her cup.)* Thank you.

*(Annick goes back into the kitchen with the kettle. Henriette gets up and goes over to the round table to get her purse, then comes back and sits down. She takes a box of saccharin tablets out of her purse and puts one into her cup. Annick comes back in.)*

HENRIETTE: Do you like going back there?

ANNICK: Oh, you know, it's either there or here.

HENRIETTE: *I* couldn't do it anymore. I mean, that *awful* narrow-mindedness, you know; I mean, I think they're all a bit retarded back there. Even my own parents still have this small-town mentality.

ANNICK: Don't you ever see them?

HENRIETTE: Oh, sure, they come to Paris now and then. My mother's still got her sister in Auteuil. Fortunately, they don't come too often.

ANNICK:   Do you have room for them?

HENRIETTE:   No, no, that's not the problem. No, they stay with my aunt, thank God. They're getting pretty old now. And then I see them every summer at our house on the coast. I mean, *there,* it's O.K. Well, at least for a week.

ANNICK:   What about your little girl?

HENRIETTE:   Malvina? She's with her dad, living in Africa. Hmm, coffee's good!

ANNICK:   Would you like some more?

HENRIETTE:   No thanks, this is fine. And you? You're not married?

ANNICK:   No.

HENRIETTE:   And yet it seems to me you were engaged, weren't you?

ANNICK:   A long time ago I was. To the Le Moigne boy. But, then my mother and his had a falling out, and so, well . . . .

HENRIETTE:   I see.

ANNICK:   Are you sure you wouldn't like a little aperitif? I've got Dubonnet, and I've got Bartissol.

HENRIETTE:   Bartissol! My God does that stuff still exist? Reminds me of the first time I ever got smashed, over at Aunt Milly's with my big brother, I musta been ten or eleven . . . .

ANNICK:   She was quite a character, your aunt Milly.

HENRIETTE:   You *remember* her?! What a bird! The black sheep of the family, that's for sure. I must take after her!

ANNICK:   So, a little Bartissol, then?

HENRIETTE:   No, no, really; thanks all the same.

ANNICK:   Oh yeah, I forgot! I have some whiskey. I always forget, since I don't drink it myself, but would you like some?

HENRIETTE:   I wouldn't turn down a shot of Scotch. *(Annick goes back into the kitchen. Henriette glances at her watch, rummages in her purse, and takes out a pack of cigarettes.)* Damn! Do you have any cigarettes?

ANNICK:   *(from the kitchen)* I don't smoke.

*(She comes back with a bottle of cheap Scotch and a glass.)*

HENRIETTE:   Christ, I finished the pack! I should've bought some on the way over. How dumb!

ANNICK:   You want me to go get some?

HENRIETTE:   That's O.K., my friend'll be here any minute. He'll have some.

ANNICK:   Here, have some Scotch. *(She pours.)*

HENRIETTE:   Not too much *there* that's fine thanks.

ANNICK:   Ice?

HENRIETTE:   Please. Two's fine. I think I'll take this off; I'm awfully hot.

ANNICK:   Here, I'll put it on the bed.

HENRIETTE:   No, here is fine.

*(She takes off her coat and puts it on the chair opposite. Annick, sitting in the other chair, pours herself some Bartissol. Henriette is wearing a beautiful black crew-neck sweater with broad, billowing sleeves.)*

HENRIETTE:   It's funny, I think I actually like this coat better without the belt.

ANNICK:   It's beautiful.

HENRIETTE: It'll do. Bartissol. . . . Just for fun, I'd like to play a trick on my brother. You know where I can get some?

ANNICK: Well I always buy mine back home from Christiane Jobic.

HENRIETTE: I'm sure you can find some around here.

ANNICK: I don't know. I do all my shopping back home. Even my bread. I figure, what the hell, somebody's got to help out the small businessman.

HENRIETTE: You never buy anything here?

ANNICK: Never.

HENRIETTE: What about clothes?

ANNICK: Depends. Sometimes at the Penny Pincher in Guingamp, sometimes at the French Lady in Lannion. Sometimes at Elise Daougabel's.

HENRIETTE: Elise Daougabel. Good God! There's a name I'd completely forgotten. So why don't you just go back and live there?

ANNICK: I got a good job here.

HENRIETTE: Oh? What do you do?

ANNICK: Little of everything. Secretarial, bookkeeping, all that.

HENRIETTE: In what field?

ANNICK: Cleaning materials.

HENRIETTE: That's nice.

ANNICK: I like it. Except I don't have a regular schedule.

HENRIETTE: How's that?

ANNICK: Well, most of the time I finish at seven instead of five. Sometimes eight.

HENRIETTE: But aren't you paid overtime?

ANNICK: You kidding?

HENRIETTE: You have a union, don't you?

*(Annick shakes her head.)*

What?! You're not union?! How can that be?

ANNICK: There's just four of us at work, including the boss.

HENRIETTE: So? That doesn't make any difference.

ANNICK: I get lots of benefits. Month bonus, six weeks vacation, sick time, presents. Last Christmas I got my record player.

HENRIETTE: Paternalism, watch out for it, that's right-wing! We actors, you know, are unionized.

ANNICK: Really.

HENRIETTE: Oh, yes. I've become fairly aware politically, you know. It's very important. After May '81 I wasn't quite as active, but ever since the Right got back in power I've been carrying on the struggle. . . . It's been over five minutes, hasn't it, since I called?

ANNICK: Yes, I think so.

HENRIETTE: Well, then, where the hell is he? He can be a real pain sometimes.

ANNICK: Maybe he got lost.

HENRIETTE: No way. He knows Paris like the back of his hand. He was born here.

ANNICK: Is he an actor, too?

HENRIETTE: No. A writer, journalist. *(She gets up, goes over to the window, and spreads the curtain.)* How horrible, it's still raining!

ANNICK: It never stops.

HENRIETTE: Just like back in Bretagne. *(She picks up a framed photograph beside the record player.)* I recognize that; that's your brother who got killed in Algeria.

ANNICK: Yes.

HENRIETTE: Taken in the Sahara.

ANNICK: Colomb-Béchar.

HENRIETTE: Good-looking guy next to him.

ANNICK: That's my boss.

HENRIETTE: Ah, that explains how you came to Paris!

ANNICK: After the factory shut down, I went two years without work.

HENRIETTE: Nice-looking guy. *(She puts the photo back down, then stoops over to flip through the records.)* Julio Iglésias, Julio, Julio, Julio, Julio, Julio; you're all set up there. You ever go to the theater?

ANNICK: I saw Line Renaud.

HENRIETTE: Ah yes, in *Crazy Amanda.* Did you like it?

ANNICK: Not very much. I think she's vulgar. Excuse me; I'll be right back.

*(She gets up and goes into the bathroom, locking the door behind her. Henriette grabs her untouched glass of Scotch and goes into the kitchen to dump it in the sink. Then she returns and puts the empty glass back down on the table. She goes over to the telephone, dials a number, and waits. The sound of a toilet flushing, then of tap water. Annick comes out of the bathroom. Henriette hangs up.)*

HENRIETTE:   Your plants are just gorgeous!

ANNICK:   They're plastic. Everybody thinks they're real.

*(Henriette goes over to the glass display case.)*

HENRIETTE:   Have you been to Venice?

ANNICK:   Yes, last year. It's filthy!

HENRIETTE:   Yes, but *so* beautiful!

ANNICK:   It was hot and stinking.

HENRIETTE:   Is this headdress here from back home?

ANNICK:   No, from Fouesnant.

HENRIETTE:   And that one?

ANNICK:   I don't remember. Madeira, I think.

HENRIETTE:   Don't know it.

ANNICK:   It's very clean and flowery.

HENRIETTE:   Do you go away every year?

ANNICK:   Yes, usually a two-week tour.

HENRIETTE:   That's nice. This one here is what, Tunisian, Moroccan?

ANNICK:   No, Greek.

HENRIETTE:   Oh, of course, how stupid of me! Do you know North Africa?

ANNICK:   I work at Barbès; I can see Arabs any day.

*(Henriette comes back to the sofa and sits down, glancing at her watch. Annick sits down in the same chair.)*

ANNICK:   Care for some more whiskey?

HENRIETTE:   No, thanks; one's enough. Do I look pale to you?

ANNICK:   No.

HENRIETTE:   Really. And yet I *feel* absolutely wiped out.

ANNICK:   Are you acting in a play now?

HENRIETTE:   Not at the moment I'm not and it's killing me.

ANNICK:   You always did like that, acting. I remember when you were little, you were always in the Christmas play.

HENRIETTE:   I just love it. It's my whole life, the theater and Paris.

ANNICK:   I never see you on that program "Tonight at the Theater."

HENRIETTE:   I'm not into that kind of theater; I'm more into your avant-garde — well, not really that either, it's rather hard to explain, but *I* call it the theater of *expression* because in it one *expresses* something very, very powerful.

ANNICK:   You never act in Paris?

HENRIETTE:   Oh yes, from time to time. My friend — you'll see him in a minute — he's written this fabulous play which I think is going to be produced this year, and, well, he absolutely insists that I play the lead role.

ANNICK:   What's it called?

HENRIETTE:   It's called "Absence of Words."

ANNICK:   I saw you in that detergent commercial on TV.

HENRIETTE:   Oh my God you actually saw me in that horror? Had to pay my taxes.

ANNICK:   You were funny.

HENRIETTE:  So I'm told. This is unbelievable! What the hell is he doing?

ANNICK:  Oh, by the way, your mother gave me an envelope for you and some mushrooms.

HENRIETTE:  Oh, right, she told me on the phone.

*(Annick gets up and goes over to the entryway, where she hung up her handbag coming in. She takes out an envelope, goes over to the round table, and points to the plastic sack.)*

ANNICK:  It's right here.

HENRIETTE:  Don't let me forget them. I'm good at that, leaving things behind. *(She takes the envelope from Annick, opens it, glances discreetly inside, takes out a note which she reads quickly, then tears it into little pieces, which she puts in the ashtray. Then she puts the envelope in her purse.)* You don't hear the neighbors here.

ANNICK:  Thank God! I'm the only French person on the whole floor. The rest are all Chinese.

HENRIETTE:  Ah, the yellow peril!

ANNICK:  No kidding. Apparently they chop up their dead in little pieces and burn 'em in the oven.

*(The doorbell rings.)*

HENRIETTE:  Well, it's about time!

*(Annick goes to open the door.)*

MAN'S VOICE:  Is Alexane there?

HENRIETTE:  Babe? So what's going on?

*(A man of about thirty with slicked-back hair enters, followed by Annick.)*

JEAN-FRANÇOIS:  Just before I left, Jerôme called about the article. Says he saw the play and doesn't agree. I'll tell you all about it later. You know where this place is we're going to?

HENRIETTE:   Me? How would I know?

JEAN-FRANÇOIS:   I'll have to call Maud. What's her number again?

HENRIETTE:   45 47 17 11.

JEAN-FRANÇOIS:   Where's the phone? Jesus, I'm starving! Mind if I use the phone?

ANNICK:   Go right ahead.

HENRIETTE:   We're disturbing you, Annick.

ANNICK:   No, no.

JEAN-FRANÇOIS:   I'll just be a minute.

*(He goes over to the telephone and dials the number.)*

HENRIETTE:   You were probably planning to go out.

ANNICK:   I hardly ever go out.

JEAN-FRANÇOIS:   Hello, it's Jeff. . . .That's just it; you know the address? Fuck!. . .Yeah. . . .Yeah. . . . *(He signals to Henriette for a cigarette. She shakes her head.)* So what do we do?. . .Who?. . . Best thing's to call me right back, O.K.?. . .Wait a sec'. . . . What's the number here?

ANNICK:   45 84 49 87.

JEAN-FRANÇOIS:   45 84 49 87. A friend of Alexane's. We'll wait. . . .O.K. Ciao. *(He hangs up.)* What a circus! Maud doesn't know the address; she's waiting for Jeanine and she'll call us back.

HENRIETTE:   What a drag!

JEAN-FRANÇOIS:   Where's the john? I gotta take a leak.

HENRIETTE:   Through that door; switch is on the right.

*(He goes into the bathroom, leaving the door open, and pisses.)*

I was counting on you for cigarettes.

JEAN-FRANÇOIS: *(offstage)* There was nothin' open.

ANNICK: You want me to go get you some, Henriette?

HENRIETTE: No way!

ANNICK: The little café downstairs, they've got some.

HENRIETTE: No, no, really.

*(Jean-François comes out of the bathroom.)*

JEAN-FRANÇOIS: Anyway, I hope they run my article tomorrow.

HENRIETTE: Hello, you.

*(He goes over to her, gives her a kiss, then sits down on the sofa.
Ever since Jean-François's arrival, Annick has remained standing.)*

JEAN-FRANÇOIS: I'll read it to you; it's very short. Shit, where
is it?

ANNICK: Would you like a Scotch?

JEAN-FRANÇOIS: Sure, thanks.

ANNICK: I'll get another glass.

HENRIETTE: He can drink out of mine.

ANNICK: It's no problem.

*(She goes into the kitchen. Henriette shows the bottle of Scotch to
Jean-François, who gives her a horrified look. Annick comes back
with a glass. She sees them snickering.)*

JEAN-FRANÇOIS: Here it is.

*(He pulls a sheet of paper out of his pocket. Annick sits down in
her chair and serves him some Scotch.)*

Whoa, *whoa*, that's *way* too much; I'll never drink all that!

ANNICK:   Ice?

HENRIETTE:   He likes it neat.

*(Jean-François rummages through Henriette's purse and pulls out a cigarette pack.)*

HENRIETTE:   Don't bother; it's empty.

JEAN-FRANÇOIS:   Fuck!

ANNICK:   Listen, I'll run downstairs and get you some; it'll just take me a minute. What kind do you smoke?

HENRIETTE:   Oh, whatever they've got, American if possible. Here, let me give you some money.

ANNICK:   That's O.K., I have some.

HENRIETTE:   See you in a minute, then.

*(Annick is in the entryway getting dressed.)*

JEAN-FRANÇOIS:   Listen to this. *(He reads.)* "The mirror has a face. Forged in the flames of Shakespearean passion, the Liverpool Theater Company has surprised, disturbed, and delighted us with this year's production of *The Mirror*, by the young playwright David Hartwell. You remember their production of *Richard II* and *Macbeth* a few years ago at the festival of Nancy, with costumes and sets by Léon Bakst. Well, these days the look has changed. The stage is bare, the costumes black, and the hairdos punk. From Purcell and Britten, they have moved right on to Boy George and The Clash. . . . As soon as you enter the theater, you are suddenly plunged into the dark — dark as pitch-black night, of a night as dark as life itself in a Hartwell play. Then, slowly, ever so slowly, a dim light gradually rises, until we notice a huge mirror occupying the entire rear stage. Night dissolves, and the stage, thanks to a lighting design as brilliant as any we have seen, the stage is alternately transformed into an abandoned loft, a vacant lot in moonlight, and finally, a Liverpool dock. . . . The children of the Beatles are now twenty; they're unemployed, desperate, violent; and they scream — they scream their hunger, scream their despair, scream their rage. As he transports us beyond the mirror, Hartwell strips us of any illusions of egotistic happiness. . . . The actors evolve upon this enormous, empty stage with an extraordinary sense of movement and gesture. Space itself is reduced by the integration of speech, and speech is itself then placed in space. The text is simple and direct and slaps you right in the face. This is a play at once sublime and terrifying. Even if you don't know English, hurry, don't miss it. I think you'll see that in the land of Lady Di, the theater is still king."

HENRIETTE:   Very, very good. Really, while you were reading I practically saw the whole thing over again.

JEAN-FRANÇOIS:   It's not too long?

HENRIETTE:   No; really, it's very, very clear.

*(During the reading, Annick went into the bathroom to fetch her raincoat. At the moment she's standing in the entryway.)*

ANNICK:   I'll be right back.

*(She leaves.)*

JEAN-FRANÇOIS:   Jerôme doesn't like it.

HENRIETTE:   Jerôme doesn't like anything we do; let's face it, the guy just isn't like us, that's all. *(The sound of locks being turned in the door.)* What the hell? The crazy bitch has locked us in!

JEAN-FRANÇOIS:   What on earth is *that* contraption?

HENRIETTE:   See what fascinating places I take you?

JEAN-FRANÇOIS:   This is un-fucking-believable! Have you checked out the décor?

HENRIETTE: You kidding? I've been stuck here over an hour and believe me, I've seen the whole bit. The dime-store furniture, the doll collection, the records, you name it. I was starting to get the creeps. Plus the whiskey.

JEAN-FRANÇOIS: Enough, please, it's killing me. Who is this chick, anyway?

HENRIETTE: I told you, a girl from back home. I mean, we must've gone to kindergarten together.

JEAN-FRANÇOIS: Hmm, I *thought* there was some resemblance there.

HENRIETTE: Creep! I don't imagine she has a very happy life.

JEAN-FRANÇOIS: I can imagine. Straight out of Zola. Alcoholic father and cripple mother.

HENRIETTE: You're not far from wrong. Her father hung himself.

JEAN-FRANÇOIS: Ah, you see?

*(He gets up and goes over to the window. She takes a compact out of her purse and goes over to the telephone seat to put on her makeup, using the mirror there on the little table.)*

HENRIETTE: She's actually a very nice girl.

JEAN-FRANÇOIS: I don't doubt it, my dear; we could take her down to Avoriaz with us this year.

HENRIETTE: Oh, sure, she'd go over great at the festival. I can just see it: *The Yellow Peril,* introducing Miss Annick Nédélec.

JEAN-FRANÇOIS: I bet she just loves this neighborhood.

HENRIETTE: She was going on about it when you got here. And before that, I got the whole Arab bit.

*(He moves away from the window and goes over to the record-player stand. He looks at the photo of her brother, then puts it down on the turntable.)*

JEAN-FRANÇOIS:   I figured as much: a perfect example of your working-class girl turned petty bourgeois. Totally alienated, right-wing, natch. And on top of that, she's servile! Did you catch that cigarette shit? *(Now he's next to the bed, searching through her shelves. He takes a packet of letters out of a small tin box and reads one, laughing.)*

HENRIETTE:   Yeah. And what about that Julio Iglesias poster in the bathroom?

JEAN-FRANÇOIS:   Hey, she's liberated, man! She shits, pisses, and strips right in front of him.

HENRIETTE:   She's got all his records.

JEAN-FRANÇOIS:   Freaks me out!

*(Henriette returns to the sofa and puts her cosmetics back in her purse. She takes out a spray bottle and begins to perfume herself.)*

HENRIETTE:   Did you check out the medicine chest? It's full of Valium, Librium, Seconal. . . .

JEAN-FRANÇOIS:   No shit?! Man, I could sure go for a Valium with my Scotch. *(He goes into the bathroom, taking his glass with him.)* Hey, Julio, it's me again, just passing through.

*(He comes back into the living room and looks at a painting above the plants. He gives a low whistle. Henriette raises her head.)*

HENRIETTE:   Far out!

JEAN-FRANÇOIS:   Pouaah! *(He spits out his whiskey and empties his glass on one of the plastic plants, spilling some on the floor. Then he sets his glass down on the round table.)* Oh fuck! *(He gets a towel from the bathroom and wipes the carpet.)*

HENRIETTE:   Don't worry; it'll dry.

*(He tosses the towel into the bathroom, goes into the kitchen, and starts rummaging through the cupboards. He finds a slice of ham in the refrigerator and eats it, leaning against the sink. Meanwhile, Henriette has gone into the bathroom. She picks up a hairbrush over the sink, smells it, grabs a towel and wipes the brush with it, then brushes her hair.)*

JEAN-FRANÇOIS:   This kitchen curtain, it's like right out of a Pagnol film.

HENRIETTE:   Classy, huh? That'd be wild, wouldn't it, to have my résumé photos taken here? I'd put on this heavy-duty, super-hard look, you know? Hair sticking straight up, I mean like real cold, real speedy-like. Can you imagine? With an Yves Saint Laurent evening gown in this setting?! I think it'd be absolutely fabulous!

*(She comes back into the living room. Jean-François is leaning against the kitchen doorframe, playing with the Breton doll.)*

JEAN-FRANÇOIS:   Or you could put on some of her duds. I mean, did you notice her style?

HENRIETTE:   You kidding? I know it inside out.

*(Jean-François is standing next to the display case. Henriette grabs a magazine from the record stand and starts flipping through it as she leans against the back of the sofa.)*

JEAN-FRANÇOIS:   Holy shit! The gondola!

HENRIETTE:   Too much.

*(He goes over to the closet next to the bathroom door, opens it, and looks inside.)*

HENRIETTE:   Where the hell is she, anyway? She's taking forever! What are you doing? *(She goes over to him.)*

JEAN-FRANÇOIS:   Nothing; just looking. It's the anthropologist in me.

*(Together, they rummage through the linen closet. He hangs a pair of panties on one of the plastic plants.)*

HENRIETTE: Could you make it with her?

JEAN-FRANÇOIS: Sure.

HENRIETTE: Really?

JEAN-FRANÇOIS: I've always had this weakness for social rejects.

*(He opens the closet in the entrance and examines the dresses hanging inside. He takes one down. It's dark green, with a round neck and little white collar. Henriette has returned to the sofa, where she sits reading her magazine.)*

JEAN-FRANÇOIS: I could just see you in a dress like this!

HENRIETTE: How horrible!

JEAN-FRANÇOIS: Go ahead, put it on.

HENRIETTE: You gotta be kidding!

JEAN-FRANÇOIS: Come on.

HENRIETTE: You're crazy!

JEAN-FRANÇOIS: Just for me, okay, babe?

HENRIETTE: But she's gonna come back!

JEAN-FRANÇOIS: Okay, fuck it; what the hell I'll just keep all the coke for myself.

HENRIETTE: You bastard! Are you holding?

JEAN-FRANÇOIS: I got a little.

HENRIETTE: Boy, I could sure use some now!

JEAN-FRANÇOIS: You got a mirror?

HENRIETTE:   No, but we can chop it on the toilet seat. You got a razor blade?

JEAN-FRANÇOIS:   Sure do.

HENRIETTE:   Man, that's just what I've been needing all day. C'mon, let's hurry.

*(She hurries into the bathroom, followed by Jean-François. On the way, he hangs the dress on the display case. Then he, too, goes in. They speak offstage.)*

HENRIETTE:   Leave the door open so we can hear her.

JEAN-FRANÇOIS:   Great, it's black!

HENRIETTE:   What is?

JEAN-FRANÇOIS:   The toilet seat.

HENRIETTE:   Is it good stuff?

JEAN-FRANÇOIS:   Pure crystal.

HENRIETTE:   We gonna do it all?

JEAN-FRANÇOIS:   Yeah.

HENRIETTE:   It looks hard.

JEAN-FRANÇOIS:   Exactly. You got a bill on you?

HENRIETTE:   In my purse. *(She comes back into the living room and looks through her purse on the round table.)* Ah. Here's one.

JEAN-FRANÇOIS:   *(offstage)* Roll it good 'n' tight.

*(She goes back into the bathroom, carefully rolling the bill.)*

JEAN-FRANÇOIS:   *(offstage)* You do the honors.

*(The sound of intense sniffing.)*

HENRIETTE:     (*offstage*) Here, take your razor blade; I gotta pee.

(*He comes out of the bathroom, stops, runs his thumb along both sides of a razor blade, rubs his gums, then puts the blade back in his wallet.*)

JEAN-FRANÇOIS:     I'm gonna call Maud back.

HENRIETTE:     (*offstage*) 45 47 17 11.

JEAN-FRANÇOIS:     Busy.

HENRIETTE:     (*offstage*) That's Jeanine.

(*He goes back toward the bathroom, stops in front of the display case, and takes down the dress, leaving the hanger behind. Henriette comes out.*)

HENRIETTE:     You're not gonna start on that again, are you, babe?

JEAN-FRANÇOIS:     Quick, O.K.?

(*She goes back into the bathroom. He leans against the doorframe, watching her.*)

JEAN-FRANÇOIS:     No, not like that; take off your clothes.

HENRIETTE:     You're mad!

(*A moment later, she steps out of the bathroom and walks up and down the living room.*)

JEAN-FRANÇOIS:     Fantastic, absolutely fantastic! Look in the mirror.

(*She looks in the mirror above the telephone seat.*)

HENRIETTE:     Not bad; not bad at all.

JEAN-FRANÇOIS:     Wait a sec'.

HENRIETTE:     Now what?

JEAN-FRANÇOIS:   Shoes.

*(He goes over to the closet in the entrance and takes out two or three pairs of shoes, chooses one, and has Henriette put them on. She walks up and down the room. When she turns around, Jean-François is rubbing his crotch. She goes over to him, unbuttoning her dress, and leans up against the display case. He starts fondling her. Then, the noise of locks being turned.)*

JEAN-FRANÇOIS:   Oh my God, how horrible!

*(They dash into the bathroom and shut the door. Annick enters.)*

ANNICK:   I locked y'all in. Must be habit.

*(She turns one of the locks, then comes into the room holding a pack of cigarettes. Giggles can be heard coming from the bathroom. Annick removes her rain-cap, drapes it over the back of a chair, and puts the cigarettes on the round table. She unbuttons her coat, takes it off, and goes to hang it up in the entrance. She notices the shoes, gathers them up, and puts them back in the closet. Jean-François comes out of the bathroom, closing the door behind him.)*

JEAN-FRANÇOIS:   Alexane's in there primping for this party we're going to.

ANNICK:   This is all I could find.

JEAN-FRANÇOIS:   Great, great. *(He takes out a cigarette and lights up.)* Is it still raining out?

ANNICK:   I think so.

JEAN-FRANÇOIS:   We're disturbing you.

*(Annick goes over to the coffee table, gathers up the bottles, and takes them into the kitchen. Henriette comes out of the bathroom, turns off the light, and shuts the door.)*

HENRIETTE:   I used your hairbrush, Annick.

*(With gestures, Henriette asks Jean-François what he's done with the dress. He answers likewise that he put it "under a cover." Annick comes out of the kitchen.)*

HENRIETTE: You have the cigarettes, hon'?

JEAN-FRANÇOIS: They're over on the table.

*(She takes out a cigarette and lights it up. Annick picks up the bottle of Scotch.)*

ANNICK: Can I put away the Scotch now?

HENRIETTE: By all means, thanks.

*(Annick returns to the kitchen. New gestures between Henriette and Jean-François: she, asking if Annick suspects anything; he, reassuring her.)*

HENRIETTE: What the hell are those girls up to anyway? Maybe I should call back. Annick, can I use the phone?

ANNICK: *(coming out of the kitchen)* Yes.

*(She picks up the glasses and the ice bowl on the coffee table. Henriette dials the number.)*

HENRIETTE: Busy.

*(Annick goes back to the kitchen.)*

HENRIETTE: It'd be quicker just going by their place — otherwise we'll be here all night.

JEAN-FRANÇOIS: Let's do it.

*(Annick reappears.)*

HENRIETTE: We'll be leaving you now, Annick. My coat.

*(She puts it on, while Annick goes over to the round table to collect the glasses there.)*

Now let's see. My purse.

*(She picks it up. Annick goes back into the kitchen.)*

Umbrella.

*(She picks her umbrella up off the round table. Annick comes back out of the kitchen.)*

That's it; we'll be off now. Thanks for everything, Annick; say hello to your mother. Oops, almost forgot my trumpets!

*(She picks up the plastic bag, which was left on one of the chairs. Annick crosses in front of them and opens the door.)*

'Bye-bye now, and thanks again!

JEAN-FRANÇOIS:   So long, a pleasure knowing you.

ANNICK:   Goodbye.

*(Annick shuts the door, locks all three locks, and turns out the light in the entrance. She spots Henriette's long leather belt draped over the back of a chair, picks it up, returns to the entrance, opens all three locks, and goes out onto the landing.)*

ANNICK:   Henriette!

*(Annick returns, locks all three locks again, puts the belt down on the round table, picks the pair of panties off the green plant, and goes into the bathroom to toss them into the dirty clothes hamper. She gathers up the pair of shoes next to the bathroom sink, comes back out, notices the whiskey stain on the carpet, then puts the shoes away in the closet. She notices the magazine that Henriette left on the sofa. She picks it up, folds it carefully, then places it back in the record stand. She puts the photograph of her brother back in its original place, picks up the letter, which she reads, then puts it back into the little tin box. She straightens the bed a bit, takes a rag from the kitchen, and starts wiping the coffee table. The telephone rings. She walks over to the telephone seat, picks up an ashtray left there by Henriette, then, without answering the telephone, goes back to the coffee table, continues wiping it, and takes the ashtray and rag into the kitchen. She turns off the gondola lights and notices the hanger*

on the display case, with the belt belonging to the green dress still hanging on it. She takes it down and goes to the closet to hang it back up, then notices that the dress isn't there. She starts to look for it. Meanwhile, the telephone is still ringing. She looks in the bathroom hamper, in the other closet, under the bed, behind the record stand, then finally in the kitchen. She opens all the cupboards, then the garbage pail. The telephone stops ringing. She looks inside the oven, then dashes into the bathroom, lifts the toilet seat, and removes the partially wet dress, which she hangs on the shower partition. Then she goes back into the entrance, picking up on the way Henriette's belt from the table. She returns carrying a stepladder, which she places in the bathroom. Then she climbs up on it. From the noise, we gather that she's looking for something, but we see only her legs. Suddenly the stepladder tips over, her legs dangle momentarily in the air, and then Annick falls to the floor. The telephone starts ringing again. She sits motionless on the floor for a moment, then gets up painfully and goes over to answer.)*

ANNICK: Shit!

*(She hangs up; sits down on the telephone seat; removes her shoes; puts them away in the closet; puts on her slippers; returns the stepladder to the entrance; grabs Henriette's belt, which is still hanging in the bathroom, then takes it into the kitchen and tosses it into the garbage. She goes over to the record-player and puts on a Julio Iglesias record.)*

RECORD:
Vois... C'est moi qui fait ce soir le premier pas
On s'ennuyait un peu mon coeur et moi
On revient près de toi

Vois... Rien qu'un instant je ne vais pas rester
Je prends de tes nouvelles et je m'en vais
Je ne fais que passer

Moi... je te retrouve au milieu de tes fleurs
Chez toi la vie a toutes les couleurs
Et le goût du bonheur

Moi... En noir et blanc je vois passer les jours
Comme un brouillard qui tournerait autour
Des choses de l'amour

Je sais en amour il faut toujours un perdant
J'ai eu la chance de gagner souvent
Et j'ignorais que l'on pouvait souffrir autant

Je sais en amour il faut toujours un perdant
J'ai eu la chance de gagner souvent
Je t'ai perdue... Pourtant.[3]

*(Annick takes a placemat out of the closet to the right of the bathroom and sets it on the round table in front of the "green plants." Then she goes into the kitchen, returning with glass, plate, and silverware, which she sets on the placemat. She returns to the kitchen to prepare her meal, and as Julio Iglesias sings the final stanza, she joins in at the top of her voice, singing: "Il faut toujours un perdant...." The curtain falls very slowly.)*

ς

# TRANSLATION OF LYRICS

## [1]"J'ai de la valse dans ma musette..."

*Got a bit o' waltz in my knapsack*
*To the joy of my accordion*
*When I knit a little song*
*With my ten fingers I'm a champion*
*Got a bit o' waltz in my knapsack*
*To get you over the big chill*
*It's in the depths of eyes*
*We watch the grass lamps glow*
*And when the waltz is over*
*We can sneak away*
*And explore the lawn.*


## [2]"Deprime" (French lyrics set to the music of *Sweet Dreams* by The Eurythmics)

*Blues, what's the sense of you?*
*You and your aspirin airs*
*No use wasting your time*
*There's nothing eating at me*
*My morale is high and my thoughts are clean*
*For he is my medicine*
*My antidote my cure-all*
*Nothing contaminates me*
*I've got a fool-proof smile*

*Blues, what's the meaning of you?*
*You and the joys you kill*
*Be on your way, you're looking bad*
*Your image is on the decline*

*Not feeling so good?*
*That's just fine*
*What's wrong with you?*
*Everything's fine* (Repeat.)

*For he is my medicine*
*His love is the one cure-all*
*Blues, I refuse you*
*You're holding a losing hand*
*You no longer take first place*
*I'm sending you back to your pits.*


### ³"Il faut toujours un perdant"

*See... Tonight it's me who makes the first advance*
*My heart and I, we'd grown a little tired*
*And so return to you.*

*See... I'm only going to stay a little while*
*I'll see what's new with you, then go away*
*I'm only passing through.*

*Me... I find you once again in all your flowers*
*Your life has always glowed in every shade,*
*And the taste for happiness.*

*Me... I watch the days go by in black in white*
*Much like a fog revolving all around*
*All involving love.*

*I know in love there must always be a loser*
*Often enough I've had the luck to win*
*And never knew that one could suffer so*

*I know in love there must always be a loser*
*Often enough I've had the luck to win*
*But I've lost you... nevertheless.*

## NOTES ON THE CHARACTERS

ANNICK. In her forties, the youngest of three children. Daughter of Germaine Le Balch, housewife; and Pierre Nédélec, worker, deceased.

Spends the first twenty years of her life in Britanny, in the little town where she was born. Public school until the age of sixteen, when her brother, Jean, is killed in Algeria. Secretarial school in the neighboring village, which she attends each morning by bus. Upon the completion of her studies, she obtains a position as typist in the paper factory where her father works. Her sister, Madeleine, marries Henri Le Fur, owner of a local bar.

Annick is twenty when the factory closes. Some of the workers (the youngest) are rehired in the Sarthe (a department in the Loire), but not the secretaries. Unemployment. Her father does some yardwork for a few village notables. The factory and the adjoining workers' houses are sold to a Belgian company, and the workers evicted. One morning, Annick finds her father dead, hanging from the door of the washhouse. Following this episode, the local authorities find a job for her mother in the village retirement home, as a maid. Several months later Annick leaves for Paris as a secretary in the small business managed by Bernard, her brother's war buddy.

She's been working there for nearly twenty years, over eight hours a day, without being asked to. She likes her boss very much and is even perhaps secretly in love with him.

Every Friday night she goes to Britanny, and every Monday morning she returns to Paris. During her month's vacation, she always takes a two-week organized tour (to Sicily, the Canaries, Madeira, Greece, etc.). She spends her two remaining weeks with her mother.

In Paris, she has no friends. Occasionally she goes to a movie with a colleague or eats out at a pizzeria.

At work, she's been nicknamed the "spinster," but she "doesn't give a damn." She'd rather live alone than "argue like some couples do" which she sees around her.

**HENRIETTE-ALEXANE.** Two years older than Annick, a native of the same little town in Britanny. Daughter of Jeanne Guillou, without profession, and Paul Bothorel, Attorney-at-Law. Has a younger brother, who is a physician in Brest. Elementary school with the nuns in her village; secondary education as an intern at the Bossuet Institute in Lannion. After her Bac in philosophy, she enrolls in law school at the University of Rennes. She remains there two years. At the same time, she takes drama classes at the City Conservatory. Law doesn't interest her; "she'll be an actress." She decides to go to Paris to take classes at a theater school directed by Clarence, a friend of her mother's sister. At first, she lives in Auteuil at her aunt's. Very soon, thanks to Clarence, she gets small parts on stage and on TV: Henriette Bothorel becomes Alexane Horel. She falls in love with a young classmate; they get married and have a daughter, Malvina.

With May 1968, she discovers a passion for politics. She separates from her husband and her daughter to live with Alain, an actor who is an activist of the far left.

Ten years later, she breaks with politics and romance to "devote herself to her career." She's still always "onto something," and does a little film.

She meets Jean-François, theater critic for a left-wing newspaper. Alexane gets more work (never starring roles) and is completely integrated into the milieu, which she adores. Her meeting Jeff has been "fabulously important," he's a "fabulously intelligent guy and *very* good in bed."

Malvina lives with her father, who is now a cultural attaché in Africa. Mother and daughter never see each other.

In twenty years, Henriette-Alexane has gone back to her childhood village only once, for her grandmother's funeral. She sees her parents either in Paris or at their summer resort.


**JEAN-FRANÇOIS.** Known as Jeff, in his dynamic thirties, with a "Paris — Les Halles" look [or "New York — Soho"?]. Eldest of three boys; parents divorced. Mother an antique dealer at a fashionable location in Paris; father, a "leftist" lawyer. Born in Paris, he's a child of Saint-Germain-des-Prés.

After pre-school, he attends private school (collège Stanislas), where he remains for ten years. He's a lively student, brilliant, turbulent, sometimes even arrogant. Family upbringing is liberal, bohemian, bourgeois. At ten, his parents separate. He lives with his mother and brothers on rue de Lille. His father moves to rue de Verneuil with a well-known actress who might well pass for the twin sister of Michèle Mercier, the unforgettable interpreter of *Angélique, marquise des Anges.* In May 1968, he's sixteen years old. Stanislas, where things never change, closes. Jean-François joins the students in the streets. He exchanges rue de Lille for rue de Verneuil, where he is better understood, "Angélique" having given way to Martine, a young leftist lawyer.

Next year, while a philosophy student, he attends numerous meetings of the far left and meets several journalists, musicians, and actors.

That summer, after "brilliantly" passing his baccalauréat, he departs alone for the United States: two months in New York, six in California, a year and a half in Mexico, working at odd jobs here and there. In Mexico, he lives for over a year in a mostly American theatrical community. Discovers marijuana, peyote, LSD. Writes articles on the American underground theater which are often published in France.

When he returns to his father's house, he's barely twenty years old. He writes a play that will never be produced, *Absence of Words* (the interior monologue of a schizophrenic).

Little by little, he manages to carve out a place for himself in the theatrical world as a critic. He contributes to several journals, then finds a permanent position with a daily paper.

He sets up in a loft on rue Faubourg Saint-Antoine. He has a very busy nightlife, and wherever it's to his advantage, he's there to be seen.

Colomb-Béchar, June 10, 1959

Dear Annick,

Sunday when I got back from my assignment I found your two letters and mom's package.

Right away me and my buddy Bernard polished off the sardines with bread and butter, they really were good, too, it's a shame the bread wasn't from home. Tell mom not to send any more crêpes, by the time they get here they're all mildewed. I'm doing okay, my health is good, except when it's hot. You won't believe this, but it gets up to 113 here in the shade. It's hard to imagine it's raining back home. Summer's on its way, pretty soon you'll be able to go down to the river for a swim. Can't wait to get home for my Xmas leave. I'll spend the first night in Paris with Bernard who says hello. We got back from Constantine exhausted where one night we danced the java and had a lot of fun. Around here it's a lot quieter, you can assure Mom there aren't any rebels around. I'm glad your steno-typing classes are going well. Pretty soon you'll have a skill and can earn a living. Tell Pop I thought about him on his birthday but was off on assignment and couldn't send a card. Tell the folks I'm going to write them soon. And tell Madeleine I'll be there for the marriage. Say hi to Yvon Le Moigne when you see him. Tomorrow I'm off, I think I'll go into Palmeria with some buddies, all except Bernard who's on guard duty.

Okay, I've got to go now or else my letter won't make the mail truck. Say hi to all the family, give mom and pop a big hug for me and Madeleine too, Aunt Francine and Uncle Louis. Keep writing, it really does me good to hear from you.

Love,

Your brother Jean

Michel Vinaver

# THE NEIGHBORS

Translated from the French
by **Paul Antal**

This English translation of *The Neighbors* was given its first reading, directed by **Virlana Tkacz,** at the French Institute/ Alliance Française Tinker Auditorium, on March 25, 1988, during the "Ubu International" festival.

**MICHEL VINAVER** was born in Paris in 1927 and was educated at the Sorbonne and at Wesleyan University, where he studied English and American literature on an international exchange scholarship. The author of fifteen plays, Professor of Theater at the Sorbonne, novelist, essayist and translator/adaptor, for twenty-seven years Vinaver also pursued a successful business career as a general manager for the Gillette Company in Europe. His plays have been directed by the most prominent French directors—Roger Planchon, Jean-Marie Serreau, Antoine Vitez—and have been produced throughout Western Europe. Vinaver's essays on theater were published in 1983 as *Ecrits sur le théâtre,* and his complete plays have just been published in a new edition by Actes Sud/L'Aire. His 1981 play *L'Ordinaire* (now entitled *High Places* in English) was first presented in the U.S. in a staged reading by translator-director Gideon Y. Schein at the O'Neill Theater Center's 1983 National Playwrights Conference. It was also presented in a reading, directed by Virlana Tkacz, during Ubu Repertory Theater's 1987 festival "Double Visions: France/U.S.A." Vinaver's short plays *Dissident, Goes Without Saying* and *Nina, It's Different,* both translated by Paul Antal, were also presented in readings at Ubu Repertory Theater and have been published by Performing Arts Journal in *DramaContemporary: France. The Neighbors* received unanimous critical acclaim when it premiered in France in 1987, and Vinaver was hailed as a French Chekhov.

**PAUL ANTAL** has taught French, Italian and Humanities at Reed College and the University of Minnesota. He has translated works of Italian essayists, the complete correspondence of Descartes and Elizabeth of Bohemia, and works of Louise Labé and Francis Ponge. His translations of Michel Vinaver's *Dissident, Goes Without Saying* and *Nina, It's Different* were published in *DramaContemporary: France.* For Ubu Repertory Theater Publications, he previously translated *Madame Knipper's Journey to Eastern Prussia* by Jean-Luc Lagarce. He currently teaches at St. John's College in Annapolis, Maryland.

## CHARACTERS

BLASON
ALICE, his daughter
LAHEU
FELIX, his son

*The work is played without intermissions.*

*The first and third acts are in real time. The second act covers a period of one year and consists of ten sequences which are played without interruption except for a lowering and raising of the stage lights in one movement like the dropping and rebounding of a ball. No other music except the Andante of Mozart's* Divertimento K. 563, *and this only during the changes between acts.*

## ACT ONE

*(The backs of two identical houses. In the foreground, their common patio. Blason and Alice are setting a table for four. A summer evening. The two houses are symmetrical, each with a double French door leading to the living area and another door leading to the kitchen.)*

BLASON:   Missing

A little over eight hundred thousand francs

*(Barely perceptible sound of a bell.)*

It's theirs isn't it?

Their telephone ringing?

*(Alice hesitates, rushes into the house at right. She returns calmly a few seconds later.)*

ALICE:   Felix

BLASON:   It's for Felix?

ALICE:   For him

Personally

One of his customers

BLASON:   Daphne?

ALICE:   You're right she again

Urgent

Remind me to tell him to call her back

BLASON:   Take a piece of paper and write down Felix return Daphne's call

When they arrive we'll all be so upset we might forget the champagne glasses they should be rinsed out since they've been sitting so long in the china cabinet up to the last gasp

He stroked her

ALICE:   *(writing)* Felix

BLASON:   Is still reeling

ALICE:   *(writing)* Return Daphne's call

BLASON:   You can add it up the first two thirds of his life put to rest today seeing that we celebrated his twenty-fourth birthday last month

And she was born on this patio sixteen years ago

ALICE:   Oh I remember and that? Those black beads that's caviar? Real caviar?

Elsa

BLASON:   Put on your glasses and read what's printed on the label

In tiny letters Alice on the right at the top

ALICE:   Imported from Iran

Felix and I terrified

We were crouched down on the ground in this corner holding hands while Suzanna was delivering

That red stuff what is it?

BLASON:   Salmon roe relatively speaking it's not as rare some people find it tastier

As it's half the price I took twice as much

ALICE:   And you brought out the old pink napkins edged with lace

BLASON:  Embroidered by your mother

A year before her accident

ALICE:  You always say her accident you were there so was I

BLASON:  The difference is you and I are still here today

ALICE:  Today yes

And yet

Isn't it our accident?

They're almost twenty years old

BLASON:  The plates with the ivy garland in the center are
maybe a hundred

The service came down from my great great-grandparents
it's genuine Limoges

Give them a little wipe Alice before setting them down

The little knife to the left of the big one

ALICE:  When Felix and I have our restaurant

I'd like the food to be served on plates

Not anything like this precious china but pretty porcelain
all the same

A service with character

BLASON:  Something classy exactly

If you want to attract the proper clientele you'd better

But in any restaurant even supposing you have a high-volume
dishwasher as you'll no doubt want

However careful you both will be the problem is the amount
of handling you have no idea how much breakage does occur

You have to count on an eleven-month turnover

ALICE:   What does that mean?

BLASON:   That each plate has an average life of eleven months

ALICE:   How do you know that? Do you have that many restaurants among your clients?

I didn't know that restaurants also take out insurance on dish breakage

BLASON:   Theoretically you can insure against anything just a question of cost

In practice I mean in day-to-day circumstances of running the business breakage of dishes is not in fact something that the companies insure against

You see I regularly go through twenty or so trade periodicals so whenever a new client calls I know in advance what his problem is

Statistics will tell you a lot if you know how to read them

Butter dish next to the toast it's beyond me

ALICE:   You do love figures

BLASON:   They're part of me

Percentages stick with me

Look here

*(Laheu and Felix enter. Sudden and long silence. Blason smiles.)*

Laheu take him for example

Statistics are not his cup of tea figures make him cringe

He says they suck the life out of things

*(Silence.)*

LAHEU:   Take Blason as far as he's concerned things become real only when he puts them in columns

For him they just don't come to life otherwise

BLASON:   Consider Laheu

Now Laheu's only interested in something if it's unique

But a unique thing just doesn't exist

Things only exist insofar as they form series

And the man knows it full well

*(Felix and Alice, holding hands, observe the pair of men. Laheu smiles.)*

LAHEU:   It's simply unbelievable

In order for him to get a grasp of something it has to stop existing in itself has to dissolve in the magma of big numbers

BLASON:   A particular case is nothing more than a particular case

LAHEU:   An average is nothing

BLASON:   God almighty just listen to him

This man is supposed to be the quality control manager at Universal Biscuit

Dare I ask what method you use at your job?

LAHEU:   I suppose when the day's over at the factory I switch off whereas you

Felix look at what they've laid out for us here

BLASON:   Or is it that you control one cookie after another?

LAHEU:   You've never tasted such things have you?

ALICE:   Me neither

FELIX:   Well there you have it

ALICE:   Felix he says there you have it

FELIX:   I've taken my largest order

LAHEU:   Caviar champagne for us Felix all these delicacies just think

ALICE:   Largest ever?

BLASON:   When a loved one departs leaving us in sorrow

LAHEU:   And not an ordinary one either

Moet et Chandon Felix

FELIX:   The largest since I've been traveling for Christophle an order for 65,000 francs from Madame Daphne

She's on her way to doubling the floor space of her store

ALICE:   Makes me think about it Felix

BLASON:   Didn't I tell you to jot it down?

ALICE:   Return her call

BLASON:   Don't let's call it a banquet

However rather than crying

FELIX:   Madame Daphne called?

BLASON:   Just call it a small celebration

ALICE:   We can celebrate his big order too

FELIX:   Well I better attend to it

(He goes into the house on the right.)

LAHEU:   Felix is still in shock

BLASON: Where did you bury her?

LAHEU: A corner of the woods she used to love covered with pine needles and cones

ALICE: I know the place

BLASON: Well now help yourself

LAHEU: Yes

He used to go there all the time with her and Alice

He'd throw a pine cone she'd leap at it bring it back you could have come along you know

ALICE: Felix said no he said it was something between father and son

Besides I thought that Papa would need me to get everything ready

*(Felix returns.)*

Having to do with men it's a question women keep asking

Should we listen to them?

FELIX: She called to add four Trianon fish services eighteen hundred each

That amounts to an order of nearly 70,000 if I add in the fish services

BLASON: And you planted something? No? The punch this Daphne has

Particularly if you consider that young people today tend to marry less and less forty-three percent of couples under twenty-five live together casually compared to twenty-eight percent just ten years ago if it were only marriage as an institution but everything is going to pieces wherever you look they've uncovered

An 800,000-franc gap in the books at Macassin Brothers

A firm dating back to 1873

I suppose you think that surprises me?

LAHEU:   We dug at the foot of a stone that had a flat surface

Felix engraved her name on it

BLASON:   One day or another it was bound to happen

ALICE:   Elsa

FELIX:   There you have it

ALICE:   Felix he said it again there you have it

FELIX:   Madame Daphne says so she says that young people
are going back to marriage bridal registries are picking up

She says the trend is reversing better days

BLASON:   On the horizon?

LAHEU:   Like the two of you talking about going down to city
hall if I understand correctly

BLASON:   I keep telling them go out and look just to be sure
not to make a mistake why those two have never known
anybody but each other

ALICE:   The grave Felix

Will you take me to it?

FELIX:   It sure is visible today

Your scar

ALICE:   Whenever I've been crying

It comes out and you know yesterday I finally asked him
for it Monsieur Fabre

My raise

Monsieur Fabre it's been two years my pay hasn't budged

If my performance has been unsatisfactory please say so

Alice why certainly dear I must think of doing something about it

The problem is all he thinks about is Monsieur Delorge

Monsieur Fabre I said to him my salary's actually decreased with inflation

Listen Alice he says Delorge has practically planted his tent in the lobby of the Ministry of Trade fortunately I do have a few friends myself at the top closer friends possibly

However never underestimate your foe Alice he wants my project torpedoed I smell a machination

What I'm being paid is not an executive secretary's salary Monsieur Fabre it's an entry-level typist's salary

Of course Alice do remind me next week won't you? But all he thinks about is how to get Delorge to hit the dust

LAHEU:   Scare him Alice

I'm slamming the door in your face Monsieur Fabre

BLASON:   I'm going over to Monsieur Delorge

LAHEU:   With all your secrets

ALICE:   He'd kill me

BLASON:   Serve him right

LAHEU:   The swindler is asking for it

BLASON:   He's no ordinary crook though

He's a hot shot

LAHEU:   I'll help myself to seconds with your permission

BLASON:   Champagne? Felix what about you?

Doesn't hear a thing stands there like a stick of wood with his empty glass

LAHEU:   A swindler all the same

BLASON:   A winner

Drink Felix come what may

FELIX:   Alice and me we're off I'm going back

BLASON:   To the grave?

FELIX:   I left my pocketknife there

*(Felix and Alice exit.)*

LAHEU:   An exploiter

Anything in order to win or make a fast buck

Shameless ruthless

Yet you admire them

You should've been a serf in the Middle Ages

BLASON:   Hit hard to get to the top is what he's done

Fabre is a great man whichever way you look at it

Not only in the Middle Ages throughout history great men have always

LAHEU:   Trampled everything on their way

BLASON:   That's the way it goes that's the way it should be

LAHEU:   You saying this? Scrupulous as you are?

Come off it

Thirty years we've been living side by side Blason

BLASON:   The fact is I'm no entrepreneur

I move slowly

But I do move

Have a look

LAHEU:   What's that?

*(Blason gives him a small package which Laheu starts to unwrap.)*

BLASON:   Heavier than it looks eh?

I acquired it yesterday

Haven't said a word to Alice yet

LAHEU:   Wasn't Felix real proud

With his huge order?

BLASON:   Nor is he Laheu

Nor will he ever be an entrepreneur

An ingot a kilo Laheu my fifth

Give me a hand will you we've got to lift this

LAHEU:   I see you're persevering?

BLASON:   The savings of the last three years lucky thing you're there

Without you I'd never be able to lift the damn trapdoor you know I've never been able to do anything with my hands

*(Laheu takes a crowbar out of his toolbox, goes about lifting a flat slab in the patio floor.)*

LAHEU:   All the same who'd believe it? You dealing with financial matters all day long ought to know

Money is made to bear fruit

BLASON:   You're the one who says so you haven't got any

LAHEU:   If I did

BLASON:   Which will never happen

LAHEU:   I'd have it bear fruit

BLASON:   The future isn't worrying you simply because you never think about it I can't get it out of my mind

I have this house I have Alice and I have you as a neighbor but everything else is going to pieces

Insecurity's gaining ground all around so much so that I can't shut my eyes at night

You have the privilege of being blind and deaf to all that's going on in this world

LAHEU:   I beg your pardon not that way at all I read the papers

We're rolling in a cart and there's always been bumps but the world's still there more than ever right there and you just need to equip yourself with a good pair of shock absorbers

One front one rear

BLASON:   No hope of ever understanding one another

At least admit that to start out in life one's got to pay an admission fee

LAHEU:   I don't know what you're talking about

BLASON:  Since they've got this restaurant thing in their heads
I've been thinking that just shy of half of what's there under
our feet could buy them a roof

Because no matter what you think Laheu it really does bear
fruit down under there

The first kilo when you helped me bury it remember fourteen
years ago today it's worth twenty times

Neither stocks nor bonds nor real estate has brought in a
better return

It bears fruit quietly and war can break out and banks can fold

LAHEU:  I think you're mad as a hatter

BLASON:  It's beyond me how dense you can be

LAHEU:  Maybe you're right maybe I'm the one that's cracked

BLASON:  No doubt I'd be happier if I were you

LAHEU:  The fact is

In your business you're bound to look at everything from
the point of view of the risk involved

BLASON:  You think it's just by chance I'm in insurance?

There's no such thing as chance

LAHEU:  You think everything is determined?

The accident?

BLASON:  Everything

LAHEU:  And your wife's death? You think it was predeter-
mined that she'd be killed in the accident?

Your fatalism is monstrous

My wife dumped me because I gave her good reasons to do so and to fall in love with somebody else

Why don't you drive anymore? If everything's determined couldn't you drive again?

BLASON: It's written somewhere I don't know where

That my driving days are over

LAHEU: Not so

The car stirs things up in you and frightens you

Suppose there was a robbery tomorrow?

Suppose Felix found another girl?

*(The two men burst out laughing and touch wood. Alice and Felix have reappeared. They are still far off, standing in an embrace. They approach and look in the trapdoor with curiosity. A wink passes between the fathers. Night falls.)*

*(Lights Out)*

## ACT TWO

*(Same set but with this difference: a good fourth of the patio has been dug up — in the area where the trapdoor was located — and presents a disordered appearance. Laheu and Felix are setting the table for four. Late afternoon.)*

FELIX:   Another order from her an even larger one

Eight complete Pompadour settings six Anthony & Cleopatra lunch settings four silverplated Chambord ice buckets four trays three cut crystal salad bowls two vases from the House of Daum four pairs of Chenonceau chandeliers twelve plate liners and just the tureen you figure a Beauharnais tureen by itself not counting tax

LAHEU:   Felix

FELIX:   Three thousand eight hundred twenty francs

LAHEU:   Come off it my boy

Knives on the other side you should know better

To the right it's the basics of the trade

How do you account for the fact

That we heard nothing?

FELIX:   If only Elsa had still been there

LAHEU:   Blason prefers Bordeaux

I brought a bottle up from behind the woodpile

But what scares me

FELIX:   She'd have barked

LAHEU:   But look it must have made a hell of a racket

They couldn't have done it without making a terrific noise

Why

But even harder to understand

How did they know?

*(Alice enters.)*

ALICE: Papa's late

FELIX: *(with a laugh)* She's put slippers on

LAHEU: But how could they have known

ALICE: At least they left me my slippers

LAHEU: Your papa stayed calm Alice I admired him

I really did but what I fear is

Oh I can't make it out

ALICE: I wonder why they didn't take away this pair of slippers

They took my suede boots my white leather Italian sandals right down to my last pair of shoes

All of Papa's shoes all his suits his shirts all my things my underwear my comb my little clock *Gone with the Wind* I had just started it it was open on my bed

*(Blason enters.)*

LAHEU: Dinner's ready

ALICE: They tore my mattress apart

BLASON: They call that taking your deposition

LAHEU: Look Blason first things first a seventeen-year-old bottle

This is an area where your expertise beats mine Felix says it should be decanted do you think that's right?

BLASON:   Absolutely you decant it after an hour and a half answering their questions

I'll be damned not an ordinary wine this Laheu

You still had that in the cellar? One just doesn't find the likes of them anymore

Trouble is they don't believe you

LAHEU:   Felix made boiled chicken with rice

FELIX:   The last one I cooked

BLASON:   I remember

FELIX:   But this one is a new recipe

BLASON:   Is that so?

They end up making you believe

LAHEU:   You wonder if it isn't you who've done it

BLASON:   You're the guilty one that's right

LAHEU:   Yes you're the one

FELIX:   Madame Daphne placed an even larger one with me

BLASON:   Don't say

They'll come and ask you to testify too

You'll have to loosen that tongue of yours a little bit

ALICE:   That's going to hurt won't it Felix?

You're under suspicion Felix

LAHEU:   You and I we're the prime suspects

Monsieur Blason kept no secrets from us did he?

BLASON:   That's what they asked me and that's what I told them

LAHEU:   Sure

Pass me your plate

I had the key I knew of the existence of a hideaway

BLASON:   You knew about the slab and what was underneath

You knew

LAHEU:   Where it was located on the patio

BLASON:   And how to lift it

I myself couldn't for the life of me

LAHEU:   You? Too clumsy to do it yourself

*(Laughter.)*

Blason your glass

BLASON:   An army of vandals has been through the place

LAHEU:   One day or another we'll find out

ALICE:   All the same

LAHEU:   Alice your glass too

ALICE:   As if madness came over them that urge to destroy

FELIX:   They had axes I'm certain of it it looks like they went in swinging axes

ALICE:   Breaking everything they couldn't carry off

BLASON:   Apart from what she's got on her back

You're naked Alice you have nothing left

ALICE: The hideaway if they hadn't found the hideaway but they found it didn't they Papa they got what they wanted

Then why

Tear apart the drapes rip up the carpeting?

BLASON: Who knew?

Tell me who?

ALICE: You too

Not a shirt left not a pair of pants

BLASON: No shirt no pants

No breach of domicile the insurance

LAHEU: Won't pay?

BLASON: No chance
　　*(Laughter.)*

It's what's called total loss and not a single clause you can base a claim on

Forwards and backwards I can recite them to you

FELIX: Bell rang

LAHEU: No doubt come for me we'll each of us have our turn to be grilled I guess

Look Blason don't you have some idea? Not the slightest?
　　*(He enters the house on the right.)*

FELIX: In the meantime Monsieur Blason Alice and you

Papa said you move into our house all we have is yours the money you know where it is take what you need to replace whatever's necessary

I'll sleep in the attic Alice is taking my room and Papa got his ready for you he moved his things into the study

Elsa would have barked if she had been around

*(Fade out and in 1.)*

*(Blason and Laheu, seated at the table, are having breakfast.)*

BLASON:   Mind you to get her raise she had to resort to heavy artillery she handed him her resignation in proper form at which point he must have said to himself

*(The two men chuckle.)*

LAHEU:   She's switching to Delorge

BLASON:   Pretty good don't you think

This black-currant jelly

LAHEU:   And she finds time to make preserves I tell you you won't see me complaining 'cause it's a lucky chance for that boy but Felix isn't up to her level

BLASON:   Nonsense you shouldn't talk that way you made him after all and now you look down on him he feels it so he folds up

The bird's not quite out of the shell you wait and see he's going to surprise us he's going to fly high

LAHEU:   Every year you tell me

For twenty years now

BLASON:   We parents tend to get impatient besides a girl steps out faster it's a well known fact

Eighteen percent and she got it retroactive to the first of January if it had been me

I don't think I'd have had the nerve to ask him for it Monsieur Fabre yielded on all fronts

He must have feared

*(The two men chuckle.)*

LAHEU:   She'd switch to Delorge

BLASON:   Privy to all his secrets

By the way Fabre has just made a fabulous coup

Haven't you heard?

Delorge had obtained the official permit to construct now the permit has just been cancelled

LAHEU:   You mean the eight extra stories to his hotel?

BLASON:   You're way off Fabre couldn't care less about the hotel extension

I'm talking about the shopping center

*(Alice enters.)*

Because you know that was his great dream from the beginning right Alice?

That there be a shopping center downtown with his name flashing in big letters on top of it

And here comes onto his own turf this former bicycle racer

Winning the Tour de France two or three times is one thing intruding into Fabre's territory is another

Alice we're going to be able to move back to our place

I don't mean to say you can't be a champion and also a clever businessman

LAHEU:   There's no hurry

BLASON:   Not that we haven't enjoyed sharing your home

No matter tomorrow the repairs are completed

LAHEU:   Alice I want to congratulate you

BLASON:   You sure as hell got us out of this pinch

LAHEU:   That raise you deserved it all right

Just ask Felix

We'll miss you

Yes

*(Felix enters.)*

BLASON:   Yes it all goes to show ordeals can be of use you
find out the kind of man your neighbor is

LAHEU:   Come on what you really find out is who you are
yourself because with regard to your neighbor you knew
didn't you?

BLASON:   Alice and you my boy?

Coffee?

ALICE:   Love one thanks

And you Felix?

FELIX:   My best customer took a dive

LAHEU:   Daphne?

FELIX:   She was overdue in the remittance of her last invoice

Didn't worry me too much

ALICE:   You didn't answer if you wanted coffee

FELIX:   The store is under legal seal and she

They arrested a gang of teenagers in the midst of a break-in red-handed and one of them ratted

Clean sweep that's the headline in this morning's paper they confessed a series of burglaries and that Madame Daphne

BLASON:   Well

    *(Silent pause.)*

Well well

FELIX:   She was the brains behind it and that's how she financed her expansion because she got twenty percent of every take

They've locked her up

BLASON:   Well then

                                *(Fade out and in 2.)*

    *(Toward evening. Blason, alone, sets the table for four. Alice and Felix enter.)*

ALICE:   You know I think we've found it

BLASON:   I didn't expect this of you Alice you left me to get everything ready by myself

You haven't kept your word

ALICE:   Our little restaurant

BLASON:   Hadn't you promiscd?

We tell Monsieur Laheu there will be a celebration and you were supposed to make the souffléed potatoes

ALICE:   Dear Papa when you hear the reason why

FELIX:   Sorry the fault is mine Monsieur Blason I'm the one that drew her out there

The little farmhouse you see the one I mean? The one up on the hill after the turn right at the outskirt of the woods

ALICE:   Where Elsa is buried

FELIX:   We didn't think it would take that long we went on our bikes

ALICE:   From up there you take in the whole countryside this morning Felix as he was going to visit her grave he went by it and they had just put out a sign "for sale"

FELIX:   I went and picked up Alice when she got off work we went up and asked to visit it

ALICE:   There aren't two like it for twenty miles around it'll be grabbed up

You have to act fast

*(Laheu enters.)*

LAHEU:   Hey what's everybody so worked up about?

BLASON:   Dinner's going to be late

That it should happen on the very day of the celebration of Monsieur Laheu's hospitality

Laheu I'm sorry

No matter tell about it

ALICE:   The dream

BLASON:   But not a cent to pay for it

ALICE:   I can borrow

Monsieur Fabre often told me he'd be glad to help me

BLASON:    And you'd put yourself in his claws? Laheu you tell
me if I'm right or wrong these kids are losing their marbles
Felix

Pop this cork for me the last bottle of champagne we had
together was in honor of poor Elsa's memory

Open the fridge Alice bring out the foie gras Monsieur Bordier
Laheu you recall don't you? I've spoken to you about him
sometimes and always in the best terms

LAHEU:    Your old head accountant, isn't he?

BLASON:    Has been with us for thirty-five years Monsieur
Macassin fired him without notice and he committed suicide
none of which explains the missing eight hundred thousand
francs

*(The telephone rings. Alice goes into the house at left.)*

They wanted a scapegoat

And light the oven

Foie gras filet mignon souffléed potatoes the Chambertin's
at room temperature mind those potatoes

She does have a knack for making them crunchy

Felix what are you waiting for? Tell us about it

Cheers

Well really this is to thank you

LAHEU:    Who's to be thanked? You've given us a lesson in
courage

Cheers

You didn't flinch under fire

BLASON:    Now let's not let these kids do anything stupid

I drink to the example you set

LAHEU:   Your health

BLASON:   Your health

(*Alice returns.*)

The foie gras Alice

ALICE:   The gold Papa

BLASON:   Well

What? The foie gras I'm telling you

ALICE:   And I'm telling you the gold

They've recovered part of it

At Madame Daphne's they've conducted a search

The police chief wants to talk to you

(*Fade out and in 3.*)

(*Night. Blason and Laheu seated, glasses of beer in front of them.*)

BLASON:   Because in the first place if you want my opinion
the police are a bunch of morons

Look here put yourself in Daphne's place

Now you're not a detective story reader are you?

They find a gold ingot at her place they identify this gold
ingot it belongs to Blason at Blason's house there's been a
burglary O.K.

What's she got to lose? She's already admitted she's running
this gang of youths doing all the burglaries in the area

The key fits the lock hard for her to pretend she doesn't know
anything about the burglary at Blason's house

The police put the heat on her she must have had an informer
no breach of domicile and how would she have known there
was a trapdoor in the floor of the patio?

So she thinks of Felix who calls on her from time to time
to take an order

Felix who's the son of Blason's neighbor you follow me?

And the cops gobble it up

LAHEU:   Put yourself in their shoes

BLASON:   Why sure

Couldn't suit them more nicely

LAHEU:   Because the story does hang together

BLASON:   Considering their mental make-up it does

LAHEU:   So you don't believe it?

BLASON:   Laheu you and I look we have to keep our heads clear

Felix is innocence itself a boy who thinks the world around him
is as pure as he is and Daphne was handing him hefty orders

The smile in his eyes when he was bragging about it

Stop looking like the bottom's dropped out

Bordier committed suicide you know why? The cops push
their pawns they have to fill in each little square and Bordier
I can tell you he was integrity itself

The trouble with him was he trusted people too much

You think I don't know what pocket the eight hundred thousand francs landed in? Come on

Like father like son you're just simpletons you don't see what's
staring you in the face you're made out of the same clay

At least one of the five ingots is being retrieved which is
what I wanted to talk to you about

That little farm up there on the hill what do you think?

Monsieur Fabre's money smells avoid it like poison

*(Fade out and in 4.)*

*(Early afternoon. Laheu alone. Felix enters.)*

FELIX:   It's been sitting vacant for eight years when you roam
around inside

LAHEU:   Nothing surprises you does it

FELIX:   Like what?

LAHEU:   For example that Madame Daphne

For once I want you to listen to me

FELIX:   The smell stays in your nose

Goat or cow by the way when the last of the animals were
gone it wasn't even scrubbed

The scrubbing will have to be done never mind all four of
us could get at it together

The beams are going to be quite a job they'll have to be
scraped bare

LAHEU:   You listening to me?

The lock wasn't broken and who had the key?

FELIX:   I don't know

Alice wonders too

If the cow shed would better be turned into the dining room
or should it be the horse stable

Assuming it's the horse stable

Because restaurant guests really enjoy it if they have a view to look at between courses

Leisurely

Alice says

Or even between mouthfuls while they're eating if it's the cow shed we'd put in two large bay windows

It's a big beautiful shed it could accommodate business seminars and be used as a banquet room they'd find it attractive

LAHEU:   At the police it lasted all that long did it?

FELIX:   All morning

At four I have to go back it isn't over

In the courtyard there's a huge tree a maple in fair weather we can serve outside

Corporations we'll be aiming at primarily

They appreciate a country setting for their meetings and you can charge them a good price

Between the cow shed and the horse stable there's a barn not that big

Our minds are almost set Alice and I the kitchen

We're thinking of installing the kitchen in the barn right between the shed and the stable

LAHEU:   Your mother was the same way

She wouldn't answer

What's got hold of you Felix?

FELIX:   I'm explaining

LAHEU:   The gold you and I knew that there was gold nobody else

The slab you and I we knew where it was and Monsieur Blason hadn't told anyone else

The key you and I

FELIX:   You playing police too?

Let them do their job we do ours

LAHEU:   Why you have to go back?

FELIX:   They want to confront our testimonies me and Madame Daphne

LAHEU:   You know what she testified

She testified that you often called in at her place

Not just in her store but in her apartment

She stated

So they're going to confront you

What's got hold of you Felix what's got hold of you?

How could you have

Listen

Deny

Even if they claim you've got your fingers in it deny understand?

Play dumb like you know how

Like your mother used to do

Dumb right to the end

Deny

FELIX:   I'd rather you didn't talk to me that way

LAHEU:   I'd rather you hadn't done that

FELIX:   What have I done?

*(Laheu goes out. Felix, alone, makes a very special kind of whistle. Alice enters.)*

ALICE:   That's the way you used to call Elsa

FELIX:   She was born here right in this corner

ALICE:   I remember we stood right here you and I

First there was a still-born one then another and then that little moving tuft of hair

FELIX:   Elsa

ALICE:   You said Elsa and it stuck

Elsa

It sounded like Alice I thought

FELIX:   Didn't really think

ALICE:   But suppose it had been a male dog?

You're beautiful Felix

I can't stop thinking you're as beautiful as a dog

Yesterday your father asked me what I saw in you

He's at a loss he can't understand it

Now I can tell him now I know

You are beautiful and now I'm going to tell you that a thousand times

Even if you say nothing

No matter

Stroke me

The way you stroked Elsa's belly I was almost jealous that evening though I realized she was dying I was a little jealous nonetheless

Stroke me here

*(Blason enters, visibly distraught.)*

I can die now

BLASON:    There's got to be an explanation but now you have to tell me Felix

Look it's a photocopy of a sheet of graph paper they found at Madame Daphne's

With a map of this patio on it

A cross where the slab is

An arrow pointing at the cross and the word "treasure"

In your handwriting at least they say they've ascertained that it's in fact your handwriting

FELIX:    A minute ago it was Papa

Now you too?

*(Felix backs away slowly and leaves. Alice follows him. Blason remains, stymied. Laheu enters.)*

BLASON:    You were right

It's him

LAHEU:  What do you mean I was right?

BLASON:  This map look it's all there

LAHEU:  So what?

BLASON:  It's in Felix' handwriting

LAHEU:  Felix' writing really?

Is that what you're telling me?

BLASON:  You saw it all clearly before I did

I didn't believe you

LAHEU:  What am I supposed to believe?

I don't understand you

BLASON:  Now I've come around I'm with you

LAHEU:  Absolutely nuts

BLASON:  Who? me?

*(The two men, still facing one another, step apart. They look at one another, bewildered.)*

*(Fade out and in 5.)*

*(Early morning.)*

FELIX:  If we'd only left a deposit right away

Now it's been sold

LAHEU:  It's no loss

FELIX:  Alice and I had drawn up plans

It was bought by Monsieur Fabre

LAHEU:  Nothing in life is ever a loss Felix

FELIX:  To make shade

LAHEU:  It can all turn around to our benefit

FELIX:  I don't know of any other tree in the region I could compare to it unless it's the oak at Monsieur Viaux's

I know the surroundings well

LAHEU:  Because one has to defend oneself and that's what you've done

A lot of things we took for granted have blown up now our eyes are wide open yours and mine

The Viaux property has been put up for sale Delorge picked it up for a song

All becoming clear

Daphne Blason

Your beautiful Madame Daphne and our neighbor Monsieur Blason

FELIX:  He's going to set up a foundation the Fabre Foundation

He's planning to tear down the shed the stable the barn and put up a small office building in mirrored glass

LAHEU:  I have it on good authority

That there was a long-standing affair between those two

You follow me?

Ha ha one by one all the threads come together

*(Fade out and in 6.)*

*(Evening.)*

BLASON:   A scheme Alice

You wouldn't imagine it

ALICE:   You didn't keep your promise

BLASON:   Never mind the little farm

ALICE:   With the maple tree

Sold

BLASON:   What time is it? What's he doing?

There's a light in his room

Will he have the nerve?

ALICE:   You're in such a state

BLASON:   Delorge is in that house

There aren't a dozen orange Mercedes around and there's no mistaking his chauffeur's silhouette

ALICE:   Even if he were there

BLASON:   The two of them are in collusion and Delorge's got friends in the right place

The order to dispose of the case came from high up

Matter closed

Forget it all

ALICE:   It's better that way

For Felix it was hard

BLASON:   Oh it was hard for Felix was it?

But don't you realize what it all leads to?

ALICE:   Things I see

BLASON:   Those two are parading now

  The field is theirs

  *(Laheu enters.)*

  Has he gone?

LAHEU:   Who?

BLASON:   Your visitor

LAHEU:   Since when are you interested in who visits me?

BLASON:   You do me a favor so I do you one that's the way
  friendships are knitted and maintained

  I had no inkling that you had such excellent and intimate
  relations with Delorge

  Maybe even Monsieur Fabre is unaware of them

  What do you figure Alice?

LAHEU:   In point of fact I was coming to ask you

BLASON:   By the way didn't you race bicycles years ago?

LAHEU:   Just out of curiosity

  Is it a fact that Daphne used to be a dance hostess in a bar
  in Pigalle called Hot Nights in Madrid

  At the time you met her and never up to this very day have
  you strayed far from her tracks

  Then what a lucky idea you had to entice her to come and
  open a gift shop in this very city

  China silverware bridal registries and the like all by chance
  of course

But then there's no such thing as chance am I right Blason everything is determined isn't it? Fate

BLASON:   As fate would have it

Too bad for you Laheu

Sometimes what a person says comes back to haunt them

Fate had me see his chauffeur walking back and forth

I've got friends too

It's just possible that a journalist might want to investigate the circumstances in which a judge signed an order of nonsuit

Whereas the dossier was

Rarely has there been a dossier so utterly crushing and I know no more than you do about Madame Daphne's background she may have been a bar hostess as I've also heard people say that she's been a shepherdess watching sheep

What clearly emerges is the wretched gesture of a father taking advantage of the fact that his son is a little bit backwards

ALICE:   Felix?

BLASON:   You pushed him into the sticky sheets of that woman

LAHEU:   What is it you're saying?

BLASON:   Knowing that woman has a weakness for young boys with peach fuzz she initiates them starts their apprenticeship teaches them the elements of the trade

Then when they're ready for service

LAHEU:   That's an interesting theory allow me Blason I have another

We could sit down

BLASON:   Fine

And drink something

Alice suppose you bring us a bottle

*(Felix has entered without being seen.)*

FELIX:   I can bring you one if you'd like

*(He goes out, returns with a bottle and two glasses. The two men take their first sips of wine in silence.)*

LAHEU:   We've been through a lot together Blason I think I know you

You've been thick with that woman Daphne since before your marriage you were her first sweet young man her first trooper

Getting married was a good management decision on your part since you had no capital and your wife had just inherited this house

The shared patio bothered you but we'll see later

Madame Blason dies very conveniently in an accident about which nothing is known except that you were behind the wheel with no traffic ahead or behind straight line then all of a sudden the car swerves a few barrels as a souvenir on the pretty face of Alice who was four at the time a scar

But you couldn't stand this common patio you figured that out of these two houses side by side it was possible to make one you knock down the adjoining wall open up a large living area

Only thing is there's Laheu and his son Felix so with Daphne you figure she's the one who comes up with the idea

The gold the slab the break-in the map of the patio in Felix's handwriting carefully faked

The Laheu family is trusting we must profit from it

*(Blason is on his feet, livid.)*

BLASON:   You rotten swine

LAHEU:   A rat

You

Period

*(Fade out and in 7.)*

*(Night.)*

FELIX:   Their differences are getting deeper

ALICE:   It's just a stage

*(Fade out and in 8.)*

*(Early morning.)*

BLASON:   What were you doing last evening?

LAHEU:   I was washing my car

BLASON:   Really?

LAHEU:   The windshield after that storm

Couldn't see out

BLASON:   Like something to drink?

*(They pour drinks.)*

Alice quit her job with Monsieur Fabre.

LAHEU:   She resign?

BLASON:   Something wasn't ticking

LAHEU:   I've noticed yes

She's not her usual self

Felix is having his share of problems at Christophle's his sales are down

BLASON:   Well sure

Since Daphne's place closed

You're going to face a surprise soon Laheu

I'm not entirely without a hand in it

LAHEU:   All the better

You know I often think about the suicide of that poor fellow Bordier

I have a notion about the missing eight hundred thousand francs

BLASON:   You do?

LAHEU:   You said one or two words too many

BLASON:   Too much talk ruins

Universal Biscuit doesn't do all that well right? Competition is getting just a little too rough

This size of operations is no longer viable now that the business is getting more and more concentrated in the hands of a few conglomerates you explained this to me

One's got to diversify and of course you know that Monsieur Fabre has already made a few acquisitions in the food industry

He's gone a long way just think his father had this tiny butcher shop on Market Square and now lo and behold

In two months' time the Fabre Shopping Center will be opening its doors two hundred and ninety thousand square feet

I thought it was right for me to call his attention at a Rotary meeting one evening to the situation at Universal Biscuit basing myself on what you had told me about its potential and its plight all the inside dope

That didn't fall on deaf ears

Fabre has taken over Universal Biscuit it'll be in the papers today

The first thing he'll do as he usually does is to draw up a list of employees he can do without

You now for certain you've got nothing to worry about

Now if by chance something did happen to you you'd always be able to get a job at Delorge's wouldn't you?

However in the event some bad luck should come along

The house you occupy I'm the taker

*(The two men glare at one another.)*

*(Fade out and in 9.)*

*(Early evening.)*

FELIX:   The personnel manager called me he told me maybe I wasn't cut out for this line of work

ALICE:   Not cut out for

FELIX:   Yes he said these two things

Not cut out for

And

Lack of punch

ALICE:   I didn't say anything to Monsieur Fabre

I who never missed a day

One morning I didn't show up

I knew I couldn't go back

FELIX:   Let's do something together Alice

ALICE:   Let's

A franks and french fry stand

FELIX:   Franks and fries

   *(Laheu enters.)*

ALICE:   Today's the anniversary of Elsa's death.

It's nice on the patio this evening

LAHEU:   Hours after the inauguration

The shopping center burned

   *(Blason enters.)*

ALICE:   I thought we might eat a little something together this evening

LAHEU:   Fabre suspects Delorge

BLASON:   It would take more for a man like Fabre to give up I can tell you

LAHEU:   So you got fired?

Did you go back?

   *(Felix and Alice set the table.)*

FELIX:   Just now

BLASON:   The stone is still there?

LAHEU:   With her name engraved?

ALICE:   Cold chicken

It was her favorite meal she would grovel until you gave her the leftover bones

BLASON:   Some bread please Felix

ALICE:   Don't you think it's nice here together?

Wine?

LAHEU:   That's true it's nice

BLASON:   From secretary to secretary information gets around

Mine found out that there was a letter from you in Macassin's mail

LAHEU:   Beg your pardon I didn't write

I phoned to ask for an appointment with Monsieur Macassin

BLASON:   You phoned?

LAHEU:   Just so

The secretary wanted to know the subject of the call I told her I had data that might interest him relating to the gap in their books

BLASON:   What? What have you dreamed up now?

Without so much as a shadow of proof

LAHEU:   He kept me in his office for an hour yesterday

I told him I had no proof

Circumstantial evidence only

BLASON:   Macassin is a gentleman

Waste an hour of his time listening to sheer nonsense

LAHEU:   He took notes he seemed to find it of interest

Especially the story of the gold and Daphne

A little more chicken? Filet?

Frankly I'd be surprised if he felt he could keep on someone who had done what I told him you'd done

BLASON:   Wait till Monsieur Fabre

LAHEU:   I'm not worried

BLASON:   I spoke to Monsieur Fabre about you in considerable detail

LAHEU:   The suicide of a fine man like Bordier ought to weigh on anyone's conscience

BLASON:   In turn Monsieur Fabre asked me one or two questions he particularly wanted to know how Delorge uses you

LAHEU:   Monsieur Fabre is a not a man to give credence to a tissue of inanities the circumstances of the death of your wife especially struck Monsieur Macassin

He impressed me as an extremely upright sort

*(Blason overturns the table, yelling.)*

BLASON:   The spite

For years you've been dying of spite and envy

You don't bother to put away a penny in the meanwhile I save

I trust you I show you everything and I let you share

But pride has a grip on you you think you're smarter than I am so you have to strip me clean

You're an engineer you know how to devise a booby trap

Before you skin me what do you do? You strip and humiliate your wife you kick her out on the sidewalk

Look at Felix this boy with his lips sewn shut it's because he hasn't forgiven you

You think I haven't figured out why you're trying to get him to marry Alice? It's so she'll belong to you it's to take her away from me

You're smart all right but you're lazy and therefore a failure one solution destroy me ruin me

LAHEU:   The hideous snare you've set the fool I've been to let myself be caught in it

BLASON:   You have the nerve

LAHEU:   You wanted a victim

BLASON:   What didn't I do for you

LAHEU:   The shame

BLASON:   Shut up

   *(They fight.)*

   *(Lights Out)*

## Act Three

*(In the background the backs of two sheds side by side and in the foreground an area of beaten earth with an irregular surface. An old mini-van. It is spring. Daybreak. No one on stage. Bird songs and sounds of insects against a backdrop of leaves stirred by the wind and the occasional passing of a car in the distance. Suddenly a small dog barks. Pause. Felix enters.)*

FELIX:    Shush

Wretched

*(He whistles in his peculiar manner.)*

Where are you?

Gone

Obviously

You rush in and wake everybody up then run off on a spree

*(Alice appears.)*

Wretched animal

ALICE:    I slept like a log and you?

Shall I bring you coffee?

FELIX:    Runs like a devil now

His paw's fine

ALICE:    The week's receipts Felix I've added it all up

It was a big week

FELIX:    People are beginning to know about us

Alice an idea I had during the night

ALICE: Two thousand four hundred this is the first week we've gone over the two thousand franc mark

FELIX: Now that they've opened this new building site

Franks aren't popular with the North Africans

Alongside the franks we could sell merguez an additional source of income

*(He whistles.)*

I don't know if you agree anyway the thought occurred to me

ALICE: Have you noticed? A clientele of elderly people is starting to form

Suppose we make a bench a lot more of them would be attracted

FELIX: And lovers too

ALICE: Two benches then

FELIX: Easy

You're always going too fast Alice

ALICE: Having worked that long for Monsieur Fabre it rubs off on you

*(Blason has appeared.)*

BLASON: True you went to the right school

FELIX: He runs you'll notice

BLASON: Besides

You're a born entrepreneur Alice

Go go

FELIX:   Like a rocket he plunges every which way didn't you say we shouldn't keep him he'd be better off dead you used to say

I can tell you his paw is like new

BLASON:   Wasn't five in the morning when he burst in yapping in my ears no way of getting back to sleep

FELIX:   You got back late didn't you?

*(Laheu has appeared.)*

BLASON:   Past midnight ninety miles driving just to bring back this heap of wood

LAHEU:   It's quite clear the used furniture business is nothing but your excuse for eating up the road miles

ALICE:   You could spend the rest of your life hanging on the steering wheel

LAHEU:   Blason the new gasoline addict

BLASON:   On and on she couldn't stop talking

This woman they were forcing her to move over to that nursing home

And she'd go on and on till the middle of the night her son was dead and her husband it had been thirty years since he passed away the grandchildren held a family council they decided she was insane

It was so they wouldn't have to pay her monthly maintenance so they got a medical certificate

How can you fight that? She told me it was a medical accommodation certificate one of her grandchildren is a member of the city board and the mayor is a physician get it? But me she said I'm just fine right where I am and you tell me if I'm incapacitated or senile or crazy I'm not afraid of dying but I'd like to die with my furniture around me and I don't bother anyone but it quite obviously bothers them to put those eight hundred francs each in my account every month

*(Alice has brought in the coffeepot, mugs, bread. They eat while they unload the mini-van.)*

Not exactly what you'd call fine merchandise

Laheu what I've brought back is mostly work for you have a look see what I mean? It's falling to pieces

It held together in her rooms so long as you didn't touch it except for Madame Ufize mornings with the feather duster

She waxed

Not a speck of dust

ALICE: A lot of character

This sideboard door has

I think so anyway

FELIX: Look

A bench Alice

LAHEU: The whole works

How much?

BLASON: I offered three she wanted ten I said to myself five maximum and I got soft

Six

LAHEU: Six thousand francs?

BLASON: I pictured her there in that nursing home with the canteen where you can buy sweets for a little extra and the little gifts you have to give to the aides if you want to survive for a while

ALICE: Monsieur Fabre would have stuck by his first offer he would have hauled the whole works away for three thousand

Three thousand three hundred he would have yielded ten percent and she'd have felt proud to squeeze a concession out of him

BLASON: I'm not Monsieur Fabre

LAHEU: That's not a bad cargo Blason not by a long shot

Quite a bit of work has to be done on it to be sure once restored we could get fifteen to eighteen thousand out of it

Figure I've got a week's job

*(Laheu has already started with it.)*

It was just about time too

How much was there left in the till?

BLASON: Six thousand

LAHEU: You should have stopped at five thousand five

What are we going to live on this coming week buddy?

BLASON: Alice told me that she and Felix had a good week

FELIX: We'll give you an advance Monsieur Blason

LAHEU: Make a note of it Alice

I don't want the accounts mixed up

A handsome piece of furniture that sideboard it's made of solid walnut

All by itself

Shining new

Go for five thousand or so

FELIX: We're off Monsieur Blason

ALICE: We're going to the grind Monsieur Laheu

(*Alice and Felix exit.*)

LAHEU: Accounts are something we'd better have a talk about you and I

BLASON: Precisely what I was telling myself driving back such matters better not be left vague

LAHEU: Driving really does you good

BLASON: I seem to recall you used to suffer from conjunctivitis didn't you? You've gotten rid of it since you've been working with files and hammers all blessed day

LAHEU: Let me tell you something

At Universal Biscuit there was air conditioning

It dries out your mucous membranes

BLASON: At Macassin Brothers after years of bickering Monsieur Macassin made a decision windows could not be opened in the summer except on one side of the building on account of the fact that papers would fly all over the place so that settled the problem except that the office air became unbreathable

LAHEU: You do what you have to do you forget what you love to do

BLASON: I used to think I loved what I was doing

LAHEU: Felix and Alice now they knew what they wanted

BLASON: A maple

LAHEU: Can be planted

Would you please lean forward so I can tip the back of this sideboard your way?

I want to see underneath

Something intrigues me

As far as arrangements between you and me are concerned

BLASON:   Half and half on the profits

That's how I see it

I buy and I sell I'm in charge of marketing

You disassemble and reassemble you put together a piece with a chairback here and a legframe there you give it the finishing touch

You're in charge of engineering and manufacturing

LAHEU:   There's also the financial and administrative function

You mind getting down on all fours for a second?

BLASON:   We could take charge of it jointly

The general management function likewise

LAHEU:   Have to think about it

BLASON:   Yes think carefully

LAHEU:   Seems to me you've got it all figured out already

BLASON:   I'm not trying to impose it's just an idea to start with it's up for discussion

The important thing is for each one to do what he knows best

LAHEU:   Regarding the profits

BLASON:   And

Have enough to eat

Do the sort of work he's cut out for

LAHEU:  Do what he loves to do

BLASON:  And have enough to eat

LAHEU:  You know what?

Step back from there look underneath

There's something strange that I can't make out

When I push this drawer it reaches all the way to the back

The other one is shallower and so doesn't go in so far and yet it hits

Somewhere in there there's an empty space

An inner space unused

BLASON:  Maybe a secret hiding place

LAHEU:  Half and half I wonder if that's fair

For example this piece is going to cost me a good week's work and it's my labor that ups the value from six to eighteen thousand

BLASON:  Suppose you tried lifting?

LAHEU:  I thought maybe by forcing a little

But it doesn't give an inch

BLASON:  Once the cabinetmaker got to his last drawer he must have run out of wood

Maybe pressing on it

LAHEU:  Let's try

Nothing

BLASON:   The oak bed I brought in last week

How much time did you spend on it?

None or just about

Is it fair to say

That it was resold as is?

And for double what I paid for it?

LAHEU:   I rubbed it down polished it

I added fresh lustre to it

BLASON:   Hardly worth mentioning but see it's typical of you drawing conclusions out of a unique case

LAHEU:   It's hollow can you hear? I knock and there's a resonance

BLASON:   Circumstances do vary but on average

And on the side

LAHEU:   On the side?

BLASON:   Try to shove it a little on the side

LAHEU:   There you go with your averages again

You do have a bee in your bonnet

BLASON:   You want us to be rational about it?

Then the matter has to be addressed statistically there's no other way

Let me try

*(They change positions.)*

Say

Inside the empty space there's something

Hear it?

If I hit it there's something flies around inside

One times one week one times two hours and you take the average let's suppose fifty operations in a year to form an idea you take the average

The point is as a buyer I might spend a month two months to locate a potentially worthwhile seller feel him out overcome resistance negotiate a good price

That aspect of the business is something a manufacturing man usually fails to size up

And with regard to selling

Two months three months can go by at our stand in the flea market before I hit upon a customer who makes up his mind and meanwhile the number of times you miss a sale the young couple comes around they argue they bargain she wants to he's not sure he wants to she no longer wants to

LAHEU:   How did you do it?

*(Blason is holding the secret drawer in his hands.)*

BLASON:   It pivoted in my hands

LAHEU:   I did try to get it to turn

BLASON:   I must have given it a slight push here in the left-hand corner

Suddenly the back rotated

LAHEU:   A hidden spring

Feel it's incredible all shiny

Still moist with the original grease

*(Alice comes in.)*

The absolute beauty of it

ALICE:   When I hear a thing like that

Here are your franks and fries

BLASON:   Felix has to see this too

ALICE:   The stand can't be left unattended especially this time of day

Business is booming with the men on the building site admittedly the fries sell better than the franks

By the way Felix had an idea

Help yourselves

*(She gives each of the men a frank with fries. Laheu gives her the object that was in the drawer: a ball of loose wool.)*

LAHEU:   Here

ALICE:   What's this?

BLASON:   Take it apart

LAHEU:   Open it

ALICE:   A woollen sock

*(She catches gold coins in her hand.)*

Come what may I'm going to get him Felix has to see this

*(She places the gold on the hood of the van which has been the lunch table, wraps the sock around her neck and disappears on the run.)*

LAHEU:   What do you think it's worth?

BLASON:   You still have that old scale?

*(Laheu disappears around the shed on the right and reappears with an old fashioned beam scale. While they carry out the weighing procedure Alice returns, followed by Felix.)*

Three hundred eighty grams assuming the scale is still accurate

The price per gram is in the area of one hundred francs that would make thirty-eight thousand francs

*(The atmosphere has become thick. None of the four seems able to break the silence.)*

FELIX:  I closed the stand

But I'd better go back

The customers wouldn't understand

LAHEU:  Half and half I reckon

ALICE:  Felix wait

BLASON:  Would seem fair to me

FELIX:  Why wait?

ALICE:  You might have your say

LAHEU:  Are we sure it's ours?

BLASON:  According to law it belongs to us

LAHEU:  According to what would it not belong to us?

BLASON:  Law decides

LAHEU:  So it's ours?

BLASON:  Nobody else's

LAHEU:  The old lady?

BLASON: A thing is sold with everything it is deemed to contain

LAHEU: Deemed?

BLASON: Deemed or not deemed

LAHEU: The old lady was not deemed to know

BLASON: Somebody died without having the time to tell Madame Ufize her husband her father her grandfather maybe Madame Ufize's father didn't know even her grandfather didn't know in the event it was the great-grandfather

*(The atmosphere starts to relax.)*

FELIX: I'm going back

ALICE: Wait Felix

BLASON: One can share and not share

I mean we share but each leaves his half in the common pot

LAHEU: That becomes the capital of the business

BLASON: With two shareholders at fifty percent

LAHEU: And that constitutes the working capital

Felix have you seen?

The spring the bottom pivots fffit

It could have stayed inside another thousand years

FELIX: That wouldn't have been a bad thing

BLASON: The spurt this gives to the business

FELIX: I'm going back

*(He goes out.)*

LAHEU:  Everything's picking up speed

BLASON:  With this additional cash I buy

LAHEU:  The more we buy

BLASON:  The more we sell

Cash snowballs

Laheu

LAHEU:  Yes

BLASON:  No

LAHEU:  What no?

BLASON:  I find it hard to come to terms with it somehow

ALICE:  I'm going back too

Something wrong with Felix

I'm worried about Felix

*(She runs out.)*

BLASON:  Makes me dizzy

If Madame Ufize had it

LAHEU:  Something wrong Blason

With you too?

BLASON:  We don't need that

*(He climbs into the van, starts the engine.)*

LAHEU:  What are you doing?

BLASON:  Going back

*(Blason sits still, hands on the steering wheel. Laheu puts the coins back into the sock, slowly, one by one.)*

LAHEU:   One thing I didn't tell you Blason

You're worth your weight in gold

*(He brings the sock over to Blason.)*

BLASON:   Suits me fine

Being here with you

I thought I'd tell you

LAHEU:   Suits Alice one can see that

BLASON:   How many times have I told you about Felix

That one day he'd break out of his shell not a single morning he doesn't wake up with some new idea

Did he tell you of his idea about the merguez?

*(Alice appears bearing Felix on her shoulder. He is bleeding.)*

ALICE:   His pocketknife he always carried it in his pocket

Didn't manage to drive it down into his heart I don't think so anyway

*(First aid. Barking of a small dog.)*

∽